THE DAY OF THE
DINOSAUR

THE DAY OF THE
DINOSAUR

L. Sprague de Camp &
Catherine Crook de Camp

BONANZA BOOKS

NEW YORK

This 1985 edition is published by Bonanza Books,
distributed by Crown Publishers, Inc. by arrangement with
L. Sprague de Camp & Catherine Crook de Camp.

Manufactured in the United States of America

Library of Congress Cataloging in Publication Data
De Camp, L. Sprague (Lyon Sprague), 1907-
The Day of the dinosaur.
Reprint. Originally published: Garden City, N.Y.
Doubleday, 1968.
Bibliography: p.
Includes index.
1. Dinosaurs. 2. Paleontology—Mesozoic.
3. Paleontology—History. I. De Camp, Catherine
Crook. II. Title.
QE862.D5D4 1985   567.9′1   85-14937
ISBN: 0-517-47682-7

h g f e d c b a

Au professeur François Bordes et à sa femme,
Denise de Sonneville-Bordes, en témoignage
de nombreuses années d'amitié.

Contents

Illustrations in Text

List of Tables

Plates

Acknowledgments

For help with this book—obtaining books and pictures for us, answering questions, and reading and criticizing parts or all of the text—we are grateful to Edwin H. Colbert, A. W. Crompton, Mary R. Dawson, Bern Dibner, Barthold Fles, Richard M. Foose, C. Lewis Gazin, F. Hallowes, Nicholas Hotton III, Edward M. James, J. A. Jeletzky, Wann Langston, Jr., L. S. B. Leakey, Willy Ley, John Mackintosh, Reginald McMahon, P. Schuyler Miller, Samuel Moskowitz, John H. Ostrom, Richard W. Pohl, Craig Rice, George H. Scithers, George Gaylord Simpson, C. M. Sternberg, William Lee Stokes, A. D. J. Whiting, and Conway Zirkle.

For the use of drawings and photographs, many of them copyrighted, permission is gratefully acknowledged to the Academy of Natural Sciences, Philadelphia; the American Museum of Natural History, New York; the Bettmann Archive, Inc., New York; the British Museum (Natural History), London; the Burndy Library, Norwalk, Conn.; the Carnegie Museum, Pittsburgh; the Chicago Natural History Museum; the *Illustrated London News;* the *Journal of Paleontology;* Roy Krenkel; the London County Council; the Museum für Naturkunde, Berlin; the National Museum of Natural History (Smithsonian Institution), Washington; the Pratt Museum of Amherst College; and David Williams III. Drawings and photographs not otherwise credited are by the senior author, as is the poem preceding the first chapter.

The Dragon-Kings

About the margins of the lush lagoons,
During the ages that the dragons reigned,
The sauropod, through endless afternoons,
Perambulated, huge and tiny-brained,
On swampy plants of somber green sustained.
His monstrous, snaky neck and little head
Arose and dipped, as if by cables chained,
As, half-submerged, upon the reeds he fed;
He lumbered down the years with elephantine tread.

Along the sandy shores of lakes and seas
Grew palmlike cycads, gaudy blooms displayed
Upon their barrel-trunks, and fernlike trees
With fronds like frozen jets of liquid jade.
Upon the sand, like logs at random laid,
Slept crocodiles. Above, through twilit air,
There soared and swooped in aerial glissade
A horde of little lizard-bats, on bare,
Sharp-pointed, leathern wings, pursuing insect fare.

Like some reptilian fiend, the carnosaur
Through woods of redwood, ginkgo, larch, and pine
Did stalk his prey—some hapless herbivore—
With head asway and golden eyes ashine;
Thus reptiles swarmed the land and air and brine.
A hundred million years they ruled, then died.
We hairless apes, who think ourselves so fine,
Should not contemn the dragons in our pride
Until we shall, one-tenth as long as they, abide.

THE DAY OF THE
DINOSAUR

1

The Day of the Dinosaur

The earth is old—inconceivably old. It is as hard for us to compare its age with anything in our may-fly existence as it is to compare the distances to the stars with the earthly distances of our daily lives.

To give an idea of the earth's age, let us set 6,000 years as the time that has passed since the rise of urban civilization. Since civilization arose very slowly and gradually, there is no exact date of its birth; but that figure will do. Then let us suppose that we could shrink the earth's time scale down to periods that we are familiar with.

Assume the entire history of life on earth, since the first "proto-plasmal primordial atomic globule,"[1] be compressed to four twenty-four-hour days. Then the time that has passed, since animals evolved hard shells and began to leave abundant fossils, would be represented by *one* twenty-four-hour day. And the lapse of time since the rise of human civilization on this scale would be represented by *one second*.

During the immense span of time since life began, many things have changed. The positions of rivers and mountains and the very outlines of the continents have altered. Plant life and animal life have changed so much that, if we were snatched back to a former geological era, we might think that we had landed on another planet.

Let us in fancy take a time machine, like the one that H. G. Wells wrote of in his story of that name. Let us not go back all the way to the days when there were only protoplasmal globules, which would prove rather dull company. Let us, rather, set the dial back to 120,-

000,000 years ago, to the beginning of the Cretaceous Period. On our compressed time scale, this equals about five and a half hours. Off we go . . .

The smaller stars wink out; a band of pallor spreads across the eastern skyline, above the saw-toothed bank of blackness that sunders water from sky. Mirroring the growing light, the surface of the lagoon pales likewise. As the sky changes from black to deep blue, small, shadowy things dart and whirl on pointed wings across the celestial dome.

The light waxes. A stripe of apple-green takes form along the eastern horizon and, rising, gives place to a band of lemon-yellow, followed in turn by one of tangerine. The whole sky lightens, revealing that the sable, saw-toothed strip, surrounding us in all directions but south, is the edge of a forest, which crowds to the margins of the lagoon and the mighty river that feeds it.

Northward, the river's several mouths wind sluggishly amongst the reed beds, silently pouring their fresh floods into the brackish waters of the lagoon. Southward stretches the lagoon, dotted with sand bars and banks of reeds, extending to the horizon. Thither the skyline is fenced by rows of far-off, palmlike trees, which stand along the keys that separate lagoon from sea. But the sea is too distant for sound of surf to reach us, save in the stormiest weather. And this dawn is quiet and clear. The air is damp and mild and still, with only a hint of the steamy heat of the coming day.

There is little sound except the buzz and chirp of unseen insects and the lapping of wavelets from the lagoon. Now and then the sharp-winged little fliers overhead emit faint, high-pitched cheeps. Out in the lagoon, a fish goes *splash,* with a spray of diamond droplets and a widening bull's eye of circular ripples.

The final stars depart. The bands of celestial color merge into the growing blueness of the sky-bowl as, above the ebon treetops, rises the scarlet buckler of the morning sun. The level rays touch the darting fliers with crimson. When one swoops close, its eye flashes in the sunlight like some mystic ruby.

This sparrow-sized creature is not a bird, nor yet is it a bat, despite its short, soft coat of russet fur. The head, mounted on a thread-like neck, resembles that of a lizard, with slender, tapering jaws and tiny teeth. The pointed wings are delicate webs of skin, extended by a single oversized finger along its leading edge, not spread umbrella-wise by four such fingers as with a bat.

Suddenly, the bat-lizard jinks in flight; its jaws snap shut upon a bulky, blundering moth. With tiny crop bulging from its morning foray, the little flier zooms off towards its favorite tree, to hang upside down in blissful digestion throughout the long, steamy day.

Glowing redly through the hazy, pollen-laden air, the sun rises clear of the forest, whence something sends forth three sharp squawks like the caw of a crow. Individual trees and shrubs stand out, each twig and leaf and frond revealed in the coppery light.

Along the beaches and on the islets that stipple the spacious lagoon grow palmlike cycads, their barrel-trunks dotted with large, curious flowers. Among them stand clumps of tree ferns; masses of jade-pale fronds spray like fountains from the tops of their palmlike trunks.

Back from the shoreline, in the forest proper, the overwhelming mass of trees are somber, needle-bearing evergreens: pines and cedars, firs and spruces, yews and larches, hemlocks, cypresses, and gigantic redwoods. The only broad-leafed tree in sight is an occasional ginkgo, its little fan-shaped leaves close-set upon thick, tentacular boughs.

On the ground grow smaller herbs and weeds in vast variety. But there is no grass. Nor are there flowers, save those on the trunks of the cycads.

As the sun turns sluggishly from red to yellow, the swooping little insect-hunting fliers streak off one by one, until none is left. In their place, a pair of larger lizard-bats—gull-sized, with fangsome beaks—skim the watery mirror. Back and forth they glide, a hand's breadth above the surface, scarcely moving their wings save for a languid flap at the end of each glide. This enables them to rise above the aqueous pavement far enough to permit a banking turn. Back and forth they go, tracing grids of parallel lines with reptilian patience.

At last one swerves and snaps; the mirror is riven in a spray of droplets. The fisher has caught a three-inch, minnowlike fingerling, quivering with the hurt of needle-fangs that pierce it through and through. The flier stirs its languid, leathery pinions to gain altitude, jerks its head, and tosses its captive high in the air above it. With coördination a human juggler would fail to match in a lifetime of practice, it catches its minnow in a wide-gaping maw and gulps it down. Then back and forth again.

A little breeze springs up, ruffling the surface of the lagoon. The yellow sun shines down upon a sand bar at the mouth of one of the river's many branches. No trees grow upon this bar; however, scattered helter-skelter upon it, we notice several tapering trunks of tree ferns or cycads, in length from three to twenty feet. But wait! One of these logs opens narrow, many-fanged jaws and closes them again. Then it rises to four stumpy legs, **quietly** walks to the water's edge, slips in with hardly a ripple, and disappears. The other crocodiles remain recumbent on the sand, as immobile as creatures cast in lead.

Except for the ever-flitting fishers, all is still again. On one of the narrow, sandy beaches, where the forest marches to the borders of the lagoon, a flash of motion catches our attention. A tiny mammal, mouselike in size and appearance, dashes out from the cover of the forest litter and races a few feet along the sand. After it scuttles another of its kind. The first mammal, as if suddenly aware of the enormity of showing itself in broad daylight, whips into the shadows again, with the other in close pursuit. This incident is part of the never-ending struggle for territory among members of the same species; for the pursuer is evicting a trespasser from his private worm-and-insect hunting preserve.

Presently, another crocodile crawls to the water. As it slithers in, another clambers out, strides stumpily ashore, drops its scaly belly to the sand, and in turn becomes a piece of leaden statuary.

The whitening sun climbs slowly higher, with intensifying glare. After a quiet interlude, another movement manifests itself. Down the beach, where the river mouth joins the lagoon, a small creature deliberately picks its way. A yard long and lizardlike, it walks bipedally on hindlegs much longer than its forelegs. As the little dinosaur (for such it is) progresses, it bobs its head forward and back, as does a walking pigeon. Its walk is like that of a chicken, searching the ground before it for its food.

A tiny true lizard now scurries across the sand. The little dinosaur dashes after it. With a flirt of its tail, the lizard streaks into the trees and scuttles up the nearest trunk.

Foiled, the little dinosaur returns to the beach and renews its stalk. Something at the water's edge catches its eye or nostril. It runs to where a dead crustacean lies decomposing upon its back. The dinosaur walks around the corpse, looking at it cautiously first with one eye and then with the other. Then it plants a foot firmly upon the small cadaver and, with jaws and fore-claws, begins to tear it apart.

With a crackling of trodden twigs and a swish of leaves, a heavy body moves through the forest. The little dinosaur jerks up its head and prances about, watching for danger. The shrubbery parts as a heavy, twelve-foot reptile lumbers out on four stout limbs upon the sand. Its hindlegs exceed its fore in length, so that its back rises to a height of five feet over its hips. Its small, nondescript, reptilian head is set upon a thick, dewlap-dangling neck. The scales along its back and heavy, trailing tail are keeled, like those of a crocodile; over its neck and shoulder the keels are prolonged into three-inch spikes.

Prepared to flee, the little dinosaur dances back from its dead crab; but then, seeing that the new arrival is a harmless eater of plants, it returns to its feast. The larger dinosaur, ignoring the smaller, drinks at the water's edge and shambles back into the woods.

The sun climbs higher. Another crocodile lumbers out of the water to join its fellows in slumber on the sand bar. The fishing lizard-bats have gone away, perhaps to seek smoother water on which to ply their trade. For a long moment, nothing moves except the little dinosaur, tearing at its carrion.

Three loud squawks again resound from the woods; this time the squawker appears. It is a crow-sized bird—but a very strange bird indeed, with a lizardlike head, jaws full of small, sharp teeth, and a long reptilian tail, from which large feathers sprout in a row down each side, reminding one of the tail of a kite. The lizard-bird issues from the woods and flaps heavily across the river, as if barely able to maintain altitude. It crashes clumsily into the nearest tree and scrambles actively up the trunk, using claws on the leading edge of its wing joints to help it along. A couple of roosting bat-lizards squeak angrily at the bird, drop from their perches, and soar away to other trees.

A watery sound from the west has been rising so slowly that we have only just now recognized it: a sound of splashing and dripping, as if large animals were moving leisurely about in the shallows. Then they appear around a bend in the shoreline of the lagoon—first one, then another, then a whole herd. They are sauropod dinosaurs: creatures that seem to combine the body and legs of a super-colossal elephant with the head, neck, and tail of a gigantic snake.

There are fourteen of these monsters in the herd. Four are full-grown, exceeding sixty feet in length and standing more than fifteen feet high over the hips, although we do not at first realize this height because they are wading half-submerged. The rest are smaller, ranging down to a couple only fifteen feet long.

All are grazing on the reeds. A neck comes down; the jaws of the little head open, revealing a battery of peglike teeth. The animal pulls up a few mouthfuls of water plants before the neck rises so that gravity can help the food on its way to the gizzard. For a few minutes, we can watch the bulge travel down the beast's interminable throat, until it is lost in the mass of the colossal trunk. Then down goes the neck again. All fourteen sauropods constantly raise and lower their heads as they feed, reminding us of a battery of dredges clearing a silted river bottom.

The sauropods laze along the shore, eating, eating, eating, and now and then taking a step or two. As they reach the bend in the shoreline where the river joins the lagoon, they halt, peering dim-wittedly this way and that. Then, moved by some mysterious instinct, they all set out at an active amble towards the other side of the river, with water boiling around their tree-trunk limbs. Where the bottom shoals, they rise until only their lower legs are submerged. With each step, their colossal feet sink deeply into the mud and come out of the holes thus made with loud, sucking gurgles. They move at a steady, plodding walk, which covers ground faster than we realize because of the enormous length of their strides.

Where the water deepens again, the sauropods keep moving. Some of the smaller ones are forced to swim, and this they accomplish with calm competence. In half an hour or more, we see them marching eastward along the shore of the lagoon away from us. They feed as they go, their heads and necks still rising and falling, until they shrink with the distance and finally vanish around another point.

Now the sun is high and hot. Again the leaves rustle with the passage of heavy bodies, and three more large dinosaurs appear from the forest. These are bipeds, built somewhat along the lines of the little carnivore—now finishing its crab—only on a much larger scale. The largest measures twenty-five feet in length and carries its head twelve feet or so above the ground. Like the little flesh-eater, it stalks on its hindlegs, its tail rising like a rigid boom to the rear to balance the weight of its head and nearly horizontal body. Its forelimbs end in hands with four fingers and, in place of the thumb, a sharp, horny spike set at right angles to the axis of the limb. The big dewlap that hangs down from its throat sways from side to side as its moves its head. Its massive build and ponderous movements suggest a plant-eater.

Resting their tails on the sand behind them, the three iguanodons squat down on all fours and bend their heads to the water. Their muzzles touch the surface, sending out circles of ripple as they drink: *shloop, shloop, shloop.* It takes a long time to fill their bulging paunches; but at last they rise and return to the woods.

The midday hush descends. Insects buzz; the crocodiles slumber. A turtle crawls out upon a log to sun itself. The little flesh-eating dinosaur completes its meal and disappears into the forest. For hours, nothing whatever happens under the burning sun.

The sun moves slowly down the arch of its path towards the western horizon. High in the deep, blue sky, a thin layer of mackerel cloud moves like an awning athwart the sun, making the light hazy and illusive. Perhaps it is going to rain before long. A big bat-lizard flies overhead, several hundred feet up, moving purposefully on business of its own. More lizards scuttle briefly across the glowing sand.

A crash of shrubbery heralds the arrival of a herd of plant-eating dinosaurs. Seven burst out of the forest and make for the water. They are bipeds—like the little flesh-eater and the three iguanodons—but of intermediate size, five to seven feet in length with heads two to four feet from the ground. They move quickly and nervously, looking this way and that. At the water, they do not drink their fill with noisy imperturbability, as did their predecessors. Instead, they sip a swallow, raise their heads to glance about, and then snatch another mouthful of water.

While they are so engaged, another reptilian biped bursts out of the woods and advances upon them with long, aggressive strides. The newcomer—as we can see from its sharp claws and great, curved fangs —is a flesh-eater. Fifteen feet long, it carries its head six or seven feet above the ground. Its huge hindlegs end in toes equipped with talons like those of some monstrous bird of prey. Its forelegs are likewise armed but so much smaller as to be of no use in locomotion.

The carnivore—a kind of dinosaur called a carnosaur—comes on with a steady, pounding rush, swaying its head from side to side to keep its balance. One of the plant-eaters emits a honking cry of warning, and the herd bursts into frenzied motion. Some splash into the water; others dash along the beach in either direction, at right angles to the carnosaur's line of approach.

In the first frantic scramble, one of the plant-eaters caroms into a fellow-creature and falls down. It is instantly on its feet again, but the delay proves fatal. Before it can sprint for safety, the carnivore's jaws open like those of a power shovel and slam shut upon its victim's back.

The prey honks madly, kicks wildly, and lashes its tail. Sand is thrown in all directions. But its attacker sinks its fangs deeper and shakes its head violently from side to side, tearing open the herbivore's leathery hide. Blood spatters the sand. Still keeping its original grip, the big carnosaur hoists its victim into the air, slams it down upon the hot sand, hoists it up, slams it down again.

At the first sounds of conflict, the turtle drops off its log. Several of the crocodiles have opened their eyes; a small one slips into the water. And still the massacre goes on: *slam, slam!*

Little by little, the struggles of the plant-eater grow feebler and less coördinated. At last there is only a spasmodic twitching of limbs. The carnosaur, whose jaws have never released their original hold, plants one clawed hind foot upon its prey and starts to pull and wrench at it. Tirelessly, it worries at its repast, clawing at the hide with its taloned hands, until at last a whole section of the victim's back tears loose. Blood pours over the sand, making crimson puddles, saturating the ground, then running on to form another puddle.

Slowly, with repeated gulps and jerks of its head, the flesh-eater works the bloody mass of hide and meat back into its throat. The piece looks too large for the eater's gullet; but the creature manages to swallow, although its flexible skull has to give a little here and there to enable it to do so. A final effort squeezes shut its big, yellow, gemlike eyes, and the gory gobbet is downed. The reptile's throat bulges to the limit of distension and then shrinks back to its normal, wattled form.

The killer does not go at once for another mouthful. Its eating, like its other actions, is governed by the sluggish rhythms of reptilian life. For some minutes it stands, braced on its hindlegs and tail, swinging its big head this way and that, while its throat-skin ripples as the muscles work within. Watching for others who might want to rob it of its hard-earned meal, the carnosaur pensively picks its teeth with the claws of one forelimb.

Soon, would-be robbers appear. The first to come is the little, yard-long carnivore (a coelurosaur, to name it rightly) who ate the crab. After it, another of its kind tiptoes towards the slayer and the slain. With a sonorous grunt, the carnosaur suddenly lurches towards them, and the two little fellows scurry away along the beach. The big one returns to its prey, which still twitches and writhes a little from time to time.

The killer is just downing a second huge mouthful when another carnosaur appears across the river. The newcomer is of the same species as the killer and a little larger. Since the river is shallow, the new arrival wades, splashing vigorously, across the bottom towards the slayer.

The latter watches the newcomer with big, bright, golden eyes. The approaching carnosaur slows and halts, thirty feet from its rival.

The two reptiles glare at each other. Again the killer utters that resonant grunt; the newcomer grunts back. For several minutes they stand, heads outthrust and jaws open, grunting. Their great jaws open and snap with sharp reports.

The sun, shining sallowly through thin, high clouds, slides down towards the horizon. The two carnivores still stand, grunting. At last the killer explodes into action. Head outstretched and jaws agape, it strides towards its antagonist, splashing into the shallows. Although the other has the advantage of size, it does not await the attack. It backs away. When its pursuer pauses, it wheels and hastens back across the river and vanishes into the trees. Its tiny brain does not harbor many thoughts, but it does know that it was trespassing upon another's turf.

The killer returns to shore, pausing to roar at the two little coelurosaurs, which have run up to the carcass to snatch a mouthful before the owner returns. As they flee, the killer pursues for a few paces and then goes back to its repast.

One more interruption. From the woods comes another plant-eater for a drink. This is a heavily built quadruped, like the one that appeared earlier in the day but larger—about fifteen feet long—and more formidably armed. Along its back, from head to mid-body, runs a double row of huge, hornlike spines, slightly curved like the horns of African cattle. There are seven pairs of these horns, the tallest a yard in length. Aft of the spines, a huge shield of bone covers the entire hip region, while down its long, heavy tail runs a double row of erect, sharp-edged plates.

Instantly aware of the newcomer, the killer raises its head. The plant-eater is slow; it moves its head vaguely about, near-sightedly peering. Seeing the killer, it halts stock-still. For some minutes, unmoving, the two stare at each other. Again the flesh-eater bends over the carcass, while the herbivore placidly drinks and returns to the woods. Its instincts tell it that, safe in its armor, it has little to fear.

The carnosaur has now torn loose and swallowed four big bites of its prey. Soon it will reach a comfortably sated state, lie down across the carcass (to make sure its booty is not stolen) and go into a disgestive torpor that will last for days. But this happy state is not to be attained. Out of the woods, fifty yards upstream, comes another carnivore, belonging to an even larger species. It is a massive monster well over thirty feet long, weighing as much as an elephant.

Along the winding beach, the two reptiles stare intently at each other. Then the larger approaches with ponderous strides. From the nearby sand bar all the crocodiles, most of whom have lain unmoving since dawn, slip quickly into the water.

As the hijacker comes on, the killer gives its challenging grunt. The newcomer answers with a deep, booming bellow. When the big fellow is only a few yards from its adversary, it lunges out, its huge jaws snapping shut with a noise like a slamming door.

The roaring and grunting of the two dinosaurs drowns out all other sounds. From the noise alone, one would expect to see a bloody battle joined; actually, while the two roar and lunge and snap in terrifying fashion, neither touches the other. And, as the new arrival comes closer, the killer begins to back away. It grunts and snaps in a frenzy of rage, but still it backs.

Then, just as the hijacker aims a terrific snap at the head of its foe, the smaller carnivore jerks away, wheels, and pounds off down the beach. The larger monster lumbers in pursuit, but not for long. As it is too heavy to run fast, the other soon outdistances it.

Meanwhile, a few feet from the mangled carcass, the narrow snout of a crocodile rises from the water. While the new conqueror is chasing the killer along the beach, the wily crocodile crawls partway out on land. With head and forelegs out of the water, its muzzle reaches the carcass. A quick snap fastens its jaws upon the bloody mass, whose limbs give a final twitch. Then its powerful tail backs water with a reversed sculling motion. Crocodile, carcass, and all slip back into the water, leaving only a few incarnadined eddies to mark its departure.

When the hijacker returns, there is no prey to be eaten. The astonished carnosaur weaves its head about, scanning the landscape. With a bellow of frustration, it paces heavily up and down the beach. It splashes into the shallows, striding back and forth. But its meal has disappeared. For half an hour it continues, with dumb persistence, to hunt for its dinner, as the sun vanishes behind a bank of low clouds and the light dims. At last the hungry hijacker gives up and crashes off through the woods in search of other prey.

Above the band of crimson in the west, the silver sickle of a new moon shines, like the fingernail paring of a god. As the moon in turn sinks towards the mass of clouds boiling up in the west, a few bright stars shine dimly through the high veil of cirrus overhead. Nocturnal insects strike up their evening song. Aloft, the little, insect-eating lizard-bats swirl and soar once more on narrow, pointed, leathern wings. Across the dim beaches, the mouselike mammals run.

Darkness falls . . .

The day that we have just spent along that sandy beach of 120 million years ago belongs to a period when the dominant animals of land, sea, and air were reptiles. Among these reptiles, the dinosaurs were the most spectacular, although they were by no means the only kind of saurian. So many and so varied were the reptiles then that they have given their name to a whole era of geological time. The first of the dinosaurs trod the earth as much as 175 million years ago; the last of them departed about a hundred million years later, leaving whole quarriesful of fossil bones and petrified footprints to mark their passing but no certain evidence to explain their extinction.

Nothing outside of our wildest nightmares can compare with these bizarre creatures, of which, for the most part, only fragments have come down to us. Still, during the past century and a half, we have learned much about dinosaurs—their appearance and their habits— because a few dedicated men have gathered their remains, pieced together their shattered bones, and unraveled the story of their lives.

In this book, we shall meet some of the lumbering dragons of the Age of Reptiles and some of the scientists who found and studied them. There is drama and humor in the search for their bones and much keen detective work in the reconstruction of their shapes and their environment. Besides meeting the dinosaurs and their discoverers, we shall see how the fossils of these reptiles confirm the belief that the simpler forms of life develop into the more complex, and how, traveling the long road of evolutionary development, man himself came to bear the form he has today.

2

The Finding of the Dragons

To re-create the giant reptiles of a hundred million years ago takes more than a fertile imagination. It requires an understanding of how rocks were formed, laborious digging into sandpits and quarries, long hours of piecing broken bones together, and the reasoning power to infer from a jawbone or a footprint what kind of life some vanished life form led. To comprehend the labor that clothes each skeleton with the aura of life, we, too, must know something of geology (the science of the earth) and paleontology (the science of fossilized animals found within the earth).

For more than twenty-five centuries, men have found fossils and sometimes recognized them for what they were. The first man known to have mentioned them was Xenophanes of Kolophon, a Greek philosopher from Asia Minor who lived six centuries before Christ and who spent his last years in Italy. Xenophanes correctly inferred from the presence of fossil sea shells on the Italian mountain tops that Italy had once risen out of the sea.

A hundred years later, Xanthos the Lydian explained fossil shells in Asia Minor in the same manner. A few years afterwards, when the historian Herodotos visited Egypt, he likewise reasoned that the sea must once have covered most of that land because "I observed that there were shells upon the hills."[1]

Xenophanes, Xanthos, and Herodotos thus showed better sense than many later thinkers. During the Middle Ages, dinosaur fossils found in Europe were thought to be the remains of mythical fire-breathing dragons, or of Hannibal's elephants, or of the giants mentioned in Genesis vi, 4. Some people asserted that fossils were not even relics of living things, but were "sports of nature"—that is, blobs of minerals that happened to look like bones or shells. Others claimed that fossils were pseudo-bones that were formed from the rocks by some mysterious generating power in the earth or by the influence of the stars. Still others said they were models, which God had made when he was practicing for the Creation. Professor J. B. A. Beringer of the University of Württemberg even averred, in the early eighteenth century, that they were a divine hoax to test men's faith.

In the seventeenth century, several men of science like Nils Steensen of Copenhagen (who Latinized his name to Nicolaus Steno) argued convincingly that fossils were the remains of living things, citing such examples as fossil sharks' teeth shaped exactly like the teeth of modern sharks. After that, people who studied fossils little by little came around to the belief that fossils were indeed the relics of bygone organisms.

The word "fossil" first was used by a sixteenth-century German physician, Georgius Agricola,[2] who wrote about the earth and its products. Scientific knowledge in those days was so slim that Agricola, who composed the pioneer treatise on mining, also wrote a perfectly serious work on gnomes in the earth and how to get rid of them. He used the word "fossil," from the Latin *fossum,* "dug," to cover anything dug out of the earth—coal, minerals, and ores. Gradually, the word came to be limited to objects, found in the earth or its rocks, that were the remains of living things.

In later centuries, the word "fossil" has been stretched to cover such traces of former life as fossil eggs, footprints, excrement, the burrows of worms and rodents, and the perishable parts of plants and animals preserved by drying, freezing, or chemical action. In addition to footprints hardened into sandstone, casts of the skin of dinosaurs have been found, as well as the soft parts and even whole bodies of comparatively recent mammals.

Fossils may consist of the original material of the animals or plants, or of this material more or less changed. For example, coal consists of masses of fossil vegetation from which the lighter elements have departed, leaving only the carbon. Although, in most mine coal, the remains are a formless mass, sometimes a whole fossil tree transformed into coal still keeps its shape. Sometimes, soft-bodied animals are likewise preserved as thin black films of carbon.

Often, plants and animals are more or less mineralized. Sometimes, as the soft parts decay, the hollows they leave are filled with a mineral such as sandstone, while the hard parts remain much as before. Sometimes the hard parts, too, are slowly replaced when water seeps through rock, taking away the original substances atom by atom and replacing them by atoms of minerals. These minerals may preserve the form of the original with the utmost fidelity, down to its microscopic cell structure; or they may make only a rough copy of it. Bone resists replacement more stubbornly than wood or shell. Hence fossil bones—even quite ancient ones—are apt to contain much of the original bone substance.

Sometimes an animal is buried in a compact material that solidifies before the animal decays. Thus is formed a hollow space or *mold* shaped like the original animal. This mold may remain hollow, or it may fill up with another mineral to make a *cast*. An extraordinary mold found in Oregon proved to have the form of an extinct rhinoceros. The beast had been caught in a volcanic eruption and covered with lava; the lava had hardened around its body before the body had disintegrated. This hollow space not only preserved the shape of the animal but also still held a few charred bones. Similar molds of several people and one dog were created in A.D. 79, when a rain of volcanic ash from Mount Vesuvius buried the Roman provincial town of Pompeii.

For a living thing to become a fossil, it must have the luck to be buried soon after death, so that oxygen and oxygen-breathing organisms cannot reach it. On land, such burials may take place in quicksands, bogs, swamps, and small, stagnant bodies of water. Although some animals are fossilized after they have drifted about in the waters of rivers and lakes, such animals are less likely to be preserved whole.

Some swamps are better at preserving their victims than others. Much depends upon the local chemistry of the soil and the water. Some mudholes are almost sterile and hence excellent burial places, while others teem with life or have chemical action that causes rapid decay.

In dry regions, sandstorms often bury and preserve animals. In the Gobi Desert, for example, whole herds of dinosaurs and early mammals perished thus and have been recovered only recently by a Polish woman scientist. One of the world's richest fossil deposits has been found in the tar pits of Rancho La Brea, in Los Angeles. Here seepage from underground petroleum beds created pools of half-liquid natural asphalt; and rain water lying on top of the asphalt attracted thousands of animals to their doom. Over the millennia, mammoths, mastodons, ground sloths, saber-toothed cats, camels, horses, bison, bears, wolves, condors, and other denizens of Pleistocene California were trapped in the tar. Thus these pits have given us a splendid picture of animal life in this area and have filled out many museum collections throughout the United States.

Some animals and plants are preserved when they sink to the bottom near the mouths of large, muddy rivers and are promptly covered with silt that hardens into sandstone. Others die in the shallows that rim many of the world's oceans and seas. If local conditions cause limestone in the water to form rocky concretions, this fine rock forms protective coatings alike around the bones and shells of ancient organisms and the sunken hulls of ancient ships.

There are also some rare fossils, such as insects preserved in amber —a fossilized pine resin found along the shores of the Baltic Sea—or the gizzard stones of plant-eating dinosaurs, which swallowed stones to act as grinders in their auxiliary stomachs.

Despite all these various ways that fossils may be created, only an extremely small fraction of all the billions of ancient plants and animals have had the good fortune to be preserved for posterity. When most living things die, swarms of scavengers, from invisible bacteria up to crabs, hyenas, and vultures, descend upon them and swiftly consume them. Scavengers soon demolish even so large a carcass as that of an elephant. The skin and entrails decay; porcupines gnaw the tusks; while the bones, which are spongy despite their size, crumble away. Smaller organisms disappear even more quickly. Birds are often swallowed whole, while the remains of larger animals are readily torn apart and scattered.

Few indeed are the plants and animals that have left recognizable remains; fewer still have had the luck to be found by fossil-hunters. Many fossils may lie in their rocks for millions of years, only to be mashed out of shape by the stresses in the earth's mobile crust. The movement of the crust may lower the bed of rock so deep that it will never see the light of day again. Or the rock may be thrust up so high that winds and rains carve it into mountains and valleys. In such eroded rock, the fossils crumble away into sand or silt, which, in time, may be redeposited to form a new fossil-bearing bed.

Therefore, the fossils that men have recovered do not give a complete or even a balanced picture of ancient life. In the great majority of the cases, the only parts that survive are the bones and teeth of vertebrate animals, the shells of mollusks, and impressions of the horny, jointed armor of such arthropods as insects, spiders, and crabs.

In any real fauna, the small animals vastly outnumber the large. But these small animals are less likely to be fossilized than the large. For one thing, their bones are more readily carried off to be gnawed than are the larger bones. For another, small skull bones are comparatively thin and fragile, so that many specimens of small to medium size are found in a headless condition. At Kindope, near Tendaguru in Africa, for instance, German scientists found 15,000 bones of dinosaurs but only six skulls.

Moreover, small, agile creatures are less likely than large, heavy, lumbering land animals to be trapped in quicksands, swamps, and bogs. Hence, fossilized birds are extremely rare, although throughout the Age of Mammals, we believe, small birds were as numerous as they are now.

Likewise, fossilized animals from lowland habitats outnumber those from upland regions, since swamps and bogs occur mostly in low-lying land, not in the mountains.

Furthermore, sea-dwelling animals are much more likely to be preserved than land forms. In point of fact, most of the actual fossil beds are marine deposits; and most of the fossils in them are sea shells.

Further to complicate the record, most practicing paleontologists are *invertebrate paleontologists*—men interested in fossil animals without backbones—and most of the published material has to do with invertebrate remains. This is not surprising when one considers that invertebrate paleontology is economically useful to oil and mining companies, whose success depends upon locating mineral deposits by means of the fossils in adjacent beds of rock.

The *vertebrate paleontologist,* who studies animals with backbones and who deals with such dramatic fossils as dinosaurs or such scientifically potent ones as man's apish ancestors, has no such secure economic base to operate from. He must become a university professor or a museum curator; and the number of such posts is limited. Or he must be wealthy in his own right. As a result of the economic factor, all the vertebrate paleontologists in the world today could probably be numbered in the hundreds or at most in the low thousands. And rare indeed in the life of one of these is the thrill of discovering a perfect fossil skeleton.

Finally, as a general rule, the more recent a geological period, the more numerous are its fossil-bearing beds. Conversely, the more ancient the period, the fewer the fossils, because the older a fossil, the greater are its chances of being destroyed by geological forces. Hence, ancient faunas are more scantily represented than those of more recent date, even though the actual life of the earlier periods may have been as rich and teeming as that of any later time.

Thus, to get a truthful picture of the life of a former age, we must correct the fossil record. We must visualize complete animals from fragmentary remains. We must imagine small animals as far more numerous than their remains would indicate. We must assume that the upland and mountain faunas were richer than their scanty fossil traces imply.

Lastly, we must bear in mind that the fossil record is uneven from age to age. We can recover only those fossils that just now happen to be at or close to the surface of the earth. Millions of fascinating fossils lie buried deep under layers of more recent rock or have sunk beneath the restless sea. And millions more have been destroyed forever by the implacable, never-ending process of erosion.

For these reasons, one who is interested in life of the past must know something about the science of geology and about the way in which the rocks have revealed their age.

The science of geology dates from the eighteenth century. Although the scientific revolution began a hundred years earlier, geology was long impeded by a nearly universal acceptance in Europe and America of the myth of the Creation, as told in Genesis.

One scientist, in the sixteenth century, died in the Bastille for suggesting that Genesis could not be taken literally; in the next century, another was burned at the stake for the same heresy. Even as late as the nineteenth century, it took no small courage to run counter to established religious beliefs and proclaim the facts about the history of the earth and the life that has dwelt upon it.

The science of geology came into being as a result of mining operations. As the need for coal, to turn the wheels of the Industrial Revolution, became more and more acute, mines grew deeper and deeper. Consequently, men urgently needed to learn all they could about the composition of the earth's crust.

The leading geologist of the eighteenth century was Abraham Gottlob Werner (1750–1817), a neat, pudgy little German with heavy eyebrows under his white peruke. Werner did more than any one other man to put the study of the earth on a scientific basis. He showed once and for all that stratified rocks were laid down in a definite order, with the more recent rocks normally lying on top of older rocks, like the layers of a layer cake.

Werner mistakenly believed that all these layers or *strata* had been deposited by water. The earth, he thought, had once been covered by a deep, muddy, soupy, world-wide ocean; and, as this ocean subsided, the solid materials in the water settled down into layer upon layer of rock. This came to be known as the "Neptunian" theory.

Against Werner's Neptunian theory, the Scotsman James Hutton, in the 1790s, put forth his more accurate "Plutonist" theory. According to this theory, only some of the rocks—those called *sedimentary*—had been made by the settling of mud. Other rocks, called *igneous,* had been formed by "fires inside the earth"—that is, by volcanic action, either near the surface of the earth or deep within it.

Finally, around 1800, the Englishman William Smith (among others) showed that the age and order of formation of the various strata of sedimentary rocks could be determined by comparing the fossil sea shells buried within them. The shells on which Smith largely relied were those of ammonites, ancient relatives of the squid and the octopus.

As the science of geology grew, geologists learned that the main classes of rock were the sedimentary, the igneous, and the metamorphic. Sedimentary rocks, like sandstone and limestone, were laid down by water—or on rare occasions by wind—layer upon layer. Igneous rocks, like granite and basalt, were formed by cooling from the molten state. The more slowly a rock cooled, the coarser its texture became. Metamorphic rocks, like gneiss and schist, developed when either sedimentary or igneous rocks were altered by heat, pressure, or other forces within the earth's crust.

Pressures like these not only altered the texture of the rocks themselves, but also often bent, twisted, folded, raised, or lowered the original rocks, sometimes thousands of feet. Forces like these caused coastal lands to rise, so that the sea shells of one period could be found upon the mountains of a later time.

With rare exceptions, like that rhinoceros buried in lava, all fossils are found in sedimentary rocks. In fact, some sedimentary rocks contain solid masses of fossils. Coal, for example, is a mass of fossil plants; while chalk and diatomite (used in making dynamite) are composed of the skeletons of one-celled organisms. Other sedimentary rocks contain few or no fossils.

The richest sources of such fossil land animals as dinosaurs are certain kinds of shale (solidified clay) and sandstone (solidified sand). In general, the finer the sand, the better the fossils are preserved. Of course, if the bed of sedimentary rocks has been subjected to the metamorphic process, the fossils within are usually destroyed or so changed that they can no longer be recognized.

As nineteenth-century geologists studied the types of fossils buried in sedimentary deposits, it soon became apparent that outcrops of rock in different parts of Europe and America bore fossils similar in kind and number. By observing the sea creatures in various beds of sedimentary rock, and by matching these beds with others of like fossil faunas and so going farther and farther back in time, geologists since Werner, Hutton, and Smith have built up a detailed and, on the whole, trustworthy picture of the order in which rocks were laid down.

People sometimes ask: Geologists date fossils by the rock formations in which they occur, and date the rocks by the fossils in them. Isn't this arguing in a circle? No, it really is not. In sedimentary formations, the more recent generally lie on top of the older. There are exceptions, as when the movement of the earth's crust bends the beds into folds and wrinkles. In such cases, however, the geological processes usually leave plain indications.

When strata are piled up in the normal fashion, with the youngest on top, fossils in them come in a definite order. For example, suppose a mollusk was evolving during a certain period, then we find it occurring in the strata as follows:

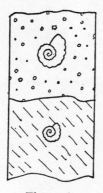

Figure 1.

with the larger type, having the larger number of turns, on top. If we find another bed in which mollusks of the same kind occur as follows:

Figure 2.

then we can match up the two sets of beds, as follows:

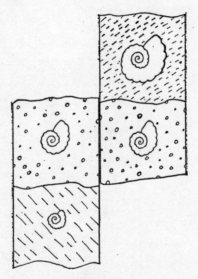

Figure 3.

Around 1800, William Smith in England, using the mollusks called ammonites, worked out this method of "stratigraphic correlation," as this matching of beds by their fossils is called.

The earth, as we have said, is old—so old that it takes imagination to gain even a rough impression of its antiquity. Not even today has it been definitely established exactly how long each era really was.

For the past two centuries, scientists have been trying to estimate the age of the earth and to measure the lengths of the epochs into which its existence is divided. The elegant French naturalist, Georges Leclerc, Comte de Buffon (1707–88) was one of the first to try to calculate the age of the earth. In his time, men had already guessed that the sun had somehow given birth to the earth, or that a single event had produced both bodies. They also knew from volcanic eruptions that, deep inside its rocky crust, the earth was hot. It seemed likely, therefore, that the earth had once been white-hot, like the sun, and had slowly cooled to its present state.

Buffon ordered a number of balls of stone and of metal to aid his calculations. One by one, he placed them in a wire holder, heated them to white heat, and allowed them to cool. From the time it took these balls to cool, he calculated that a ball the size of the earth would take 74,832 years to cool to its present temperature. It was a good first try, but—as things turned out—Buffon's answer was wildly wrong.

Some decades before Buffon's experiment, the British astronomer Edmund Halley suggested another way of computing the age of the earth. Halley assumed that the oceans started as fresh-water bodies and that salt had been dissolved out of the rocks by rain water and carried into the sea by rivers. By estimating the rate at which all the world's rivers were carrying salt to the sea, he thought, one could compute how long this process had been going on.

In the 1890s, Lord Kelvin made this calculation and concluded that the earth was between twenty and forty million years old. The geologists King, Becker, and others used the same method and estimated the earth's age from 24,000,000 to 100,000,000 years. Other scientists tried to estimate the time required for rivers to lay down the beds of silt that later turned into sedimentary rocks; but none of these calculations gave consistent results.

Early in the present century, Henry Norris Russell in the United

States and Arthur Holmes in England finally solved the problem. They fixed the age of the earth by means of radioactivity.

The dense, radioactive metal uranium, like other radioactive elements, breaks down, an atom at a time, into other substances. Each atom, after a long series of changes, ends its career as an atom of a particular kind of lead, called lead-206. This disintegration takes place at a uniformly decreasing rate. Of any lump of uranium, one per cent will change into lead-206 in about 66,000,000 years. During the next 66,000,000 years, 1% of the remainder changes into lead-206. Thus the amount of uranium in the sample constantly decreases but never reaches zero.

A piece of uranium ore always contains some lead-206. Hence we can tell the length of time that has passed since a sample of ore took solid form by measuring the percentage of lead-206 in it. The oldest uranium-bearing rock so far measured turns out to be well over two billion years old. The earth as a whole must have existed for at least three billion years; some estimates put its age as high as ten to fourteen billion.

The discovery of radioactivity also showed why the Comte de Buffon went astray in his calculation of the earth's age. The decay of radioactive elements gives out heat. One pound of uranium gives out very little heat, but all together the radioactive elements in the earth emit enormous amounts of heat. This heat replaces the heat that is slowly leaking away through the earth's crust into outer space. Therefore, the earth's rate of cooling is much slower than anything Buffon could possibly have imagined.

The uranium-lead method of dating rocks does not work for such comparatively short periods as a million years. To date events since the appearance of man, we must rely upon other methods. Some of these are chemical, some involve radioactivity, and some call for counting tree rings or the layers of silt laid down each year on the bottoms of lakes. The best-known is the radiocarbon method discovered by Willard F. Libby in the late 1940s. However, since this book is concerned with the much more ancient rocks, we need not go into the details of these other methods.

Table 1 and the charts on the endpapers of this book give the reader a rough idea of the comparative length of the major eras and their main subdivisions. It also shows how recently man has arrived on the face of the earth.

ERA	PERIOD	CHARACTERISTIC LIFE	LENGTH, MILLIONS OF YEARS	DATES, B.C.
Cenozoic	Pleistocene	Mammoths, man	2	2,000,000
	Pliocene	Two—tusked mastodonts, apelike submen	10	
	Miocene	Four—tusked mastodonts, Proconsul (common ancestor of apes and men)	15	
	Oligocene	Titanotheres, entelodonts	10	
	Eocene	Uintatheres, creodonts	18	
	Paleocene	Small, archaic mammals	15	70,000,000
Mesozoic	Cretaceous	Last dinosaurs, angiosperms	60	
	Jurassic	Dinosaurs, first birds and mammals	35	
	Triassic	First dinosaurs, cycads	35	200,000,000
Paleozoic	Permian	Mammal—like reptiles	30	
	Pennsylvanian	Finback reptiles, coal forests	25	
	Mississippian	First reptiles, large amphibians	30	
	Devonian	First amphibians, sharks, and insects	55	
	Silurian	First land plants, ostracoderms	40	
	Ordovician	First fishes	80	
	Cambrian	Marine invertebrates	90	550,000,000

Table 1: Geological eras and periods since pre-Cambrian times.

Nineteenth-century geologists, investigating sedimentary rocks, named the periods when these rocks were formed after the first formations they studied. As the correct sequence of the rocks became better known, many names were changed. Hence, today, we have some names derived from places (such as "Devonian" from Devon, England); some from kinds of rocks (such as "Cretaceous" from the Latin word for "chalk"); and some from other sources.

Geologists divided the history of the earth into a few long "eras" and each era into a convenient number of shorter "periods." When the original scheme of dividing the earth's history into Primary, Secondary, Tertiary, and Quaternary eras proved unsatisfactory, the modern scheme of chronology took form. This divides the earth's existence into the following eras: the Azoic ("no life"), Archeozoic ("ancient life"), Proterozoic ("former life"), Eozoic ("dawn life"), Paleozoic ("old life"), Mesozoic ("middle life"), and Cenozoic ("recent life"). The Paleozoic could logically be split into two eras, not only because of its length, but also because an important event— life's conquest of the land—occurred in the middle of it.

All these eras have been divided into periods, but the divisions of the eras before the Paleozoic are not well established and do not concern us. The last three eras are the only ones from which abundant fossil records have survived. Even in these, not everybody agrees upon the system. European geologists, for instance, generally ignore the Paleocene and lump the Mississippian and Pennsylvanian together under the older name "Carboniferous."

The tables and charts show the relative lengths of the three last eras and their epochs. The lengths of the more recent eras are now fairly well known, estimates varying by ten or fifteen per cent. Estimates of the lengths of individual periods, however, vary as much as 50 per cent, and there is much dispute as to just where the boundaries between them should be located. Although each year scientists add new facts to the record of geological time, many gaps remain. Most of these will be filled in once Asia, Africa, and South America have been combed for fossils as thoroughly as Europe and North America were explored during the nineteenth century.

The first signs of life appear in the Archeozoic Era. These take the form of two-billion-year-old traces of bacteria, algae, and some things of such indefinite shape that experts do not yet agree as to how they should be classified—or, indeed, whether they are the fossils of living organisms at all. Signs become more definite in the Proterozoic Era, starting nearly two billion years ago, and still more so in the Eozoic, beginning about 1,200,000,000 years ago.

Life in these pre-Cambrian times did exist, but the forms it took were either microscopically small, or soft and vulnerable, or both. Hence very few fossil remains of this life have come down to us. Most organisms before the Cambrian were mere little blobs of jelly, lacking hard shells or skeletons, and so were preserved only by the rarest chance.

Another reason for the scarcity of pre-Cambrian fossils is that most pre-Cambrian rocks have by now been eroded away or so metamorphosed that any fossils in them can no longer be recognized. Furthermore, most pre-Cambrian life was probably shallow-water life, confined to a narrow strip, a fraction of a mile in width, around the margins of oceans, seas, and lakes. Look at the map of the world and imagine such a strip around each body of water. On a world map of average size, this strip would be much narrower than the line of printer's ink that divides the land from the sea. Considering the fact that the total area, in which pre-Cambrian life was possible, forms but a tiny fraction of the earth's entire surface, it is small wonder that pre-Cambrian fossils are so scarce.

Fortunately, one good fossil-bearing pre-Cambrian bed has recently been discovered in Australia. It holds the remains of worms, jellyfish, sea pens (a kind of coral), and some small, disk-shaped animals like nothing now alive. These and other pre-Cambrian rocks also contain traces of worm burrows, fossils thought to be those of sponges, and the little, ball-shaped skeletons of the one-celled animals called radiolarians.

The first period from which we get abundant fossil remains is the Cambrian period of the Paleozoic Era, which began less than 600 million years ago. Although there were in that distant age no land plants or animals, save perhaps some minute one-celled organisms, the Cambrian seas teemed with life.

The surprising thing about Cambrian life is not that it is so primitive but that it is so advanced. From a practically lifeless earth, a varied, impressive fauna seems to have sprung into being all at once. If one could paddle around a shallow Cambrian sea with flippers and a mask, one would not find it very strange, except for the lack of fish. All the main divisions of the sea life of today, except the vertebrates, were present. There were shrimplike crustaceans but no crabs. There were snails but no squids. There were sponges, coelenterates like the modern corals, echinoderms like the modern starfishes and sea urchins, and brachiopods or lamp shells. The largest animals were trilobites—relatives of the modern horseshoe crab, which looked somewhat like oversized woodlice. The trilobites of the Cambrian Period grew up to 19 inches long; in later periods, some reached a length of 30 inches. They spent their lives crawling sluggishly over the sea bottom, eating whatever smaller creatures they came across. In the periods following the Cambrian, the first fishes, the first land plants, the first amphibians, and then the first reptiles appeared.

The eighteenth century, which saw the first discoveries about the composition and age of the earth and the first studies of invertebrate animals, also witnessed the discovery of the first of the giant reptiles.

In 1766, some workmen were digging in a sandstone quarry at Pietersberg, near Maastricht in the Netherlands. From this quarry, a gallery of rock ran under land belonging to a Dr. Goddin, Canon of the Cathedral of Maastricht. When the workmen came upon some fossil bones, an intelligent local French officer named Drouhin salvaged them and sent them to the geological museum in Haarlem.

In 1780, the same quarrymen encountered more fossil bones, including a large, well-preserved, crocodile-like skull. As the workmen talked excitedly about their find, somebody in authority stopped the quarrying and sent for the nearest scientist, a French army surgeon named Hofmann. Dr. Hofmann directed the workmen to cut free and remove from the rock gallery the block of stone containing the skull, so that he could study it and the bones lying with it.

Word of the fossil find flew about the neighborhood. Scientists dropped in to see Hofmann's fossil and ventured wild guesses as to the sort of animal the skull had belonged to. Meanwhile Dr. Goddin sued Dr. Hofmann for the skull—the best part of the find— on the ground that it had been taken from rock beneath his land. Goddin won his case, and unlucky Hofmann was forced not only to turn the skull over to the Canon but also to pay court costs.

When, two years later, Hofmann died, a Dutch anatomist and naturalist, Peter Camper, bought up the parts of the skeleton still in his possession. After examining these bones and Goddin's skull, Camper announced that together they formed the remains of a whale. A few years later, Peter Camper's son, Adrian Camper, reëxamined the bones and pronounced them the skeleton of a monitor lizard.

Canon Goddin did not keep his prize for long. In 1794, during the French Revolutionary Wars, a French army attacked Maastricht. While artillery bombarded the town, Goddin's suburb remained intact. Goddin rightly suspected that this immunity to cannon balls was granted, not to save his cathedral, but to protect his famous fossil. He was right: a committee of French scientists had asked the artillery officers not to destroy the fossil, because they wanted to seize it once the fighting was over.

Goddin artfully hid his monster in a cave. When the town fell, the French looked in vain for the skull. Then the commanding officer offered 600 bottles of wine to the finders. Soon a squad of grenadiers staggered into view, bearing the rock in which the skull was still embedded. The rock was duly sent off to Paris and set up for study by the great Cuvier in the Jardin des Plantes, where it still is.

Young Mynheer Camper proved right: the beast had been a giant lizard, closely related to the modern monitors. In 1828, a British geologist, the Reverend William D. Conybeare, named the dragon after the man who first studied it: *Mosasaurus hofmanni*, "Hofmann's Meuse-lizard."

Thus was the first dragon of old brought back into the light of day, and thus were men stirred to go forth and seek other ancient reptiles. As we shall see, there was drama in this search. There were thrills and dangers, heartbreak and worry, concern and triumph, tragedy and comedy. Because so many men have given time and money to the pursuit of these rock-bound reptiles, the world's natural history museums are now filled with the remains of creatures as bizarre as any from medieval dragon legends.

3

Out of the Sea

Even as the first-known giant reptile was being fought over, men with a scientific turn of mind were wondering how such creatures had come to be and how they had vanished from the earth. Men were also trying to classify the animals and plants of today and those of ages past.

While French science was flowering in the revolutionary ferment of the years 1790–1815, two French scientists were making notable contributions to the study of these problems, although they disagreed with each other on most scientific questions. One of these men was Jean Baptiste Pierre Antoine de Monet de Lamarck (1744–1829) son of a petty noble of Picardy. After winning honor as a soldier, Lamarck became King's Botanist and rose to the post of Keeper of the King's Gardens. During the French Revolution, the scientists working in the Jardin du Roi tactfully changed the name of the institution to the Jardin des Plantes and so avoided the risk of a wholesale purge.

After the Revolution, the fifty-year-old Lamarck became the first professor of invertebrate zoology. In fact, he created the science of invertebrate zoology by making order out of the chaotic scraps of knowledge that men then possessed about animals without backbones. He invented the word "biology" and made a valid classification of invertebrate animals.

Lamarck, unfortunately, had a way of putting his worst foot forward. He wrote ponderous philosophical treatises full of vague, meaningless phrases. Worse yet, he discussed the scientific questions of his day without having sufficient knowledge or insight. Hence, despite his genius, he usually managed to range himself on the losing side of each scientific theory that he espoused.

Although an early champion of evolution, Lamarck made the mistake of upholding the old, mistaken idea that physical characteristics acquired during the lifetime of an animal, as a result of such factors as exercise or diet, are passed on to that animal's descendants. For example, he believed that an animal's efforts to get food and protect itself could work a change in form that would recur in the creature's offspring. Thus, he explained the crane's long legs by reasoning that its forebears, not liking to get their bottoms wet, stretched their legs while wading for food. Being a humorless man, Lamarck never knew when he was carrying an argument to absurdity, nor did he realize that foolish arguments like this made even his sound ideas look silly. He died an old man, blind and obscure.

Lamarck's more-or-less-friendly rival was Georges Léopold Chrétien Frédéric Dagobert Cuvier (1769–1832): anatomist, paleontologist, politician, and courtier. Cuvier was a man of mixed Swiss, German, and French antecedents; but since France annexed the town of his birth in 1793, and since Cuvier worked most of his life in France, we may call him a Frenchman.

As a youth, Cuvier tutored and wrote observations on biology. These came to the attention of the scientists of the Jardin des Plantes, who offered Cuvier a job. A strikingly handsome little man with a lordly manner—suave, adaptable, and determined—he held numerous scientific and political posts under Napoleon and later under the restored Bourbon kings, who made him a baron.

Cuvier turned out a prodigious amount of work by organizing it with fearsome efficiency. In his study he kept eleven desks, each fitted out with the stationery, manuscripts, and reference books for one project. When Cuvier felt like working on a certain book or article, he went to the right desk without wasting seconds shuffling

1. Late Jurassic scene in Europe, similar to that described in the first chapter, showing *Rhamphorhynchus*, a pterosaur or flying reptile; *Archaeopteryx*, a primitive toothed bird; *Compsognathus*, a small carnivorous dinosaur; and cycads. *Courtesy of the Chicago Natural History Museum.*

2. Model of a Cambrian sea bottom, showing the invertebrate life of the time: algae, sponges, jellyfish, trilobites (left foreground), and shrimplike crustaceans (right). *Photo from the Smithsonian Institution.*

3. Model of an Ordovician sea bottom, showing the invertebrate life of the time: algae, straight-shelled nautiloid cephalopods (with tentacles), crinoids (sea lilies), trilobites and corals. *Photo from the Smithsonian Institution.*

4. Cuvier's drawing of the skull of the Maastricht mosasaur (top), from his *Recherches sur les ossements fossiles*.

5. The slate quarries of the Solnhofen, in southern Germany. *Photo from David J. Williams, III.*

6. Jean B. P. A. de M. de Lamarck (1744–1829), pioneer evolutionist. *Courtesy of the American Museum of Natural History.*

7. Georges L. C. F. D. Cuvier (1769–1832), the founder of vertebrate paleontology. *Courtesy of the Burndy Library.*

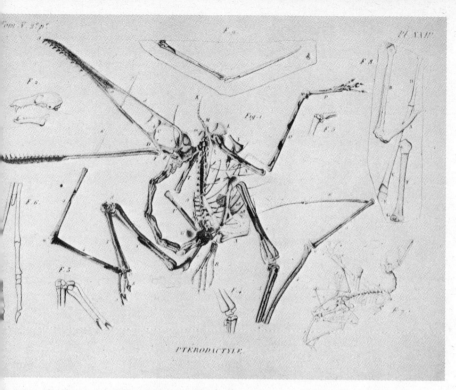

PTERODACTYLE.

8. Cuvier's drawing of the fossil of a pterodactyl or pterosaur, from his *Recherches sur les ossements fossiles.*

9. *Ichthyosaurus,* fossil from the Holzmaden slate quarries, showing the outline of the animal's dorsal fin and tail. *Courtesy of the American Museum of Natural History.*

10. Mary Anning (1799–1847), discoverer of the first known fossil ichthyosaur and plesiosaur. From a contemporary portrait. *Courtesy of the British Museum (Natural History).*

12. A Devonian forest, as painted by Charles R. Knight, showing *Aneurophyton*, a seed fern (left); *Calamites*, a horsetail (center); *Archaeosigillaria*, a lycopod (right); and *Psilophyton*, a very primitive plant (pale, slender, right of center). *Courtesy of the Chicago Natural History Museum.*

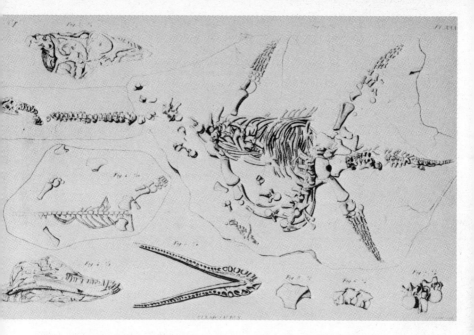

11.   Cuvier's drawing of the original plesiosaur fossil, from his *Recherches sur les ossements fossiles*.

13.   Head of *Dinichthys*, a giant Devonian placoderm. The scalloped edges of the jaws took the place of teeth. *Photo from the Smithsonian Institution.*

14.   *Eryops*, a six-foot Early Permian amphibian. *Photo from the Academy of Natural Sciences, Philadelphia.*

papers and gathering supplies. Under his chilly correctness of manner, he was a kindhearted man who aided such junior scientists as young Louis Agassiz.

Cuvier founded the sciences of comparative anatomy and vertebrate paleontology—the study of fossil animals with backbones. He established the relationships between the various animals' forms and habits: hooves for plant-eaters, claws for flesh-eaters, and bones of distinctive shape for every type of beast. Thus, he proved that the owner of the huge fossil claw, which America's Thomas Jefferson had named *Megalonyx,* was not a super-lion, as Jefferson had thought. Instead, it was a huge beast that was related to the modern sloth but that lived on the ground instead of in trees.

Once Cuvier neatly demonstrated his theory of the correlation of animals' parts before a committee of scientists. He showed them a piece of local gypsum in which was embedded the skull of a small mammal. From its teeth, he identified the beast as an opossum. Then, said Cuvier, it should have in its abdomen the small bones, supporting the pouch, which are characteristic of marsupials. Cuvier went to work with his needle, chipped away the rock, and presently found the marsupial bones. *Voilà!*[1]

Cuvier was the man who identified Hofmann's sea lizard. Another strange fossil came to Cuvier's attention—the skeleton of a little flying creature, different from anything men had ever seen. This fossil, from the slate quarries near Solnhofen,[2] Germany, was in the private museum of the Palatine Elector, where it survived until the bombings of the Second World War.

In the early 1800s, Cuvier studied a description and drawing of this small creature published by a Florentine man-of-letters named Collini, who served as the director of the Elector's "cabinet." Collini had called the winged thing an "unknown marine animal" and wondered whether it ought to be classed with the frogs and salamanders, despite the fact that its forelimbs seemed absurdly long for fins.

Fascinated by this mysterious little animal, Cuvier asked the Elector's officials to send him the fossil for study. He was told that the fossil had been mislaid. Actually, the officials did not want an outsider to get the credit for describing it; they themselves, eventually, described it as a bird.

Cuvier, undaunted, used Collini's excellent drawing to identify the little fiendlike beast correctly: it was a flying reptile, *le plus extraordinaire* of all the fossils he had seen. Cuvier named it *ptérodactyle,* from the Greek for "wing" and "finger." Nowadays we more often call these flying reptiles *pterosaurs* or "wing lizards." Other pterosaurs soon came to light, ranging in size from sparrows to turkeys.

As these and other strange creatures from the distant past came out of their rocky graves, it became necessary not only to find names for them but also to group or classify them. Both Lamarck and Cuvier did much to clear up the classification of animals, although the task has never been finished and probably never will be.

Long ago, men discovered that, to understand a set of facts, they had to group them in some logical way, with like things in the same class and unlike things in different classes. Furthermore, they had to give these classes names, so that they could easily talk and write about them.

Even in ordinary speech, we classify things in a crude way. If you own a dog named Whitey and I own a dog named Inky, we can both see that yours is white and mine is black and that they are two separate creatures. They may not be much alike; for yours may be a little Sealyham while mine is a big Newfoundland. Still, Whitey and Inky resemble each other more than either resembles a cat or a horse. Therefore, we call them both *dogs*. For the larger group made up of all the cats, dogs, horses, men, and elephants, we have the word *mammals;* for the still larger group that includes the mammals, lizards, fishes, and lobsters, we have the word *animal* to distinguish them from such other living things as grasses, flowers, shrubs, and trees, or such inanimate objects as hammers, chairs, lakes, and stars. Scientific classification of living things, however, must be more exact than the rough classification of ordinary speech.

The man who first began to classify living things was the Greek philosopher Aristotle. In the fourth century B.C., Aristotle divided animals into groups with two legs, four legs, and no legs; into animals with and without bones; into animals with and without blood; and so on. He soon found that classifying living things is not so easy as it looks. For instance, if he grouped animals according to the number of their legs, men would be classed with the birds.

Aristotle did realize that all dogs belong to one group, which we call a *species.* For a group of similar species, he used the Greek word for "family." We Latinize this word to *genus.* All domestic dogs belong to the same smaller group, or species; while all dogs— including wild dogs and wolves—belong to the same larger group, or genus.

For nearly two thousand years after Aristotle, little more was done to classify things. Then, in the sixteenth and seventeenth centuries, Caspar Bauhin in Switzerland and John Ray in England began to classify large numbers of animals and plants. To identify the groups into which they divided living things, they invented the *binomial system of nomenclature,* a system we still employ.

In this system, each species is represented by two words in Latin or Latinized Greek. The first word, a noun, is capitalized and identifies the genus. The second word, a lower-case adjective or noun, gives the species or smaller division of the genus. Hence, the domesticated dog is *Canis familiaris,* the "household dog." The wolf is *Canis lupus,* the "wolf dog." The cat is *Felis domesticus,* the "tame cat"; while man is *Homo sapiens,* the "wise human being." How we flatter ourselves!

Sometimes, in the case of a newly discovered creature, the name honors its discoverer, as in *Mosasaurus hofmanni,* "Hofmann's Meuse-lizard." If a name is repeated often in one text, we may abbreviate the genus name thus: *M. hofmanni.* When it is important to give the fullest information, we add the surname of the man who named and described the species: *"Tylosaurus dyspelor* Cope." When the animal has no common English name, we may Anglicize the genus name by omitting the italics, the capitalization, and the Latin inflectional ending, as by reducing *Mosasaurus* to a casual "mosasaur." Since any word can be Latinized, we get some strange combinations like *Szechuanosaurus,* but these need not alarm the reader. In discussing extinct life forms, we usually omit the species name unless we wish to distinguish one species of a single genus from another.

Bauhin and Ray chose Latin for the names of genera and species because, three hundred years ago, books were still being written in Latin, the language of learned men. This was a fortunate choice; for Latin is an international language, whereas men of different nationalities would never have agreed to a system of names in any one living, modern language. To us, for example, *dog* may seem to us the easy, natural word for the animal; but to a Frenchman the natural word is *chien,* to a German *Hund,* to a Spaniard *perro,* and so on through all the world's 3,000-odd tongues. Latin not only made possible a single name for a single genus, but it also gave scientists materials for making up as many new names as they needed whenever a new organism came to light.

Even this system of names is not always easy to apply. Since hundreds of thousands of genera are now recognized, nobody can keep track of them all. Time and again, a paleontologist selects a name for a new genus, only to be reminded that the name he selected is already in use. Names of extinct animals tend to be long because, extensive as were the vocabularies of the Greeks and the Romans, nearly all their short, simple, suitable words are already in service.

To make matters worse, the general rule in naming a species is: first come, first served. The name first given to a species is supposed to be retained forever. The results can prove awkward. Sometimes a name, based upon a few fragments only, turns out to be highly inappropriate when the rest of the organism comes to light. At other times, a name comes into common use; then somebody, digging into some old, dusty publication, learns that an earlier scientist had long ago given the same beast another name. However, as the second name has become common, the animal often continues to go under the second name. Although the rule is that the name first given should stand, in controversial cases the International Commission on Zoological Nomenclature has the power to modify its code in order to stabilize the currently accepted names of organisms.

A hundred years after Bauhin and Ray, the binomial system was further developed by the Swedish botanist Carolus Linnaeus (1707–78). A short, dark man with a large, hooked nose, Linnaeus became a physician in Stockholm, where he acquired a good practice. Later, he taught botany at the University of Uppsala, became a nobleman, and changed his name to the Swedish form: Carl von Linné.

Linnaeus, or Linné, became so famous for his classifications of plants and animals that his own name will be remembered as long as there are any scientists left alive in this world. His work was much needed; for, in the eighteenth century, many European scientists set out to study the flora and fauna of Asia, Africa, and the Americas. Although many of them died from the hardships of travel or from tropical diseases, the survivors sent back to Europe hundreds of specimens of unfamiliar plants and animals. As a result, the number of known species of living things grew at a dizzy rate, and many of them came to the attention of the professor of botany at Uppsala.

Although Linnaeus was primarily a botanist, in his book *Systema naturae* (1735), he classified both plants and animals more systematically than had ever been done before. His predecessors had spoken vaguely of groupings larger than the genus, such as "backboned" animals or "warm-blooded" animals. Linnaeus, however, devised a whole series of classifications, with each larger group inclosing the smaller groups of which it was made up. Such a series of classes is called a *hierarchy*.

Linnaeus recognized the species as the main unit. A group of species made a *genus*. A group of genera made an *order;* a group of orders made a *class;* and a group of classes made a *kingdom*. Linnaeus distinguished two main divisions of living things: the animal kingdom and the plant kingdom. Nowadays, many biologists recognize a third kingdom, the *Protista,* into which they pack all the single-celled organisms. Linnaeus' system was such an improvement on earlier classifications that it was quickly adopted throughout the learned world.

Even Linnaeus' system, however, had its shortcomings. For instance, a species is to some extent a natural group. The distinction between one species and another is usually (but not always) sharp. A species is a population of organisms, all freely interbreeding among themselves but not interbreeding with members of other species. Still, sometimes members of two different species within the same genus, such as the horse and the ass, interbreed and produce such sterile offspring as the mule. Sometimes, the distinction between species breaks down completely. For example, anyone would put the domestic ox and the American bison in two separate species or even in two different genera. Yet, they are interfertile and produce a fertile hybrid offspring, the cattalo.

When scientists tried to define the larger groups—genera, orders, and so on—it soon transpired that these were arbitrary, man-made groupings which did not always fit the facts. Because the relationships of living things are so much less simple and tidy than Linnaeus had assumed, later scientists have devised additional ranks for the original hierarchy: *phylum,* between kingdom and class; *family,* between order and genus; *infraclass; cohort; superfamily; suborder;* and so forth.

When, in the nineteenth century, it was recognized that all living things change or evolve over the centuries, the problem of classification became even more complex. The element of time was added to the problem. If two populations of similar animals exist at the same time, and if each population interbreeds only within itself, it is easy to see that we have two species. But suppose that one population lived hundreds of thousands of years before the other? Suppose that one was the ancestor of the other? Since these populations could never even try to interbreed, interfertility has nothing to do with the case.

Moreover, it is easy to decide that an organism belongs to one species and its altered descendant, a million years later, to another. But suppose that we dig up so many fossils that we can trace the line of descent from the first to the second, following every tiny, gradual change? How shall we divide this line of descent into species? And should the classification of an animal be determined by its ancestors or by its descendants?

Since these problems have never been solved and probably never will be, biologists struggle along as best they can; but there are almost as many systems of classification as there are classifiers. One expert divides the insects into nine orders, another into seventeen, and still another into thirty-one. However, this fact need not disturb us if we remember that a class is not something pre-existing in nature, but something invented by men for their own use. One classification is as "right" as the next; but one may be more useful than another. A classification that lumped men together with hornets, because they both build houses, would not be very useful. So, if the classification used in this book differs from those in some other books, that means only that we consider our system, not necessarily more "right" than the others, but more convenient and useful for our purposes.

And speaking of lumping, classifiers themselves can be classed as lumpers and splitters, according to whether they like to class living things in few or many groups. Lumpers, for instance, recognize only one or two species of bears of the brown-grizzly group in North America and Asia (including Europe). However, the great naturalist C. Hart Merriam, a notorious splitter, claimed there were over fifty species in North America alone.

Paleontologists often complain of splitters who erect new species on the basis of small differences in bones. These differences, they say, may be due, not to differences of species, but to differences of age, sex, or local races, or to individual variations. Alas! A human weakness enters into classification. The scientist stands to get more fame from describing a new species than from merely reporting the find of one more specimen of an old one. Therefore, in doubtful cases, he is likely to become a splitter, however firm a lumper he is in criticizing his colleagues.

On the cliff-lined southern coast of England, near the mouth of the river Axe, stands the old town of Lyme Regis. In the early nineteenth century, the town's main industries were—as they still are—stone-quarrying, cement-making, and catering to summer visitors. In Lyme Regis lived Richard Anning, a man who eked out his carpenter's earnings by finding and selling natural curios. The curios on which he most relied were fossil shells; and he taught his young daughter Mary (1799–1847) how to gather fossils, too.

In 1810, Richard Anning died, leaving eleven-year-old Mary to make her way as best she could. In time, she came to own a curiosity shop stocked with quite a variety of fossils.

Mary Anning had been on her own for only a year when she saw some bones protruding from a cliff near Lyme. The twelve-year-old girl carefully traced the outline of the thirty-foot skeleton by pecking away the rock with a hammer. Then she hired a crew of men to quarry out the huge block of stone, containing her fossil.

At this time, paleontology was the hobby of just a few well-to-do men. Among these men in England were the Reverend William Conybeare and his friend Sir Henry de la Beche. They heard of Mary Anning's monster, bought it, and published an account of it. The creature appeared fishlike, all thirty feet of it, and had four paddles or flippers and a pair of long, pointed jaws full of sharp teeth.

In many ways, however, Mary's monster was not truly fishlike. Scientists argued as to whether it was a fish or a reptile. Two authorities, Cuvier and Owen, finally decided the case: it was, they declared, a reptile with the outward form of a fish, just as a whale is a mammal with the outward form of a fish. The creature was an example of what we call today *convergent evolution.* That is a term used to describe the process whereby the descendants of two very different animals, over the ages, come to resemble each other closely. Mary's specimen acquired a home in the British Museum and the name of *Ichthyosaurus,* from the Greek words for "fish" and "lizard."

During the following years, more ichthyosaurs were found in the cliffs around Lyme Regis. In 1824, they also began turning up in Germany. The best source of ichthyosaurs was found to be the slate quarries of Holzmaden, in the extreme south of Germany; there were literally hundreds of well-preserved fish-lizards, as well as the remains of crocodiles, fishes, and invertebrates. One ichthyosaur had twelve little ichthyosaurs inside it, showing that, like some living reptiles, this creature brought forth its young alive. The remains of other ichthyosaurs showed that the animals' diet consisted largely of shellfish, for they had just eaten some ammonites and belemnites when death overtook them.

One peculiar feature showed up in many ichthyosaur specimens: the last couple of feet of the long tail was bent down sharply, at a forty-degree angle. The anatomist Richard Owen (1804–92) suggested that the tail had originally borne a leaf-shaped vertical fin and that the weight of this fin, or water resistance to it, had put a kink in the tail after the creature died. As it turned out, Owen was only partly right.

Bernard Hauff (1866–1950) owner of some of the slate quarries at Holzmaden, became interested in this problem. By offering rewards to his workmen, Hauff collected many fossils and taught himself how to free his fossils from the rock by laboriously picking the slate away with engravers' tools. Once, when he had made a bas-relief of one ichthyosaur specimen, Hauff observed a dark stain in the rock around the skeleton, as if it were a silhouette of the soft parts of the reptile. Having carefully cleaned away all the excess rock, Hauff found that he had indeed a complete outline of the sea beast and that it had bore a high, triangular dorsal fin like that of a shark. Moreover, the kink in the tail was explained. The ichthyosaur had a fishlike tail fin, with two lobes, and the vertebral column bent downward into the lower lobe, like a shark's tail upside down.

The ichthyosaur was, in fact, a kind of reptilian porpoise. Since its vertebrae did not have to bear weight, they were simple disks, like those of a fish, so articulated that the body could be bent from side to side for swimming. To judge from their streamlined form, ichthyosaurs must have moved very fast. However, since they were cold-blooded and had, in all probability, a three-chambered heart, they may have had less energy than a speedy modern porpoise.

Mary Anning kept on hunting for fossils. When she found a skeleton, she left her dog to guard and mark the spot while she rounded up a crew of workmen to quarry the specimen. Amateur paleontologists came to her shop more and more frequently for previously unknown fossils.

One of these shoppers was the Reverend William Buckland, a liberal Anglican cleric who spent his time crusading for better sanitary conditions for the poor when he was not dashing about the countryside with a big, blue, fossil-gathering bag. He once dug in a cave at Kirkdale that had housed a family of hyenas back in the Pleistocene Era. And so proved that Britain had long ago harbored beasts very different from those of modern Europe.

Among his friends, Buckland was something of a clown. At a party, he would illustrate the way fossil footprints were formed by imitating a hen waddling through soft mud. An amateur chef, he once tried to persuade his guests to eat a dinner of roast crocodile and was disappointed to find no takers.

Buckland would often visit Mary Anning. The pair could be seen scrambling about the sea cliffs of Dorsetshire, the divine in his tall beaver hat and the young maiden lady in her billowing skirts.

In 1821, Mary Anning found another sea reptile. This was smaller than the ichthyosaur and quite different in form. Again, Conybeare and de la Beche bought the fossil and named it a *Plesiosaurus,* "almost-lizard." This reptile resembled a long-necked turtle without a shell. It had a lizardlike head with jaws full of sharp, fish-catching teeth and a neck about thirty vertebrae long. Its body was compact and somewhat flattened; and the limbs were four large, powerful paddles. Inside the body, the ventral ribs formed a strong, solid structure much like the nether shell of a turtle. The tail was shorter than the neck and, in some kinds at least, ended in a lozenge-shaped tail fin.

Evidently the plesiosaur, unlike the ichthyosaur, rowed itself about with its paddles and used its tail for steering only. The paddles were so mounted that the beast could quickly stop, turn, or back water with them.

Mary Anning developed into a lean, homely woman with a tart sense of humor and a lively manner. Doggedly devoted to fossil-hunting, in 1828, she discovered the first British pterosaur. For her services to the new science of paleontology, the British government made her a substantial grant of money, which she shrewdly put into an annuity that supported her until she died of cancer at the age of forty-eight.

Among Mary Anning's last sales were an ichthyosaur and a plesiosaur to a rich, retired American physician, Thomas B. Watson. Dr. Watson bought these fossil dragons of the sea as a gift to the Academy of Natural Sciences in Philadelphia, of which he was one of the founders. Here they can still be seen.

A few years after the first plesiosaur came to light, the first of the dinosaurs emerged from the rocks in which they had lain for scores of millions of years.

In Lewes, not far south of London, lived the son of a shoemaker, Gideon Algernon Mantell (1804–92). Trained as a physician, Mantell made geology and paleontology his hobbies. One day in 1822, while he and his wife were poking around in the Lower Cretaceous beds of Tilgate Forest, Mrs. Mantell called her husband's attention to the remains of a fossil reptile as huge as any dragon of story or song. The remains, while fragmentary, indicated a monster more than twenty feet long.

Mantell found few clues, indeed, to the animal's relationships. He asked the views of a number of scientists and received an equal number of different replies. He sent teeth and bones to the famous Dr. Cuvier in Paris, who pronounced the teeth those of a rhinoceros and the bones those of a hippopotamus.

Finally, the English naturalist Stutchbury showed Mantell the teeth of a modern iguana, a large lizard from the American tropics, and pointed out how strikingly similar were the teeth of Mantell's reptile. Mantell, therefore, named his fossil *Iguanodon*, "iguana-tooth." When a triumphant account of Mantell's discovery was read before the Royal Society of London in 1825, Cuvier, with his usual objectivity, handsomely acknowledged his previous error.

About the same time, the tireless Reverend Buckland found fragmentary remains of another giant reptile near Oxford, while Mantell discovered different parts of a similar creature in his Tilgate Forest hunting ground. Although this animal was about the same size as the iguanodon, there was one big difference. The teeth of the iguanodon indicated a plant-eater; the new saurian's saber-shaped fangs could only belong to a flesh-eater. Buckland named his reptile *Megalosaurus* or "great lizard."

Mantell went on hunting the big game of former eons. In 1832, he found the remains of another monster, *Hylaeosaurus*, a low, squatty fellow covered with spines and armor plates like some gigantic horned toad.

However, Mantell's hobby now made such inroads into his time that his medical practice suffered; and his house became so jammed with fossils that his wife left him. To get money to live, Mantell had to sell his collection of fossils to the British Museum for £5,000 (about $24,500). Later, he removed to London, where he spent the rest of his life fossil-hunting, writing, and lecturing. At last account, his house in Lewes was still standing, marked by a brass plate on the door that read: HE DISCOVERED THE IGUANODON.

One of Mantell's best iguanodons came from a quarry near Maidstone. In 1949, the town of Maidstone adopted a new coat of arms, which included "On the dexter side an Iguanodon proper Collared Gules . . ."

Because of the work of these early enthusiasts, the day of the dragon transpired at last. Modern men could visualize, if dimly, the long-ago world of flying reptiles, swimming reptiles, and lumbering land reptiles.

Men began to recognize, too, that all these creatures came from a definite group of geological beds. Geologists called this group of rock deposits the Secondary or Mesozoic formations. Below them in the Primary or Paleozoic beds, the fossils consisted mainly of invertebrates, fishes, and amphibians. Above the Mesozoic beds lay the Tertiary or Cenozoic formations, of which the most impressive fossils were those of mammals.

In the nineteenth century, men were at last beginning to realize that, for a long time, reptiles ruled the earth, and that the Mesozoic Era—"the Age of Middle Life"—was also the Age of Reptiles. Reptiles lived before and after the Mesozoic, of course; but during that era, the giant reptiles in which we are interested held sway over every continent save Antarctica. Moreover, in no era but the Mesozoic did there live an array of reptiles so huge, strange, and formidable that we may apply to them the old mythological name of "dragon."

Men were also learning that, despite the common use of *-saurus* in their names, most of the big Mesozoic reptiles were neither lizards nor the ancestors of lizards. They belonged, not to any of the modern orders of reptiles, but to several distinct orders of their own. And, strange as it may seem, most of them disappeared completely, without leaving descendants, at the end of the Cretaceous Period of the Mesozoic Era.

4

Life Invades the Land

Since all animal life depends upon plants for its ultimate nourishment, animals could not move out of the water and on the land until the plants had done so. We cannot tell just when this happened, because the earliest land plants were such small, soft things that no fossils thereof have survived. But we can tell something of how the great step out of the water was taken.

After the seas had come to teem with life, hundreds of millions of years rolled by. The continents presented to the silent skies a rocky, lunar landscape of somber browns and grays and blacks, relieved only by stretches of tawny sand dunes. The sun shone, the rains fell, the snows melted on these vast deserts of sand and rock. Rivers, thick with silt and soil from the swift erosion, ran to the sea. Lands rose and sank. And still nothing lived on all those millions of square miles of rock, gravel, and sand—sand, gravel, and rock. No bird sang, no insect buzzed, no blade of grass thrust the tiniest green stem into the empty air.

Then, during the early Silurian Period—we may guess—patchy carpets of small primitive plants, suggesting the mosses, lichens, and terrestrial algae of today, spread inward from the margins of rivers and seas. Little by little, they adapted themselves to drier and drier conditions, and slowly they moved farther from the waters. Eventually, they may have covered much of the earth in zones of regular rainfall—places that now support a solid growth of grass, shrubs, and trees. We can only guess, from the habits of their remote descendants of today, how far these plants could travel from the seas, because, at best, they have left only the faintest traces in the form of fossils.

During the later Silurian and early Devonian periods, other members of the plant kingdom, driven by the forces of competition and adaptation, also surged shoreward. One kind of water plant after another learned to survive on land. Like today's marsh plants, some stood upright in shallow water; others sprawled flat across the dry ground while keeping a life-saving root in the water. Competition urged them relentlessly inland, until at last the shores were covered with reedlike, fernlike, mosslike plants, some the size of small trees.

Although there was some variation among the plants of this time, they ran more or less to one physical type. They started from a base below water level on the margin of some lake or sea and ran a horizontal stem landward along—or just under—the ground. Every so often, this stem sent up a vertical shoot into the air. Other shoots, directed downward, served as secondary roots. None bore true leaves.

Like their modern descendants, these early plants depended on a process called photosynthesis, by which a plant makes its own food from carbon dioxide, water, and sunlight. Lacking leaves, they had to rely upon the reaction of sunlight with the chlorophyll in their stems or trunks. Compared to a modern, leafy plant, this was not efficient; but it was the best they could do.

Some of these plants had naked stems; others, stems adorned with spines or scales. When these stems were no longer buoyed up by water, improvements in their design were required. The stems had to grow strong and rigid enough to withstand the pull of gravity and had to be so braced by roots that the first brisk breeze should not blow them down. Moreover, the stems required tubes and chemical pumps for raising water from one cell to the next. They had to develop a complex skin structure, so that carbon dioxide could move into the plant and oxygen could move out, without losing too much internal moisture in the process.

During the Devonian Period, real jungles developed near the

water, with trees up to forty feet high. Dominating these jungles were plants of several groups, most of which still have living members. There were calamites, related to the modern horsetails and scouring rushes. There were lycopods, akin to the modern club mosses and so-called ground pines. There were true ferns; there were also seed ferns, which looked like true ferns but which reproduced by seeds instead of spores. Some of these plants appear in Knight's painting of a Devonian forest, Plate 12.

Although many of these Devonian plants attained the size of trees, nearly all their surviving relatives are little things. One summer, along a little stream in Vermont, we saw within a few feet of one another a perfect assortment of living plant fossils from the Devonian: ferns, horsetails, scouring rushes, and club mosses. We collected samples in order to start a little Paleozoic garden in our apartment; but the horsetails, which seem to be delicate things, all died on the way to the city.

Once plants were established on dry land, animals followed them out of the water. By the end of the Devonian, the shoreline forests crawled with arthropods or jointed-legged invertebrates—spiders, scorpions, centipedes, millipedes, and insects resembling the present-day springtails and silverfish. And after the arthropods came the first land vertebrates.

The earliest traces of vertebrates are some bony plates from the Ordovician Period. In rocks of the Silurian Period occur well-preserved fossils of fishlike creatures—not true fishes—called Agnatha or ostracoderms. The first word means "jawless"; the second, "shell-skinned." Ostracoderms in many ways resembled their living relatives, the cyclostomes ("round-mouths"); that is, the lampreys and the hagfishes.

Figure 4. *Pteromyzon,* the modern lamprey, a cyclostome. (After Osborn.)

Cyclostomes are eel-like creatures with round sucking mouths set with circles of teeth. A cyclostome has, in addition, a pair of eyes on the sides of the head, a single nostril on top, seven gill slits behind each eye, and a fringe of fin above and below the tail. It has no jawbones or paired fins.

When young, a cyclostome feeds on small, bottom-living animals. When it grows up, it fastens itself parasitically to the flank of a higher fish. The lamprey sucks its host's juices; the hagfish gnaws into its body and eats its viscera. When grasped, a cyclostome ties its eelish body into an overhand knot and, by moving the knot along its body, slips out of its captor's grasp. In addition, the hagfish startles its captor and makes its own escape easier by exuding incredible quantities of slime, whence the name "slime eel." Despite their scientific interest, cyclostomes are difficult creatures to love.

Although the ostracoderms had many features in common with lampreys, they varied greatly in shape. Many were quite fishlike in appearance, with fins and tails much like those of modern fishes. Most of them were more or less armored with scales, plates, and spines. In many, the forward part of the body was covered by a solid head shield of bony plates. Besides a pair of conventional eyes, this shield often bore, on the centerline between them, a third, small, auxiliary eye, called the pineal eye. There was often a pair of armored paddles on the sides behind the head shield. The mouth was a slit on the underside of the shield, with muscles to work it but no jaws or teeth.

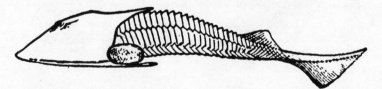

Figure 5. *Cephalaspis,* a Devonian ostracoderm. (After Osborn.)

Although there was plenty of bone in the head shield, the paddles, and the scales of an ostracoderm, there was none in its skeleton, which was made of cartilage. Cartilage is the stiffening material of

your nose and ears: a tough, translucent, flexible substance made
of cells that grow as they age. Bone, on the other hand, is hard and
stiff. Bone cells secrete chemicals, which form a rigid mass. The
final product consists of tiny crystals of calcium phosphate packed
in a matrix of the protein collagen. This is what engineers call a
two-phase substance. Like many two-phase substances, such as
bamboo and reinforced concrete, bone is stronger than either of
the two phases would be by itself. The collagen furnishes tensile
strength, while the calcium phosphate supplies strength in compression.

Once a piece of bone has been formed, however, it no longer
grows from within. Therefore, bones grow at the surface or on
the ends instead of all over like cartilage. In a higher vertebrate, the
skeleton begins in the form of many pieces of cartilage. As the
organism matures, bone little by little takes the place of the cartilage.

In the Devonian Period, the ostracoderms declined, being ousted
by the more advanced true fishes. Most of these belonged to the
class Placodermi. Many placoderms looked much like their ostracoderm predecessors, even to the armored heads and plated side
paddles.

Figure 6. *Climatius,* a Devonian placoderm.

However, the placoderms also displayed important improvements.
In many, the cartilage of the skeleton was stiffened by a deposit of
bone. But the biggest improvement lay in the development of jawbones. Each gill of an ostracoderm had a stiffening structure called

a gill arch, made of two pieces jointed together thus: >, with the point or joint aft. In placoderms, the first two pairs of the original seven pairs of gill arches disappeared, while the third pair were enlarged and moved forward. The upper member of the arch became part of the skull, while the lower formed a half of the lower jawbone.

Having jaws, these fishes no longer had to live on tiny bottom-dwelling organisms. They could now eat larger animals, including other fishes. This in turn meant that they could become larger. In the Devonian one genus, *Dinichthys,* reached a length of 30 feet. This formidable creature looked something like a giant catfish with an armored head.

While the placoderms flourished, two newer groups of fishes branched off. One, the cartilagenous fishes or Chondrichthyes, lost the bone from their skeletons, went back to pure cartilage, and became the sharks and rays. Small early sharks, looking much like modern dogfish, swarmed the Devonian seas.

The other class, the bony fishes or Osteichthyes, added even more bone to their skeletons. The bony fishes in turn split into two subclasses. The older of these was the lobe-finned or fringe-finned fishes, the Choanichthyes; from them the ray-finned fishes or Actinopterygii—which includes most kinds of fish living today—branched off.

The lobe-fins are a small group but very important in the story of evolution. They are called "lobe-fins" because each of their paired fins takes the form of a muscular flap or lobe, like a stumpy limb, whence the rays that hold the web of the fin stick out in a row to form a fringe. In ray-finned fishes, on the other hand, all the rays radiate from one point, like the ribs of a lady's fan.

For another thing, all the lobe-finned fishes either have or once had *lungs* besides their gills. At one time they all lived in small streams and pools in lands of long drouths. Lungs were evolved to help them to survive these times of peril. Even when the water did not wholly dry up, heat and stagnation might lower its content of oxygen to the point where gills alone could not keep the animal alive. When this happens, the lungfish comes to the surface and gulps air into its lungs.

The lobe-fins split into two orders, the Dipnoi or lungfishes proper and the Crossopterygii—or crossopts, to use a less awkward handle. Of the dipnoans or lungfishes, three kinds survive: *Lepidosiren,* the caramuru of South America; *Protopterus,* the comtok of Africa; and *Neoceratodus,* the dyelleh of Australia. The first two are eel-like fishes with lungs in pairs. Their lobe-fins have been reduced to mere streamers. Both can survive even if their water dries up completely. They bury themselves in mud, wrap their tails around their faces, and go to sleep until the next rain. This sleep is like hibernation, except that it takes place in summer and is therefore called "estivation," from the Latin *aestivus,* "relating to summer."

The Australian dyelleh is a larger fish, up to 5 feet long, with large greenish scales, four strong lobe-fins, a tail fin that tapers to a single point like a spearhead, and a single lung.

Figure 7.   *Neoceratodus,* the dyelleh or Australian lungfish.

As for the other order of lobe-fins, the crossopts, they, too, divided. One suborder, the Rhipidistia, came out on land; the other, the Coelacanthini, went back to the ocean. Like the ray-fins, the coelacanths converted their ancestral lungs into a swim-bladder, which functions like the buoyancy tank of a submarine. By adjusting the volume of gas in its swim bladder, the fish can make its overall density the same as that of the water, so that it has no tendency either to rise or to sink. A shark, having no swim bladder, cannot do this but must keep swimming so as not to sink into the abyss.

The coelacanths flourished through the Mesozoic Era and then disappeared. . . . Or, at least, they were supposed to have disappeared. Then, on 22 December, 1938, a trawler operating out of East London, South Africa, came into port. As soon as he came ashore, Captain Goosen got in touch with Miss M. Courtney-Latimer, curator of the local natural history museum.

Miss Courtney-Latimer had persuaded the captains of the trawlers to save rare and unusual fish for her. Now Captain Goosen had a fish as unusual as one could want. It was 4.5 feet long, weighed 127 pounds, and had snapped at the captain when hauled aboard. It was covered with large blue scales and had lobes not only in its paired fins but in two of the fins on its centerline as well, and a tail of peculiar shape. It was a coelacanth.

Miss Courtney-Latimer wrote the leading fish expert of her acquaintance, Professor J. L. B. Smith of Rhodes University. Smith, on Christmas vacation, did not get the letter until weeks later. Then he tried to telephone East London; but in South Africa the telephones are run by the postal service and close down on weekends. By the time Smith finally got to East London, the insides of the fish, despite such efforts as could be made to preserve them, had disintegrated to the point where Miss Courtney-Latimer felt that she had to throw away the guts and let a local taxidermist mount the rest of the fish.

The discovery received worldwide publicity; it was compared to finding a living dinosaur. Smith described the creature, naming it *Latimeria chalumnae.* Naturally, he still yearned for a complete specimen, so that he could study the viscera. Reasoning that the fish

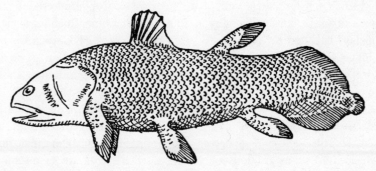

Figure 8. *Latimeria,* the modern crossopterygian, from the waters off South Africa.

probably lived in the Mozambique Channel between Africa and Madagascar, he had leaflets printed up in English, French, and Portuguese and distributed along the coasts of that region, offering £100 for a whole coelacanth.

At last, in 1952, Ahmed Hussein, a fisherman of the Comores Islands north of Madagascar, caught a coelacanth, heard of the reward, and sent word to Smith. The latter, after another struggle with the holiday-silent telephone system, persuaded Prime Minister Malan to have him flown to the Comores in a government airplane. When Smith saw the fish, laid out upon the deck of a trading ship, he knelt down and wept.

Since then, several other coelacanths have been obtained and studied by French scientists. The creature appears to lurk in holes in rocks and reefs, whence it pounces out upon its prey. The Comores natives knew it well, calling it *kombessa*. It had been overlooked by science because it lived where trawlers' nets seldom caught it.

Creatures like *Latimeria* are often called "living fossils." The meaning of this term is as follows: Now and then a life form becomes so well adapted to its environment—it fits so perfectly its niche in the scheme of things—that it can hardly be improved upon for its particular rôle. Then the forces of selection, instead of changing the species into one or more different species, tend on the contrary to keep it much as it was.

Hence some animals and plants have lasted for hundreds of millions of years, barely changing at all during this time. Such an ancient of days is called a "living fossil" (a term invented by Darwin for the ginkgo tree) because in it we see a close approximation of a life form that existed in remote geological times. Such living fossils may be common, like the brake fern, the oyster, the shark, and the opossum; or rare, like the coelacanth fish and the platypus. Often in the fossil record, we come upon some extinct animal that resembles the common ancestor of several widely different forms, which lived many millions of years before the creature in question. So this animal, too, was once a living fossil; now it is just a fossil.

As we have seen, both orders of lobe-finned fishes have living representatives: for the dipnoans, the three lungfishes; for the crossopts, the kombessa. (There is also a genus of lobe-finned freshwater African fishes, *Polypterus,* but opinions differ as to whether these fishes should be classed with the Choanichthyes.) The other subclass of bony fishes, the ray-fins, took over the lakes, rivers, and oceans; now they comprise the vast majority of living fishes, from sardines to swordfish.

The remaining suborder of the crossopts, the Rhipidistia, includes the first vertebrates to come ashore. They seem to have done so, not to pursue their prey, but to save their own lives from drouth. Even a fish with a lung could perish if trapped in a pool that completely dried up. The modern African and South American lungfishes avoid this danger by estivating in the mud; no doubt some ancient lungfishes did likewise. Some, however, adopted the more active stratagem of leaving the drying pool and crawling on land, upstream or down, until they found another with more water in it.

Several modern fishes of widely separated groups have developed the ability to move about on land. These include the common eel, the little climbing perch of India, and the mud skippers. The last, which belong to the goby family, not only come out on land but even hop about the mud in pursuit of insects, like a fish that is trying to evolve into a frog but hasn't yet quite made it.

The lobe-finned fishes had an advantage in this respect. They possessed fin lobes, with bones and muscles, which could be turned into limbs with a minimum of redesign. Several rhipidistian fishes from the Upper Devonian seem to belong on the road to land vertebrates, especially the very primitive lobe-fin *Osteolepis.* Since the

Figure 9. *Osteolepis,* a Devonian lobe-finned fish closely resembling the ancestor of the tetrapods (amphibians, reptiles, etc.). (After Romer.)

first land vertebrates already existed, none of these fishes could be
our actual ancestor. Rather, they were, in their day, "living fossils,"
which had persisted from an earlier time with little change. The
9-inch *Osteolepis,* if not our direct fishy ancestor, gives us a very
good idea of what that ancestor must have been like.

Intermediate between a fish and a true land vertebrate was
Osteolepis' contemporary *Eusthenopteron,* a 40-inch fish, conven-
tional-looking save for an unusual three-pointed tail and paired
lobe-fins, which could be turned down and used as legs. Inside each
lobe was a set of bones, wherein we can recognize some of the limb
and foot bones of higher vertebrates.

Figure 10. *Eusthenopteron,* a walking crossopterygian fish from the
Later Devonian.

The next step was an Upper Devonian animal called *Ichthyostega,* whose remains were found in Greenland by a Danish expedition. It was a salamanderlike creature four or five feet long, with a
head much like that of *Eusthenopteron* and a fringe of fin around its
tail. However, *Ichthyostega* had turned its lobe-fins into real legs,
with five webbed toes on each foot.

Ichthyostega still spent most of its time in the water; it fed and
bred in the water. But, when occasion demanded, it could get around
on land more actively than any fish. No doubt it paid for this ability
by not being so swift in the water as a fish; but then, since it lived
in swamps and pools, that did not make much difference. In such a
restricted space, high speed would be of little use.

However little time *Ichthyostega* spent on land, it was still a
competent land animal, no longer a makeshift. And however slug-

gish and ineffectual it might seem to us, it had little competition. So vertebrate life had at last, however imperfectly, conquered the land.

Ichthyostega was the oldest member, of which the fossil bones have survived, of the class Amphibia ("double lives"), which thrives today in the form of frogs, toads, and salamanders. The name re-

Figure 11. *Ichthyostega,* a primitive Later Devonian amphibian.

fers to the fact that most amphibians are hatched in water as fish-like animals with gills. Later they undergo a *metamorphosis* or change, lose their gills, and come out on land to breathe air. The metamorphosis is most complete among frogs and toads, whose tadpoles change their appearance completely on reaching maturity. In salamanders, the change is less dramatic; the animal merely loses its gills without much alteration of its outer form.

As with most groups of organisms, many amphibians do not fit any easy definition of the name "amphibian," although there is no doubt about their belonging biologically with the group. Some members of the class spend their whole lives on land; others, their whole lives in the water. The class includes the yard-long Japanese giant salamander as well as tiny eel-like and wormlike animals with rudimentary limbs or none at all.

During the next two geological periods, the Mississippian and the Pennsylvanian, amphibians dominated life in fresh water and on land. Although, during this stretch of time, land plants waxed in size and variety and pushed farther inland, the main theater of life was still the border between land and water. Here, through the

Mississippian and Pennsylvanian periods, grew the great swamp forests, of which our modern anthracite beds are the fossils.

Most of the plants were still pteridophytes: that is to say, lycopods, calamites, and ferns, as well as the transitional seed ferns. The ground was matted with creepers and vines, including creeping and climbing ferns. Lycopods reached heights of well over 100 feet. In some, the trunks and branches bore narrow, sword-shaped leaves, closely set like those of an araucaria or monkey-puzzle tree. Low on the stem, the leaves died and fell off, leaving a scaly pattern on the trunk.

The Pennsylvanian saw the rise of plants of the phylum Spermatophyta, which includes all the remaining large land plants in the world. This phylum falls into two classes. One is the Gymnospermae or "naked seeds," which includes the ginkgo or maidenhair tree, the palmlike cycads, and all the conifers—the pine, yew, cypress, and other needle-bearing evergreens.

Some early gymnosperms had tall, straight trunks with a crown of long, narrow leaves at the top. Others had branches and needle-like leaves arranged like the ribs and barbs of a feather.

The other class of spermatophytes is the Angiospermae or flowering plants, which did not yet exist in Paleozoic times. This class includes all the rest of the plants we know, from common grasses to palms, oaks, and mahoganies.

On the ground scuttled multitudes of spiders, scorpions, and insects, including cockroaches several inches long. *Arthropleura,* resembling a centipede, reached a length of five feet. Through the air flew the primitive dragonfly *Meganeura,* with a wingspread of two and a half feet.

Wallowing in the swamps, wriggling through the waters, and waddling about on land was a host of salamandrine amphibians, large and small. Some were long and eel-like, with limbs reduced to vestiges; others were bulky and bloated. Some had their heads armored with shields of fantastic form. The biggest, like the 6-foot *Eryops* and the 15-foot *Eogyrinus,* looked like a preliminary sketch for an alligator. The commonest amphibians of today, the frogs and toads, were wanting; they did not exist until the Mesozoic Era.

Like the plants, the animals that came ashore to live had to solve engineering problems. Of course, we do not mean that the problem was attacked in any conscious way. Such adaptations are a mechanical, unconscious process that works by chance: the chance that, out of thousands of unfavorable mutations or genetic changes, there shall arise, ever few thousands or tens of thousands of years, some mutation that gives the organism an advantage, however slight, over its competitors. Then natural selection fosters the helpful mutation or change, so that it soon spreads throughout the species.

In the case of land animals, the problems were those imposed by gravity and air. The backbone was no longer a mere stiffening rod to enable the animal to wriggle from side to side and thus to scull itself through the water. Instead, it became part of a truss structure, like a cantilever bridge. The legs played the rôles of bridge piers.

To keep the backbone from sagging with the weight of the body, individual vertebrae could no longer be simple disk-shaped structures; they acquired flanges and spines for the attachment of muscles and ligaments. Whereas in fishes each vertebra was made up of several parts, loosely joined together and only partly turned from cartilage to bone, in amphibians the vertebrae tended to become more solidly fused together and more completely ossified. Scientists classify amphibians largely on the basis of the construction of their vertebrae—the precise way in which the several bones making up each vertebra are joined together.

Also, living in the air, an animal had to keep from drying out. Hence it had to develop a thick skin, corresponding to the bark of trees. The cells of the skin, when they died, did not flake off at once, but clung together in a hard, leathery mass to form a more or less continuous waterproof layer.

The purposes of some other improvements are not quite so evident to us as are the changes in backbone and skin. But if they persisted, we may be certain that the changes really were of some value to the animal. For example, certain Paleozoic amphibians had teeth arranged in a way that seems odd to us. The teeth in our jaws form a single, U-shaped row, as do the teeth of most living mammals, reptiles, and amphibians. But many Paleozoic amphibians had not just one row of upper teeth, but two parallel rows. Others had teeth arranged in a pattern all over the palate.

Many of these amphibians also had a small opening in the top of the skull like a miniature eye socket, with a nerve channel leading to the brain. This opening, called the pineal foramen, is believed to have housed a small third eye—or at least a light-receiving organ of some sort, if perhaps not a fully developed eye.

What was the purpose of this pineal eye, which also occurred in many ostracoderms and Paleozoic fishes? We do not know. We can guess, however, that it controlled the animal's responses to light and dark: to day and night, or to open sky versus the deep shade of the forest.

Other animals show comparable arrangements. For example, the horseshoe crab, in addition to two large compound eyes at the sides of its carapace, has a pair of tiny simple eyes or ocelli side by side on the centerline. Recent researches show that these eyes are sensitive to ultraviolet light. Many other arthropods, especially insects and crustaceans, have similar extra eyes. Apparently, evolution finds it easier at certain stages to develop special eyes for special purposes than to combine all these functions in a single pair of all-purpose eyes like ours.

The pineal eye was common among Paleozoic amphibians and persisted in several lines of Paleozoic and Mesozoic reptiles. In other lines, as in mammals, the organ was reduced to a vestige. A working pineal eye survives today in only one species, the lizard-like tuatara.

These improvements, which appeared in the amphibians, persisted in their descendants, the reptiles, birds, and mammals. All these animals may be lumped together with the amphibians in the superclass Tetrapoda, the "four-leggers," to distinguish them from the other superclass, the Pisces, which includes the fishes, the cyclostomes, and the other legless, water-breathing vertebrates.

The amphibians of the coal age lived simple lives. They ate the insects; they ate the fish; and when they could, they ate each other. In spring, when the sexual urge came upon them, they probably grunted, croaked, and cheeped at each other as do modern frogs and alligators. Aside from the sounds of wind and water, these were practically the only sounds in this somber world—a silent, steamy, brooding, monotonously dark-green world, without flowers or fruit, without birds or butterflies, and without seasonal changes of foliage.

Then, during the Pennsylvanian Period, life took another step forward. Certain amphibians evolved an egg of a new type, the amniote egg. This egg contains three compartments. One, the amnion, holds the embryo. Another contains the yolk, which supplies the embryo with food. A third, the allantois, holds the embryo's waste products; it might be called an external bladder. A skin or shell, which allows oxygen to pass in and carbon dioxide to pass out, incloses the whole.

These egg-laying amphibians evolved into reptiles. *Seymouria,* which looked like a stout, two-foot lizard and which comes from the Lower Permian of Texas, stood on the threshold of reptilehood. *Seymouria* was not the direct ancestor of the reptiles, but a little-changed descendant of an earlier form that throve in the Mississippian or early Pennsylvanian Period and gave rise to the reptiles. Even in the Permian, *Seymouria* was a living fossil and soon thereafter became a fossil indeed.

Figure 12. *Seymouria,* an animal from the Early Permian of Texas, on the border between amphibians and reptiles.

Although reptiles like *Seymouria* spent most of their time in the water, they developed dry-land eggs to protect them from other water-dwellers. These eggs proved much safer than amphibian eggs —jellylike little blobs laid in strings, which could be gobbled up by any hungry marauder. Since no vertebrates made a permanent home on land, and since land-lying eggs had little to fear from attacks by insects, the first reptile stole a march on the rest of the vertebrate world by laying its eggs where, for all practical purposes, they were invulnerable. Thus reptiles gained the evolutionary advantage of having a larger percentage of their eggs survive to hatch.

Scientists have long argued whether *Seymouria* and its kin were "really" reptiles or amphibians. Some assert that *Seymouria* must be an amphibian because it has a sensory line system and therefore must have lived in the water. Most fishes possess a sensory line system, usually a pair of "lateral lines" running along the flank, one on each side. Nerves connect these lines with the brain.

There have been many disputes over the function of the sensory lines. Once they were thought to be organs of a chemical sense, like our senses of smell and taste. Now the prevailing opinion seems to be that the lines detect changes in water pressure, like the vibrations made when another creature swims past. Like fishes, most amphibians have a sensory line system, although in their case the lines are usually on the head instead of along the flanks. And *Seymouria* had such a system.

The trouble with many of these arguments is that they forget that classes are artificial, man-made things. If one defines a reptile as an animal that lays eggs on land, and an amphibian as an animal with sensory lines, some organisms can be reptilian and amphibian at the same time.

There is nothing surprising in this. Nature cares nothing for human definitions; creatures that bestride the dividing line between these man-made groups, or combine the features of two or more groups, are always turning up. The real argument should be, not what the animal "really" is, but where is it convenient to locate the dividing line between the groups. Should it be on one side of this particular animal or on the other?

In turning from amphibians into reptiles, the kin of *Seymouria* faced another problem, besides that of evolving an egg that could be laid on land. This was the problem of fertilizing the egg. When eggs were laid in the water, they could be laid unfertilized, and the male could then fertilize them by discharging sperm at them.

This, in fact, is what most fishes and amphibians do. Among most fishes, the males swim behind the females and fill the water with a cloud of sperm as they pass over the eggs. Among frogs, the male mounts the female and discharges his sperm at the same time that she lays a string of eggs.

Among land animals, however, external fertilization is impractical. For one thing, the shell that is needed to protect the egg would keep out the spermatozoön. Therefore, the egg must be fertilized while it is still inside the female, before it has formed its shell.

Since internal fertilization is necessary to land animals, the males of most species are furnished with a more or less rodlike organ for injecting spermatozoa into the females, who are correspondingly shaped to receive them. Although this arrangement applies not only to most land vertebrates, but also to most land invertebrates, such as insects, snails, and worms, it is not universally so. The males of many birds and of the lizardlike tuatara manage to impregnate their mates without any such intromittent organ.

After the Pennsylvanian Period came the Permian. This was a time of mountain building, of the rising of continents to great heights above the sea, of cold, dry climates, and of an ice age, which covered much of the southern hemisphere with glaciers. By no means all of the lands of the Permian were either deserts or covered by glaciers; far from it. Hot, moist zones still existed, but the temperate zones were crowded towards the equator. During the Permian, there was a greater variety of climates and topography than had existed in the earlier ages. As today, there were mountain ranges and desert belts in addition to the swampy plains of earlier times.

The Permian glaciation was not the first ice age. There had been at least one more—perhaps two—in distant pre-Cambrian times. We may be living at the end of yet another: the Pleistocene glaciation.

There has been much argument over glacial periods ever since Louis Agassiz, the Swiss naturalist, discovered them a century and a half ago. As a struggling young scientist, Agassiz worked for a while in Paris under the great Cuvier, then obtained a professorship at the University of Neuchâtel in Switzerland.

While hiking over the Alps in 1836, Agassiz heard of a startling idea set forth by a thoughtful chamois-hunter named Perraudin. This man believed that the huge ridges of gravel and long lines of boulders scattered about Switzerland had been put there by glaciers. Skeptical at first, Agassiz became convinced by his own studies that this was so. The earth, he decided, had in recent geological ages undergone a cold period, in which thick sheets of ice had overspread Europe.

At first Agassiz's older colleagues thought him slightly mad; but little by little he won them over to his belief. Eventually, he emigrated to the United States to spend the rest of his life as a professor at Harvard. He founded the famous Museum of Comparative Zoology in Cambridge and, on the coast of Massachusetts, a scientific center which became the well-known Woods Hole Marine Biological Laboratory.

Many men asked themselves: what was the cause of these glacial periods? To Eugene Dubois, the Dutch anatomist who, in 1890, found the Java ape-man *Pithecanthropus,* glaciation was simply the result of the sun's cooling. In a few thousand years, as the sun cooled further, the ice would return, covering more land than ever, and so on until the entire earth was frozen and all life extinct.

With the discovery of radioactivity and the working out of the theory of nuclear power, however, it transpired that the sun has its own atomic mechanism for keeping hot. In fact, when it does run out of fuel a few billion years hence, the result is likely to be a rapid heating up, followed by explosions of the nova type, before its final collapse. In any case, Dubois's theory of the cause of the ice age has been altogether discredited.

Then a Scot, Coll, suggested that the ice ages had been caused by changes in the earth's orbit, which made the earth circle the sun in a more elliptical path than it does now. Since a planet traveling in such a path moves fastest when it is closest to its star and slowest when it is farthest from it, the result would be a year of short, hot summers and long, cold winters. The snow and ice deposited during the winters would not be all melted during the summers. Hence the regions of permanent snows would spread, and we should have an ice age.

Others proposed that the earth's axis had changed its angle of inclination to the ecliptic (the plane of the earth's orbit). The German astrophysicist Nölke suggested that the solar system had passed through a cloud of cosmic dust, which shielded the earth from the sun's heat. The Swedish chemist Svante Arrhenius proposed that variations in carbon dioxide (CO_2), in the atmosphere caused ice ages; increases in CO_2 would warm the earth.

Later theories of glaciation involved eras of mountain building. The idea was that the earth alternated between states of mountain making and states of rest. During mountain building, the continents were high, climates cold and dry, and land bridges like the Isthmus of Panama connected the larger continents. In the resting periods, on the other hand, continents were low, flat, and partly covered by shallow inland "epeiric" seas. Lands bridges were submerged, and the free flow of ocean currents gave the world a warm, moist, relatively uniform climate.

All these schemes have been either discarded or drastically modified by the triumph of Wegener's theory of continental drift. Evidence for this belief had been slowly accumulating, until in the 1960s and 70s it all came together with a rush, leaving little room for doubt.

Early in this century, historical geologists fell into three schools: the stable-continent school, the transoceanic-continent school, and the small continental-drift school. The stable-continent geologists did not admit sunken continents; the most they allowed was the slight movement of existing lands, so as to open and close land bridges.

The transoceanic-continent school believed in large vanished land masses. This school began in the 1860s, when British geologists noted resemblances between certain formations in India and South Africa. William T. Blanford pointed out the likeness between the rocks and fossils of a Permian deposit in India, in a tract called Gondwana, and a corresponding formation in South Africa.

Thence it was thought that South Africa and India had been joined by a land bridge, including Madagascar and the Seychelle, Maldive, and Laccadive Islands. The German biologist Ernst Heinrich Haeckel used this land bridge to explain the distribution of lemurs, primitive primates found in Africa, Madagascar, India, and Indonesia. The British zoölogist Philip L. Sclater suggested the name "Lemuria" for this land bridge, after the lemurs.

Although scientifically obsolete, the name "Lemuria" was adopted by the pseudo-scientific lost-continent or Atlantist cult. Helena Petrovna Blavatsky, the founder of Theosophy, applied it to a large imaginary southern continent, which included Australia and the Indian Ocean and "broke up" less than a million years ago. Later occultists moved Lemuria from the Indian Ocean, where Mme. Blavatsky at least had the grace to leave it, to the Central Pacific, where for good geological reasons we can be sure there has never been a continent.

In the 1880s, the Austrian geologist Eduard Suess thought that, in Paleozoic times, there had been a super-continent in the Southern Hemisphere, which he named Gondwanaland after Blanford's Indian tract. He also thought that there had been two northern continents, Atlantis (North America and Europe) and Angaraland (eastern Siberia and northern China), named for a Siberian river. Little by little, parts of Gondwanaland sank, leaving the present southern continents. Last to subside was the Indo-Madagascan land bridge, the former geologists' Lemuria.

All such hypotheses have now been relegated to the discard by the confirmation of the continental-drift theory, of which more anon. Meanwhile, for over a century beginning with Jules Verne, writers of imaginative fiction have used Atlantis, Lemuria, and Gondwanaland as settings for their tales of science fiction and fantasy. This is all harmless fun, so long as no unwary reader is beguiled into thinking that there is sound scientific evidence for the existence of these lost continents.

The now dominant ice-age theory was developed in 1920 by a

Yugoslav physicist, Milutin Milankovich, who combined several previous proposals. The earth's motion has several irregularities, which vary back and forth in cycles. Some variations promote the formation of polar ice; others discourage it. The variations are not in step; therefore the glacier-promoting extremes of two of these variables coincide only at long intervals, or three at still longer intervals, and so on. When all come together at once, which happens perhaps every 250 million years, we get an ice age. These variables include the following:

The tilt of the earth's axis varies between 22° and 24.5°, with a period of about 41,000 years.

The axis wobbles in a circle, like a slowing top, making one revolution in 25,780 years.

The earth's orbit is not an exact ellipse, so that the orbit itself rotates, making one circuit in about 23,000 years.

The eccentricity of the orbit (the extent to which it departs from a true circle) varies in a cycle of 92,400 years.

Since the triumph of the continental-drift theory, it has transpired that the movement of continents also affects the formation of polar ice. The present situation, with two-thirds of the earth's land masses huddled in the Northern Hemisphere, extending well into the Arctic Circle and surrounding a small North Polar ocean, also favors ice ages. In the last two million years, the earth has undergone four periods of glacial advance, with longer mild interglacial periods. We may be heading into a fifth glaciation unless human activities, such as the large-scale burning of fossil fuels, change the scenario.

At any rate, during the Permian Period, the coal forests shrank and the plants adapted themselves to drier climates. The amphibians continued their way of life; but now the reptiles grew and radiated out from their original simple, lizardlike forms. They acquired a variety of shapes and sizes; in fact, they became the dominant animals of the time. Logically, the Permian Period should be included in the Age of Reptiles. In common usage, unfortunately, the Age of Reptiles is held to be synonymous to the Mesozoic Era, beginning with the Triassic.

Permian reptiles are mainly known from fossil-bearing beds in Russia, South Africa, and Texas. The first large group of reptiles—the immediate descendants of *Seymouria* and its kin—belong to the order Cotylosauria. These were the first vertebrates that really lived on land and did not use the earth merely as a safe place to lay their eggs. Most cotylosaurs were small carnivores. They looked like stout lizards, ranging in length from a few inches up to five feet.

Some cotylosaurs, however, evolved flat-crowned teeth and enlarged intestines for devouring plants instead of meat. Since plant food is less easily digestible, pound for pound, than meat, it calls for a more elaborate digestive apparatus. These plant-eating cotylosaurs were the first herbivorous land vertebrates. The new structures that fitted them for eating plants gave them, for a while, a tremendous evolutionary advantage, since they were surrounded by abundant supplies of food that neither ran away nor fought back. At first they did not even have natural enemies, since they were much larger than the flesh-eating cotylosaurs.

Some herbivorous cotylosaurs, called pareiasaurs, grew to be as big as a cow. They were stout, ungainly reptiles, sometimes with knobs or horns on their heads. They weighed as much as a thousand pounds and moved slowly on pillarlike legs. Their legs, although bowed, at least raised their bodies well above the ground.

Figure 13. *Bradysaurus,* an eight-foot pareiasaur from the Middle Permian of South Africa.

In the pareiasaurs, we see the first preliminary sketch of an animal design that has evolved over and over. This is the large stout-bodied, thick-limbed herbivore, protected by its size from the attacks of carnivores. This bodily form is called "graviportal" or weight-carrying. The design has been repeated, with steadily increasing refinement and perfection, down to the modern elephant and rhinoceros.

Another group of reptiles, the pelycosaurs, retained a lizardlike shape. A plant-eating American pelycosaur from the middle Permian, *Cotylorhynchus,* reached a length of ten feet and combined a massive body and limbs with an absurdly small head.

Figure 14. *Cotylorhynchus.*

Some pelycosaurs bore sail-like structures on their backs, made of elongated spines attached to their vertebrae and connected by a web of skin. Some had little crossbars on these spines, like the yards on the masts of a sailing ship. In some, the spines were flattened like a row of paddles.

These sails were long a subject for argument. One man made a most unlikely guess, that they were actually used as sails when the animals swam. Others said that the sails had no practical use but were a symptom of something wrong with the animal's evolutionary mechanism.

Nowadays it is thought that the sails somehow served in heat control. Control of bodily temperature was another problem for land animals, since the temperature of the air varies more widely than that of the water. Amphibians and reptiles are called "cold-blooded" beause they have no thermostatic mechanism, as we have, to keep their bodies at one uniform temperature. Therefore, they take on the temperature of the surrounding air. When the air is cold, they become stiff and sluggish. When it is hot—say, more than a few degrees above 100 degrees Fahrenheit—the animal dies unless it can find a pool, a burrow, or some other place to cool off.

Snakes and lizards often bask in the sun in the early morning, spreading themselves on a rock, to warm their bodies as quickly as they can to the temperature at which they are most active and efficient. Once that temperature is reached, however, the reptile goes about its business. If forced to remain in the sun on a hot day, it soon expires of heatstroke.

To avoid this danger, modern desert reptiles have evolved a whole set of ingenious adaptations. Some are active only at night, or in the twilight hours; the rest of the time they retreat into caves or burrows or bury themselves in the sand. Some live at the bottoms of narrow ravines, which the sun penetrates only briefly. Some lurk in the shade of bushes or boulders, now and then making a quick dash from one shady sanctuary to another.

The finbacked reptiles coped with temperature in another way. In the early morning they probably placed themselves at right angles to the rays of the rising sun, so that the sail should absorb as much solar radiation as possible. In the heat of the day, perhaps the sail, well furnished with blood vessels to transfer heat between the sail and the animal's body, acted as a radiator to get rid of excess body heat.

The lesson of the pelycosaurs is that one should not hastily conclude that some peculiar shape or organ of a living thing is necessarily useless, because one cannot see any obvious use for it. If such an organ exists, it probably has a use, or the evolutionary force called *rudimentation* would have reduced it to an insignificant vestige, like the four tail bones, with four muscles for wagging them, that you carry at the lower end of your spine.

*   *   *

In most reptiles, the teeth are of simple form, and all the teeth in the mouth of one animal are of more or less the same size and shape. If the animal is a flesh-eater, the teeth are sharp spikes for seizing its victims; if it eats plants, the teeth are blunt or flat-topped pegs. In either case, the teeth are more or less interchangeable. Each reptile has an unlimited supply, for, as each tooth wears out, it is shed and another grows in its place.

The pelycosaurs, however, tended to develop teeth of unequal size. The flesh-eaters, especially, bore four enlarged teeth, two upper and two lower, at the outer front corners of the jaws, where the canines of a dog or other carnivorous mammal occur. The pelycosaurs' relatives the therapsids carried this tendency even further. They evolved specialized teeth like those of mammals.

Most flesh-eating reptiles, being equipped with simple spikes only, cannot chew their prey. They have to gulp it down whole and then lie up somewhere, dozing, for days or even weeks to digest the mass. With specialized teeth like those of mammals, on the other hand, an animal can slice its meat into smaller chunks before swallowing it. Therefore digestion is faster, since the stomach acids do not have so far to go to penetrate these smaller pieces. Hence the beast need not lie around in a torpid state, easily attacked, to absorb its last meal.

The pelycosaurs were the dominant reptiles of the early Permian. Their cousins the therapsids, which evolved from sailless pelycosaurs, appeared in the Middle Permian and waxed mighty in the Late Permian, while the pelycosaurs dwindled. By the end of that period, the pelycosaurs had disappeared.

Some therapsids became large, lumbering herbivores, like their predecessors the pareiasaurs, now dwindling to extinction. Others became formidable carnivores as big as a St. Bernard dog. One group of these, the gorgonopsians, evolved a pair of long fangs in the upper jaw for stabbing their prey, just as did the saber-toothed cats many millions of years later. We do not know whether any therapsids attained such mammalian traits as hair, external ears, and body-temperature control, since these features leave no sign on the skeleton; but they did succeed to some degree in straightening their upper limb bones to a more nearly vertical position.

This position of the limbs makes walking and running far easier for a land animal. If one watches a newt creeping, one sees that the upper joints of its limbs project sidewise like oars, leaving elbows and knees sticking out. The animal has a spraddle-legged gait in which the bending of the body makes up for the lack of limberness of the leg joints. Each limb goes through a kind of rotary motion as if the animal were swimming the crawl stroke. Although their limbs are more mobile, lizards use a similar spraddle-legged gait.

However, some therapsids, and later the dinosaurs and the mammals, developed modified limb bones. The upper joints of the femur and the humerus, where they fit into the pelvis and the shoulder blade, were moved around to the side of the bone instead of remaining at its end. In this way, the limbs could be carried in a vertical position beneath the body, taking some of the load off the muscles and enabling the animal to run faster.

Despite their advances, most therapsids became extinct in the Triassic Period. Their progressive teeth somehow failed to save them. Reptiles of other kinds, especially the rising dinosaurs, crowded them out. Some small therapsids, however, survived and evolved into mammals.

As the reptiles radiated, filling one niche in the environment after another, they acquired a variety of shapes and sizes. We cannot tell much about their relationships simply by looking at them, because some closely related forms looked very different; while others, only distantly related, came to look much alike. Several different lines, for example, took on the appearance and habits of crocodiles. But only one group of these were true crocodiles; the others were imitation or pseudo-crocodiles.

To trace out the family tree of the reptiles, paleontologists have found their skull bones the most trustworthy indicators. The reason for this is simple. Such visible, external features as sharp teeth, or a streamlined form for swimming, or armor to ward off enemies, have a direct, immediate effect on the animal's survival. Hence they tend to evolve rapidly. On the other hand, it matters little to the reptile's survival just how the bones of its skull are arranged, so long as they provide the necessary space and support for the brain, the jaw muscles, and the other soft parts of the head. Therefore, these bones tend to keep the same arrangement for whole geological periods at a time.

Nowadays "a hole in the head" is a byword for something nobody needs. In classifying reptiles, however, holes in the head have proved not only useful to the reptiles themselves but also to the paleontologists. For, by considering the number and arrangement of these holes (temporal fenestrae, to use a more elegant term) scientists have divided reptiles into five main branches or subclasses. As usual, not everybody agrees with this classification, but it is good enough for our purposes.

Do not think of a "hole" as an opening that exposes the brain. In our own skulls, the brain is so large that the skull is essentially a box of bone holding the brain, with a few projections in front to support the seeing, breathing, smelling, and eating apparatus.

In a reptile, however, the brain is only a very small part of the head. A reptile's skull, therefore, consists of two boxes of bone, one inside the other. The inner box, which is closed all the way round except for the small nerve openings, holds the brain. The much larger outer box holds the eyes and other organs that make up the head. It is this outer box that has the fenestrae.

The main purpose of these openings is to allow the jaw muscles, in biting, to bulge out through the holes and thus to act more powerfully than if they were imprisoned in a solid box of bone. A reptile with such holes is a little more vulnerable than one with a solid skull, since the skin over the holes lies directly against the muscles instead of being separated from them by a wall of bone. A flesheater, however, expects to bite others rather than to be bitten by them, so this difference is not of much account. The fenestrae also lighten the skull. Many reptiles had an additional fenestra on each side of the muzzle, just in front of the eyes.

If we so classify the reptiles, the five subclasses are as follows:

1. Anapsida (cotylosaurs and turtles): no holes; a solid skull.

2. Synapsida (pelycosaurs and the mammal-like therapsids): one pair of holes, on the sides of the skull.

3. Parapsida (ichthyosaurs): one pair of holes, on top of the skull.

4. Euryapsida (plesiosaurs and placodonts): one pair of holes, on top of the skull; but the skull bones bounding the holes are arranged differently from those of the parapsids.

5. Diapsida (lizards, snakes, crocodiles, pterosaurs, birds, and dinosaurs): two pairs of holes, one on the top and one at the sides of the skull.

Note that the closest living relatives of the dinosaurs are the crocodiles and the birds. There are a few other minor groups of reptiles, not here classified, some of which we shall meet anon.

During the last half century, the biggest advances in the paleontology of the Age of Reptiles has been the untangling of the relationships among these various groups of reptiles. These advances have been concerned with dinosaurs only incidentally, for the main groups of dinosaurs—as well as pterosaurs, ichthyosaurs, plesiosaurs, and mosasaurs—were already well known fifty years ago. In this branch of study, the signal achievement of scientists since that time has been the hunting down of the scarce remains of the small, nondescript animals from whom the great dragons of the later Mesozoic descended, and determining which is related to which.

Let us look over the list of reptilian subclasses again. At the end of the Permian Period, the anapsids—except for the turtles and one small lizardlike branch of the cotylosaurs—had disappeared. The parapsids and the euryapsids were destined for careers in the sea. Hence, during the early part of the Mesozoic Era, the remaining two subclasses of reptiles, the synapsids and the diapsids, strove for supremacy on land.

To achieve this hegemony, each contestant had to become less dependent upon sources of water. The two subclasses solved this problem in different ways. The synapsids developed long, straight limbs like those of a mammal. By means of these limbs they ranged widely over the country around their water sources, returning to water to drink when they had to.

The diapsids' solution was to become thriftier with the water in their bodies, so that it did not have to be replenished so often. They developed highly efficient kidneys. These organs extracted nearly all the water from their bodily wastes, so that the wastes were excreted in semi-solid form. Hence, the water-wasting process of urination was not necessary to them.

These differences in function still persist in the higher vertebrates. Mammals, which are descended from synapsids, still have to urinate; birds, descended from diapsids, do not. This difference of function also means that the genito-excretory system of mammals differs radically in its construction from that of birds and living reptiles.

The Permian Period saw a great wave of extinction on the earth. It was like the extinction that overtook the giant reptiles at the end of the Cretaceous and wiped out most of the giant mammals at the end of the Pleistocene. We hear less about it because the organisms that died out at this time were less spectacular than mammoths or dinosaurs. Nevertheless, so many groups of amphibians and reptiles disappeared that, at the beginning of the Triassic, the number of known tetrapod genera was less than a quarter of what it had been in the Late Permian.

The Permian extinction affected not only land animals, half of whose known families came to an end, but also many land plants and things that lived in the sea. On land, many primitive plants, like the tree-sized lycopods and the tree ferns, became extinct. In the sea, some groups like the trilobites and the placoderm fishes vanished utterly. Some, like the sea scorpions and the sea lilies, practically disappeared. Some, like the lamp shells and the corals, were much reduced. Other and abler types took their places.

And so, with widespread death and usurpation, the Paleozoic Era ended and the Mesozoic, the true Age of Reptiles, began.

5

The Rise of the Dinosaurs

As the Permian glaciers melted, the climate warmed, the sea level rose, and the lofty mountain ranges raised during Permian times began to be worn down. Some 200 to 215 million years ago, the Permian Period ended and the Triassic, the first period of the Mesozoic Era, began.

Earth's hordes of shambling and scuttling reptiles, of wriggling and wallowing amphibians had no notion of this. Nobody winded a bugle, ran up a flag, or made a speech to herald the dawn of the Age of Reptiles. As far as earth's living beings were concerned, one day was exactly like the next: a simple matter of eating and avoiding being eaten. There was no sharp distinction between one era and the next; nor, even in theory, do geologists pretend that the change took place on one particular day.

As the continents sank and the climate warmed, plant life again spread from seashores, swamps, and river banks over the plains and hills. Because upland fossils are scarce, we cannot tell how rich the Triassic upland flora was, but it undoubtedly did exist.

In the Triassic, the seed ferns disappeared. The spermatophytes—the club mosses, horsetails, and true ferns—receded. Although they still flourished, the spermatophytes were smaller and fewer than in the coal age. Now the gymnosperms grew great and tall. These included the ginkgo and its many extinct relatives. They also in-

SUBDIVISIONS OF PERIODS	NEW WORLD FORMATIONS	OLD WORLD FORMATIONS
Upper (Late) Cretaceous	Lance, Hell Creek, Laramie, Montana, Colorado, Dakota, Ceará	Maastricht, Nubian, Senonian, Djadokhta, Turonian, Dohoin Usu, Cenomanian, Gault, Greensand
Lower (Early) Cretaceous	Potomac, Washita, Fredericksburg, Trinity, Bahia	Albian, Wealden, Iren Dabasu, Aptian, Shantung, Neocomian
Upper (Late) Jurassic	Morrison, Sundance	Tendaguru, Portland, Purbeck, Malm, Cirin, Solnhofen, Kimmeridge
Middle Jurassic	Navajo	Oxford, Dogger, Madagascar
Lower (Early) Jurassic	Wingate	Lias, Holzmaden, Talbraggar
Upper (Late) Triassic	Brunswick, Wingate, Chinle, Chugwater	Keuper, Yünnan
Middle Triassic	Shinarump, West Humboldt	Muschelkalk, Shansi
Lower (Early) Triassic	Stockton, Moenkopi	Bunter, Sinkiang

Table 2: Some typical, principal geological formations of the Mesozoic Era.

cluded conifers much like today's pines, araucarias, cypresses, and sequoias. Finally, they included a host of cycads.

Nine genera of cycads still exist, some looking like palms and some like ferns. The best-known cycad is the sago palm, which is not a real palm at all. It has a stumpy, barrel-shaped trunk, with fronds like those of a date palm growing in a crown from its top. Many ancient cycads had trunks of this kind, some with flowerlike structures growing here and there upon them. It is not known for certain whether these were "real flowers"; that is, devices for luring insects to drink nectar in order to brush pollen on them, so that they should transfer this pollen from male to female flowers. Nor can we tell from the fossils what sort of color and smell these flowers had in life.

If the cycads' flowers were "real flowers," this was nature's first experiment with pollenation by insects instead of by wind. The whole function of flowers is to lure insects for this purpose. It is a thriftier way of uniting the male and female germ cells than wind pollenation, if there are flying insects willing to cooperate. A plant that depends upon wind pollenation—say, a pine or a ragweed—must emit enormous quantities of pollen, in the hope that the wind will blow in the right direction to carry the pollen from a male to a female plant.

The great majority of flower-bearing plants (with a few exceptions like the dandelion and the magnolia) do not rely upon the wind for pollenation. They do not need to emit vast clouds of pollen because they use insects to carry their pollen to a neighboring plant of the same species. The function of the flower is to attract the insect. Color and smell advertise the fact that there is a bribe of nectar waiting in return for the small service of bearing pollen to the cup of another flower.

Now, such a complex relationship between a plant and an insect requires a long period of evolutionary development of both species. The plants must develop the structures to attract the insects and to brush the pollen off on them; while the insects must evolve special tongues for sucking up the nectar and the instincts to respond to the sight and smell of the flowers.

In the Triassic Period, however, there were no flowers, unless the flowerlike things on the trunks of cycads were the first experiments in this direction. We can only guess what the Triassic landscape would look like in areas where there was not enough rain to support a forest. Since grass did not yet exist, the earth between the trees, shrubs, and herbs would be either bare or covered by primitive plants, corresponding to modern mosses. If it was bare, erosion must have been rapid, so that much of the country was cut up by gullies.

Where were these lands of the Triassic? It is an ancient commonplace that land and water have traded places throughout the ages. Several Greek philosophers inferred this when they saw marine fossils upon the hills.

However, it is one thing to say that some present-day dry land was once under water and some present water dry land, and quite another thing to draw a map of the earth as it appeared in 200,-000,000 B.C. To unravel the past history of the earth's surface, we must utilize all the facts known about rocks and the fossils in them. This study is called *paleogeography* or historical geology.

If there is an exposed acre of rock and if there is a fossil-bearing bed of the necessary period in this rock, we can usually tell whether this area was land or water at the time under study. First, we study the character of the rocks. We know that limestone and chalk are laid down on the bottoms of shallow seas and lakes, that sandstone is usually deposited by rivers on deltas and plains, and that coal is made in swamps. Then, we study the type of fossils found therein, to ascertain whether they are the remains of land or water animals. Thus, from the kind of fossils and the kind of rock they lie in, we can often venture an educated guess as to what sort of terrain presented itself in the bygone era in which we are interested.

But what if the area we are studying is covered by a formation of another age, or lies at the bottom of the sea? Similarly, our problems are aggravated as we go back in time and formations become scarcer and less well-preserved. Still, we can learn much about the geography of the past by studying how the earth was built up and how living things were distributed.

Fossils themselves, by their very distribution, tell us what land bridges and water channels existed in former times, what sort of climate prevailed, and how the ocean currents flowed. To show how the opening and closing of land bridges among the continents took place, the fossils of large land animals are the best indicators, because these creatures move about actively on land but cannot cross even narrow stretches of water. Other organisms are less helpful: flying things like insects can be blown across water; small land animals may ride over on driftwood; and seeds and eggs may be carried across by birds.

When we find that in some past age the same kind of large land animal lived in two land areas, now separate, we know that these land areas must have been joined together. For instance, we know that there must have been continuous land, probably via Asia, between Africa and North America during the Jurassic Period, since we find sauropod dinosaurs of the same genus in both places. Likewise, we know that North and South America were separated throughout the first half of the Age of Mammals. About the end of the Pliocene, an isthmus appeared above the water, joined the two continents, and let the animals cross over. That is why there are armadillos from South America in Texas and jaguars from North America in Brazil today.

Another such land bridge, now closed, connected Alaska with Siberia via the Bering Strait. The American paleontologist George Gaylord Simpson has worked out a timetable of the opening and closing of the Bering Bridge by comparing the percentage of species, genera, and families of animals that lived at the same time on both adjacent continents. He found that the bridge was open for traffic during most of the Cenozoic Era, with an interruption in the Middle Eocene Period, another interruption in the late Oligocene, and a third interruption, still in effect, since the last retreat of the Pleistocene glaciers.

Many geologists agree that the main land masses have stayed in much the same places that they now occupy during the whole Cenozoic Era, even though epeiric seas have overflowed the continents and land bridges have opened and closed. Therefore, during the last sixty or seventy million years, the connections among the continents have been those you see on the map today: Bering Strait, Panama, and Suez. During that time there have been no direct connections among Africa, South America, and Australia. The first two communicated via the northern continents only, while Australia and New Guinea, although they may have been joined to each other, were separated during this whole time from the Asiatic land mass.

Before the Cenozoic Era, however, the evidence is less definite and opinions vary widely. Some geologists believe that direct connections among the southern continents existed, either by way of

Antarctica, or by land bridges across the South Atlantic and Indian oceans.

To understand the earth and its changing surface, it is important to understand the composition of the crust on which we live. At its surface, the earth consists of a skin of crystalline rock. As we go deeper, the rock becomes hotter until, 50 to 100 miles below the surface, it is a white-hot, glassy substance, called "magma." This hot magma would be molten if it were on the surface; but, because of the enormous pressure upon it, it is actually a solid, stiffer than steel.

The comparatively thin, crystalline crust above the magma is made up, in the main, of igneous rocks. These include dense rocks like basalt, made of silicon and magnesium salts, called "sima"; and light rocks like granite, made of silicon and aluminum salts, called "sial."

These rocks are not distributed at random. The land areas are mostly sial, while the sea bottoms are mainly sima. The continents are, in fact, patches of sial "floating" on a crust of sima like cakes of ice in a river. Like ice, they extend down into the medium in which they float much farther (ten to sixty miles) than they project up out of it. Sedimentary and metamorphic rocks also occur, but their total quantity is small compared to the bulk of the igneous rocks.

Therefore, when geologists find sial or "continental" rocks under water or on an island, they suspect that these may mark the site of a former large land mass. On the other hand, they believe that islands made entirely of volcanic sima, like the islands of Polynesia, must have grown up from the sea bottom by volcanic action and are not the remains of any continent.

The ocean bottom consists partly of shallow continental shelves, which are merely the submerged edges of continents; vast submarine plains, miles deep; and areas of moderate depth and broken, mountainous relief. By studying the speed of earthquake waves, geologists have inferred that the great deeps are more or less pure sima, while the continental shelves are mostly sial, and the submerged mountain ranges are partly sial. The greatest areas of deep sima are in the Central Pacific, the southern Indian, and the Arctic oceans. These are the "permanent" oceans, where no continents—past, present, or future—are to be expected.

The great submarine mountain ranges, where we might reasonably expect a sunken continent, lie in the southwestern Pacific Ocean (including the Fiji Islands and New Zealand) and the northwestern Indian Ocean. The Atlantic Ocean seems to be mainly sima, with little patches of sial here and there, and therefore never could have boasted a large land mass in its middle.

Most historical geologists fall into one of three schools; the stable-continent schools, the transoceanic-continent school, and the continental-drift school. The stable-continent geologists—including, in recent decades, most living American geologists—do not believe in sunken continents. The most they will allow is the slight movements of existing lands required to open and close land bridges.

The transoceanic-continent school, on the other hand, believes large vanished continents possible. The continental-drift school holds that the continents are fairly stable in size and shape but that they slowly drift about the surface of the earth.

The transoceanic-continent school began in the 1860s, when some British geologists noted striking resemblances between certain formations in India and South Africa. Once of these men, William T. Blanford, pointed out the likeness between the rocks and fossils of a deposit of the Permian Period in Central India, in a tract called Gondwana, and a corresponding deposit in South Africa.

Blanford and his colleagues inferred that South Africa and India had once been connected by a land bridge, which included Madagascar, the Seychelles Reefs, and the Maldive and Laccadive Islands. These observations came to the notice of the Austrian paleontologist Neumayr and the German biologist Haeckel. In 1887, Neumayr published the first paleogeographical map of the world, showing how he thought it had looked in Jurassic times. This included a great "Brazilian-Ethiopian Continent," from whose southeast corner extended an "Indo-Madagascan Peninsula" corresponding to Blanford's Permian land bridge.

Haeckel went further. He used an Indo-Madagascan land bridge to explain the distribution of lemurs, primitive primates found in Africa, Madagascar, India, and the Malay Archipelago. More than that, he speculated that this bridge had lasted well into the Cenozoic Era and was the original home of man. The British zoologist Sclater suggested the name "Lemuria" for this bridge. This name has stuck to the area and has been adopted by the modern pseudo-scientific lost-continent or Atlantist cult, although it now appears that Haeckel was wrong about this land bridge's lasting into the Cenozoic, and most paleontologists believe that they can explain the distribution of lemurs without it.

In the 1880s, an Austrian geologist, Eduard Suess, brought out an immense five-volume treatise on the geology of the world, *Das Antilitz der Erde* (The Face of the Earth). In this work he expressed the opinion that, in the Paleozoic Era, there had been one large continent in the Southern Hemisphere, which he called "Gondwanaland" after Blanford's tract in India. Suess thought that there had also been two northern continents. One, "Atlantis," was essentially North America with a peninsula reaching over to Europe via Iceland. The other was eastern Asia, which he named "Angara-land" after a Siberian river.

During the Jurassic and Cretaceous periods, according to the Neumayr-Suess school, Gondwanaland gradually broke up as its various parts sank. Australia and New Zealand separated first. This is why they have no native placental mammals, since placental mammals had not yet evolved at the time of the separation. South America was sundered next.

The last to sink was the land bridge from South Africa to India. This is the geologists' Lemuria, and is not to be confused with the Pacific "Lemuria" or "Mu" of the occultists, for which there is no geological evidence whatsoever. Likewise, Suess's "Atlantis" has nothing but the name in common with Plato's lost continent of Atlantis in the North Atlantic—a purely mythical continent supposed to have vanished in an earthquake about 11,000 years ago.

Although the evidence suggests some route for direct migration between the southern continents during the Age of Reptiles, most

geologists object to Suess's idea of a vast continent of Gondwanaland on the ground that it would have displaced so much ocean water
that the other continents would have been completely submerged.
They believe that narrow intercontinental isthmuses rather than one
great continent linked Australia, Africa, and South America in the
distant past.

If continents can rise and fall, can they not drift? Alfred L.
Wegener, who was a professor of geophysics at the University of
Graz and who perished exploring the Greenland icecap in 1930,
said: If the continents float in the sima crust like cakes of ice in
water, would they not drift about like cakes of ice? Therefore, he
assumed that back in the Paleozoic Era there had been a single
supercontinent, which included all the modern continents.

Wegener's maps showed how modern continents could, with a
little stretching and bending, be fitted together like pieces of a
puzzle. According to Wegener's theory, the supercontinent, which
he called Pangaea ("all earth"), had come unglued in the Mesozoic
Era; and its parts started drifting asunder. Europe came loose from
North America, he contended, as late as the Pleistocene Period.

Scientists found serious flaws in Wegener's theory in its original
form. For one, an erroneous surveying report gave Wegener the idea
that Greenland was moving westward at about twenty meters a year,
which implied that it had parted from Europe only within historic
times. It was even suggested that Plato's Atlantis was North America,
which in ancient times lay just over the horizon. Atlantis "disappeared" when North America drifted too far west for the primitive
ships of the time to maintain contact with it.

In addition, the centrifugal and gravitational forces that Wegener
relied upon to move his continents were much too small for the job.
Finally, how could continents, made of comparatively weak sial,
plow their way through the denser and stronger sial on which they
rested?

Hence, for nearly fifty years, Wegener's theory was laid on the
shelf, considered ingenious but not taken very seriously. Then a flood
of evidence came to light, showing that, although Wegener had many
details wrong, his basic idea was right after all. The continents do

move about the globe, although at a speed of no more than a few centimeters a year.

Back in the Permian Period, all the continents had been clustered in a single super-continent, Pangaea, reaching from pole to pole and extending about a third of the way around the earth in the east-west direction. The rest of the globe was covered by a single vast ocean, of which the Pacific is a remnant.

Moreover, continents do not "plow" through anything. The earth's crust is made up of tectonic plates, of which geologists class ten or twelve as large plates and a larger number as small. These plates move about, carried by currents in the magma beneath. (Benjamin Franklin once suggested a similar idea.) The continents ride on these plates as cakes of ice do in a river.

When two adjacent plates move towards each other, the leading edge of one is forced down into the molten interior, to be re-melted. When plates move apart, lava rises from below to fill the gap and solidify. Lately, with deep-sea submarines, lava has been seen doing this on the sea bottom, bellying up in glowing red masses, which darken as they cool and solidify. The water in contact with them does not boil because the pressure does not permit it.

The Atlantic Ocean has a submarine mountain range, the Mid-Atlantic Ridge, which passes in a serpentine curve down its length from Iceland to the Antarctic, remaining about equidistant from the Americas to the west and from Europe and Africa to the east. It includes several islands: the Azores, Ascension, and Tristan da Cunha. This ridge is actually a rift, whence the sea bottom is moving away on both sides and in which eruptions of lava frequently rise to fill the gap. Hence the often-active volcanoes of Iceland and the Azores.

Back in the Permian, as Wegener thought, the Americas did indeed fit against the corresponding continents on the eastern side of the gap. (Sir Francis Bacon had made the same suggestion in 1620.) The fit is even better if the boundaries of the continents are taken to be the edges of the continental shelves instead of the shore lines.

The prevailing present-day view is that there may well have been an even earlier Pangaea, in pre-Cambrian times, which broke up into fragments and then was reassembled by the motion of the crustal plates. Then in the late Permian or early Triassic, Pangaea separated into two supercontinents. Geologists call the northern supercontinent Laurasia and the southern one Gondwanaland, after Suess's sinking supercontinent. The two land masses were separated by a long, narrow sea, called Tethys Sea; but they came close enough in places, sometimes actually touching, to permit animals to migrate from one to the other.

During the Cretaceous, the two supercontinents in turn broke up by the drifting apart of sections. Laurasia separated into North America and Asia (including Europe). Gondwanaland fragmented into India, Africa, South America, and another piece that included Australia and Antarctica. During the following Cenozoic Era or Age of Mammals, India migrated northward and came up against Asia. The land along the line of the collision was forced upward and became the highlands of Tibet and the Himalayas. Meanwhile, Australia and Antarctica parted company. By mid-Cenozoic, the world's map looked much as it does today.

The main changes since then have been the opening of the Panama land bridge between North and South America; the intermittent opening of a land bridge between Asia and Alaska; and the separation of the Indonesian islands from the mainland. The connection between the Americas allowed the ancestors of the jaguar and other cats, of peccaries, and of llamas to invade South America, and the forebears of opossums and armadillos to migrate in the opposite direction.

Some of these migrants became established in their new homes but failed to survive the wave of extinction at the end of the Pleistocene. For instance, mastodons migrated to South America and ground sloths to North America, but all are now extinct. South America also lost an extensive fauna of native predators, which proved unable to compete with the invaders from the north. These predators included an array of giant flightless birds, and another of carnivorous marsupials, ranging from a jaguarlike marsupial sabertooth, *Thylacosmilus,* down to animals corresponding to the bears, wolves, foxes, and weasels of other continents.

Since the tectonic-plate revolution, belief in land bridges (other than the obvious ones like Panama, Suez, and the Bering Sea) has greatly declined. The tectonic-plate triumph is connected with recent discoveries about the earth's magnetism.

It has long been known that the earth is a magnet with north and south poles. These poles are connected by a space called a magnetic field. In this field, the earth's magnetism affects iron and some other substances. The earth's magnetic poles are in the same general regions as, but not very close to, the geographical poles. Thus the North Magnetic Pole is in the Boothia Peninsula at the northern extremity of Canada, over a thousand miles from the geographic North Pole.

Nobody knows for certain why the earth has a magnetic field. The most plausible explanation so far is that this field is generated by currents of molten iron in the liquid core of the earth, 1,800 or more miles below the surface. These movements set up vast electrical currents, which generate the magnetic field.

Igneous rocks, it is now known, hold a kind of fossil magnetism, a record of the earth's magnetic field in former ages. While the lava of which these rocks were formed was cooling, small crystals of iron oxide lined up with the earth's magnetic field, as does the needle of a compass, and stayed in the same positions after the lava had frozen to solid rock. By examining these rocks, scientists can tell the direction of the earth's field when the lava hardened.

Furthermore, as the French physicist Bernard Brunhes discovered in 1906, the earth's magnetism, for reasons not understood, undergoes reversals from time to time. The North Magnetic Pole becomes the South Magnetic Pole and vice versa. At such a time, the north-pointing end of a compass needle would point south. These reversals occur at irregular intervals, averaging about three reversals per million years.

During the 1960s, Ronald G. Mason and Arthur D. Raff of the Scripps Institution of Oceanography, studying the pattern of fossil magnetism on the floor of the Atlantic Ocean, discovered an astonishing fact. On either side of the Mid-Atlantic Ridge, areas of normal magnetism ("normal" meaning the kind prevailing right now) alternated with areas of reversed magnetism in a pattern of stripes, parallel to the Ridge. On either side of the ridge, these stripes formed a symmetrical pattern, like the stripes on a zebra.

Because the reversals occur irregularly, it is possible to recognize the record of a period east of the Ridge and match it to a similar record to the west. This is natural if the sea floor has moved away from the Ridge in both directions, taking with it a record of the magnetic direction that prevailed when the lava of which the floor is composed rose into the Ridge and froze.

Although the exact form of the Triassic continents is still largely unknown, we know quite a lot about the beasts that roamed these land masses.

In the Triassic, the big amphibians of the earlier periods lingered on, dwindling in numbers. The largest of all, *Mastodonsaurus,* lived in Europe in the Late Triassic. This was an animal ten feet long, a third of this length being head. It looked like an enlarged *Eryops;* that is to say, something like a cross between an alligator and a bullfrog, with a huge head; a plump body; short, stout, bowed legs; and a short tail. Fish fossils mixed with the remains of one *Mastodonsaurus* show that it was mainly a fish-eater. We might call such a creature a "crocodile-salamander," or perhaps a "crocomander."

By the end of the Triassic, all the crocamanders (members of the order Rachitomi) had become extinct. At this time, the first true frogs—the commonest modern amphibians—were evolving from predecessors of more traditional or salamandrine design. Probably the crocamanders could not withstand the competition of reptiles of several different groups, which, taking to shallow water, evolved shapes and ways of life almost exactly like those of modern crocodiles.

In addition to these pseudo-crocodiles, among the swarming reptiles of the Triassic there were also vast numbers of small, lizard-like, insect-eating scuttlers. If shown an assortment of these reptiles, the reader would instantly identify them as lizards. He would do the same with many of their larger plant-eating or meat-eating relatives, which looked much like the monitor lizards and iguanas of today.

Scientifically speaking, however, these Triassic reptiles were not true lizards but pseudo-lizards, just as many of the armored lurkers in fresh water were not crocodiles but pseudo-crocodiles. Most Triassic reptiles, in fact, could be classed as either pseudo-lizards or pseudo-crocodiles. Further to confuse us, there were also turtles and pseudo-turtles. The remaining reptiles—some leftovers from the Permian, some the ancestors of the dinosaurs and other reptiles of later Mesozoic times—did not much resemble anything on earth today.

The evolutionary principle shown by these reptiles is that of *parallel evolution.* Two groups of animals, somewhat similar in size and shape but only distantly related, can, over a long period, develop forms quite different from those they started with, but end up still looking much alike, because both have taken to the same kind of habitat and way of life. Since one particular design is most efficient for that way of life, natural selection keeps nudging both groups towards one particular form. Therefore, both approximate that form, differing only in minor details. Many cases of parallel evolution, outside the reptiles, are also known. One example is the parallelism between the wolf and the possibly extinct marsupial "wolf," the thylacine of Tasmania.

As we learned in the preceding chapter, reptiles can be classified by the number and placement of the holes in their heads. There are five subclasses of reptiles, depending on these temporal fenestrae: the Anapsida, the Synapsida, the Parapsida, the Euryapsida, and the Diapsida. During the Triassic, some of these subclasses increased in size and importance; others dwindled and vanished.

Let us consider the changes that took place in the Triassic reptiles, subclass by subclass. First, consider the anapsids, the solid-skulled reptiles. The primitive cotylosaurs were extinct, except for one small lizardlike family called the procolophonids, some of which had spikes on their heads like horned toads.

Reptiles of the other anapsid order, the Chelonia or turtles, now appear for the first time in the fossil record. Their original design must have been extremely successful, for they have continued without much change from Triassic times to the present. However, the few known Triassic turtles could not withdraw their heads into their shells. To make up for this shortcoming, their necks, legs, and tails were protected by spines. They also had teeth, which later turtles replaced by a horny beak.

The synapsids (with a pair of holes on the sides of their skulls in back of the eyes) had teeth of varying sizes and certain other mammalian features. Their kin, the finbacked pelycosaurs of the Permian, had disappeared. The later therapsids, however, survived through the Triassic.

Among the Triassic therapsids, the anomodonts were massive plant-eaters, often weighing over a ton. Those that survived into the Triassic lost all their teeth (with the exception to be noted) and grew parrotlike beaks instead. In the males of some species, otherwise toothless, a pair of tusks grew down from the upper jaw. Perhaps they used these tusks to fight each other for territory or for females. Other kinds of anomodonts had knobs or spikes on their heads, which may have served as weapons of defense.

Another therapsid suborder, the theriodonts, produced some formidable carnivores like *Cynognathus,* the size of a small bear. It carried a very doglike set of teeth, whence its name, which means "dog-jaw." Knight's picture of South African reptiles of the Late Permian or Early Triassic shows a pack of cynognaths ringing an inoffensive anomodont.

A third group of therapsids, the ictidosaurs, were smaller and even more mammalian than the "dog-jaws." They were about the size of rats and woodchucks and may have lived rodentlike lives. Some of the related forms even had two pairs of oversized teeth in the front of their jaws, like those of a rodent. In the ictidosaurs, as in all early mammals, the bar of bone separating the eye socket from the temporal opening disappeared, so that the eyeball was not walled off from the jaw muscles. (Some later mammals, such as primates and horses, grew back this dividing bar. You can feel it in your own skull between your eye and your temple.)

From certain of the smaller relatives of the ictidosaurs, mammals developed. The exact steps of this development are obscure, because, for reasons we have explained, fossils of such small animals are rare. Perhaps all mammals came from one single reptilian ancestor. On the other hand, some paleontologists think it more likely that several lines of ictidosaurs made the change to mammals by means of parallel evolution. There may have been as many as four or five such lines.

We cannot tell at what point these various groups acquired the mammalian features of fur, external ears, four-chambered hearts, temperature control, live birth, and teats, since these matters cannot be settled from skeletons alone. A number of small Triassic fossils could be the bones of either mammals or reptiles. We should have to see the living animals to decide. Even seeing them might not end the disputes; for example, some paleontologists think that hair was common among therapsid reptiles, before they had otherwise evolved towards becoming mammals. Their skulls suggest that they were equipped with vibrissae or catwhiskers; and, if they had vibrissae, why not other hair as well?

Of the evolutionary advances that made mammals out of reptiles, one of the most important was temperature control, or "homeothermy." Reptiles notoriously become stiff and torpid when chilled. This fact limits their range to the warmer climates. In the temperate zone, it also limits the seasons in which they can be active. By developing a thermostatic control mechanism, mammals keep their bodies at a uniform temperature, the temperature at which their organs operate most efficiently. Mammals and birds, which keep their bodily temperatures constant, are classed as "endotherms"; reptiles, amphibians, and fishes, which control their bodily temperatures much less effectively or not at all, as "ectotherms."

Mammals are furnished not only with heat control mechanisms but also with equipment, such as sweat glands, for cooling the animal. This is useful when the heat of the ambient air, or that generated by vigorous exercise, threatens to warm the creature's body above its most healthful temperature. So equipped, an animal need not scuttle for shade or bury itself in the ground, as most reptiles must, to avoid sunstroke in the heat of the day.

Living reptiles do have rudimentary powers of controlling the temperatures of their bodies. Some can keep their temperatures above that of their surroundings by speeding up their metabolism. Some, like the crocodiles, can sweat a little. Some pant like dogs to cool themselves, while some lizards turn a darker color on cold mornings so that the sun's rays shall warm them up more quickly. Others control their temperatures by their behavior, as by seeking shelter when the ambient air gets too hot or too cold.

Another change, in the transition from reptile to mammal, took place in the structure of the jaw. In most reptiles, the jaw is made up of a dozen or more bones, in pairs. In mammals, the three rearmost bones on each side became detached from the jaw and converted into parts of the mechanism of the ear, so that the ear of a mammal is a more complex and sensitive mechanism than that of a reptile. The remaining bones of the jaw either fused together or disappeared, giving a modern mammal a jaw composed of a single bone.

The next subclass of reptiles, the parapsids (with holes on top of their heads), include the ichthyosaurs. The earliest known Triassic ichthyosaurs were already fully aquatic, with flippers for legs. However, they were less specialized for water life than they later be-

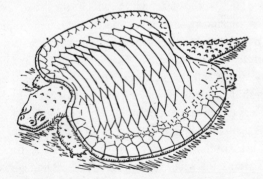

Figure 15. *Henodus,* a placodont pseudo-turtle from the Late Triassic of Europe.

came. Their tails either tapered to a single point or showed only the beginnings of the later two-lobed tail, in which the backbone bent down into the lower lobe.

The suborder of the euryapsids (reptiles with holes on top of their heads, differently arranged) included the lizardlike protorosaurs and the sauropterygians, which took to the water. Descended from the slender pseudo-lizard *Araeoscelis* of the Permian, the

Figure 16. *Nothosaurus,* an aquatic euryapsid reptile from the Triassic of Europe.

typical reptile of this group in the Early Triassic was a nothosaur. This beast looked something like a small, smooth-skinned crocodile, with a smaller head and a longer neck than a true crocodile. From the nothosaurs descended two different kinds of aquatic reptiles. These were the short-necked, mollusk-eating placodonts and the long-necked, fish-eating plesiosaurs.

As for the protorosaurs, most of them were nondescript pseudolizards. One strange group, however, is sometimes classed with the protorosaurs and sometimes with the true lizards. These are *Tanystropheus* and its relatives. *Tanystropheus,* from the Triassic of Europe, was lizardlike except for its neck. This neck was stretched out until it was almost as long as all the rest of the animal. In this respect it reminds one of the later and longer-necked plesiosaurs. However, whereas the plesiosaurs lengthened their necks by adding to the number of neck vertebrae, *Tanystropheus* accomplished the same end, like the giraffe, by increasing the length of each individual vertebra.

Tanystropheus grew to 15 or 20 feet; its long, sharp teeth suggest a diet of fish. Perhaps *Tanystropheus* crouched on the bank of a stream and plunged its head into the water when a fish came near the surface. Perhaps, on the other hand, it crept about on the bottom of small bodies of fresh water, darting its head from side to side after

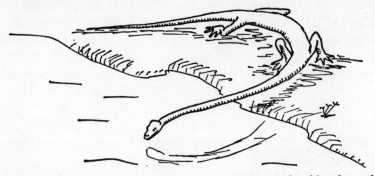

Figure 17. *Tanystropheus,* a reptile of uncertain relationships from the Triassic of Europe.

its prey then raising it to the surface by means of that fantastic neck to breathe.

The last subclass of reptiles are the diapsids (with holes on the tops and sides of their heads), the most successful of all the reptiles. The subclass Diapsida breaks into two superorders (which some people think should be raised to the rank of subclasses): the Lepidosauria and the Archosauria. The Lepidosauria are made up of three orders, as follows:

1. The Eosuchia, the ancestors of the other two orders, were small, lizardlike reptiles. Some eosuchians survived through the Triassic and evolved into true lizards. Others became pseudo-crocodiles.

2. The Squamata are the order of lizards and snakes. There is no doubt that, if the record were complete, it would show a continuous evolution from the eosuchians to the true lizards. Unfortunately, there is a gap in the record. This is easily understood when we remember that we are dealing with animals only a few inches long. As things stand, the first fossil true lizards come from the Triassic, and the first of their legless offshoots, the snakes, from the Lower Cretaceous.

3. The other offshoot of the eosuchians goes by the awkward name of Rhynchocephalia. Mostly lizardlike, they radiated in the Triassic into a variety of forms. Some lost their teeth and acquired turtle-like beaks. Some became pseudo-crocodiles. Some developed peculiar tooth structures for crushing the mollusks on which they fed, such as a bony knob at the front of the lower jaw and a socket into which it fitted in the upper jaw.

The rhynchocephalians waxed and waned throughout the Age of Reptiles; some lasted well into the Cenozoic Era. Today they are represented by a single species: the tuatara, *Sphenodon punctatum,* once common in New Zealand but now confined to a few small islands off the coast.

Although it is not a true lizard, the tuatara for all the world resembles a plump, two-foot lizard with small spines down its back. It lives in burrows, whence it sallies forth to snap up insects. It has a remarkably low metabolic rate, breathing ten to twelve times a min-

Figure 18. The tuatara, *Sphenodon*, from modern New Zealand, the last survivor of the order Rhynchocephalia.

ute at its preferred temperature of 52 degrees Fahrenheit. At a temperature four degrees lower, one tuatara did not breathe at all for an hour.

The other superorder of the diapsids, the Archosauria, comprises the reptiles most interesting to our readers: the dinosaurs, the pterosaurs, the crocodiles, and the ancestors of the birds.

We have already seen how the early vertebrates evolved one structural improvement after another to give them a greater mastery of their surroundings: the jawbones of the placoderm fishes, the lungs of the choanichthyan fishes, the legs of the first amphibians, the amniote egg of the first reptiles, and the efficient kidneys of diapsid reptiles. Now, to lead a more active life than was usual among Triassic reptiles, a better system for circulating the blood was needed; and the four-chambered heart came into being both among the archosaurs and among the reptiles that evolved into mammals.

Let us consider the circulatory system for a moment. The blood of any vertebrate passes through lungs or gills, where it takes up oxygen either floating in the air or dissolved in the water. Then the heart pumps this blood to the various parts of the body through the arteries, until the blood gives up its oxygen to the muscles and organs. By a series of complex chemical reactions in these organs, the oxygen combines with chemicals of the sugar class to furnish energy. The used-up sugar and oxygen become water (H_2O) and carbon dioxide (CO_2) which the blood carries off as waste. The blood bears the carbon dioxide through the veins and back to the lungs or gills again. There the blood gives up its carbon dioxide and takes on another supply of oxygen.

In lampreys and in most fishes, the heart is a muscular pump with two chambers. The blood from the body pours into the first chamber, the atrium, whence it is sent into the other chamber, the ventricle. Then the blood leaves the ventricle and goes to the gills, where it picks up oxygen. From the gills, it flows to all parts of the body and then back to the heart.

Lungfishes use a different arrangement. The blood traveling between heart and lungs flows around in a separate circuit, parallel to the circuit from the heart to the gills and the body. The blood from the body and from the lungs all pours into the atrium, where it is mixed and sent into the ventricle. Then this mixed blood is divided, some going back to the lung and the rest to the gills and the body.

This is not efficient. Some oxygen-bearing blood may make two or more trips around the lung circuit before it is sent to the body, while some carbon-dioxide-bearing blood may make several trips around the body before it gets to the lungs.

Among amphibians and reptiles, the heart is so arranged that *most* of the blood from the lungs goes to the body the first time around, while *most* of the blood from the body goes to the lungs. This is done by dividing the atrium into two chambers, one receiving blood from the lungs and the other blood from the body. In many reptiles, the ventricle is also partly divided.

In mammals, in birds, in crocodiles, and probably in all the rest of the archosaurs as well, the heart has four distinct chambers. With this arrangement, blood from the two circuits is not mixed at all. All the blood follows the direct figure-eight-shaped route: lungs to heart to body to heart to lungs. It is as if the animal had, not one heart, but two, one providing the power for the lung circuit and the other that for the body circuit. This system gives the animal much more speed and stamina than is the case with hearts of two or three chambers.

Long before any such advanced development as the four-chambered heart came into being, the Archosauria began with a group of small, generalized reptiles of late Permian times, called the Pseudosuchia or "false crocodiles." Varying from animals 8 to 10 inches in length up to forms four to five feet long, they resembled lizards; but lizards with a difference.

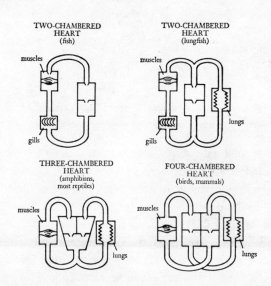

Figure 19.   Diagram showing the circulatory mechanisms of vertebrates of different kinds.

For one thing, their hindlegs were much longer and stouter than the hindlegs of ordinary lizards. (See Parker's Plate 26.) They obviously walked on their hindlegs most of the time and used their tails to balance the weight of their bodies. The forelegs, although little used for walking, were still effective in grasping their prey.

Today, two hundred million years later, several living species of lizard are developing a bipedal gait by parallel evolution. One is the frilled lizard of Australia, a yard-long reptile, which runs on its hindlegs with its tail stuck up behind it. Besides the defense of fleetness of foot, it sports an umbrellalike frill around its neck, which flaps open to startle its foes. Since its throat is bright yellow, when the creature opens its mouth and spreads its frill, the effect is astonishing.

The other bipedal lizards are the basilisks of the American tropics. There are several species, all of which belong to the iguana family.

Figure 20. *Scleromochlus,* a reptile from the Triassic of Europe intermediate between the pseudosuchians and the dinosaurs.

They are equipped with crests, frills, and inflatable air sacs on which, like the frilled lizard, they rely to frighten off their enemies. The smaller basilisks actually walk on water, beating the surface so frantically with their hind feet that they remain on top of the waves. Hence the reptile is locally called the "Jesus lizard."

The basilisk's larger relatives, the iguanas, normally go on all fours. However, one of your authors once saw a three-foot iguana dash across the road in front of his car in Mexico. Unless his eyes deceived him, this lizard made the last few feet of its sprint on its hindlegs alone, its forelegs folded back along its sides. The same gait is reported of the collared lizard of the American West.

Speedy though these bipedal reptiles are, they all retain the spraddle-legged gait of the lizard tribe. This gait is not so efficient as that of the archosaurs, which early brought their legs around under their bodies and moved them forward and backward as most mammals do.

Thus the early pseudosuchians were slender, lightly built reptiles, adapted to speed. Their skulls had large openings for lightness and lots of long, sharp teeth for catching insects and smaller reptiles. Some of their long limb-bones were further lightened by thin air sacs in the marrow cavities. Such hollow bones are characteristic of birds.

When dashing after their prey, the pseudosuchians probably bobbed their heads up and down and wove them from side to side as many birds do today. Some may even have pumped their forelegs back and forth as we do when we run.

Not all pseudosuchians were such agile little sprinters, however. The stock early put off several branches, which evolved in different directions. Some became pseudo-crocodiles. One group of these, the chasmatosaurs, had a curious hook on the end of the upper jaw. Another group developed a generally crocodilian form, but with more armor and less jaw than a proper crocodile. These, it is thought, were carrion eaters. The American *Typothorax* had armor all over its back, with a row of short spines down each side. Its relative *Episcoposaurus* had, in addition, several pairs of long spines, the last like backward-curving horns, growing out of the sides of its neck and shoulders. This was an effective protection, because a larger reptile would have had a hard time swallowing such an animal.

Another offshoot of the pseudosuchians were the phytosaurs.[1] These were very successful pseudo-crocodiles. In fact, they are among the most common Triassic vertebrate fossils. The plainest distinction between phytosaurs and true crocodiles is the position of the nostrils. Crocodiles have their nostrils at the end of the snout; phytosaurs have theirs farther back, just in front of the eyes.

With a few exceptions, crocodiles and their imitators live in fresh water. Although they can swim fairly fast by wagging their tails, they

Figure 21. *Episcoposaurus,* an armored pseudosuchian from the Late Triassic of North America.

are less swift than such beautifully streamlined sea beasts as the tuna, the porpoise, and the ichthyosaur. In general, they depend less upon speed than on stealth to catch their dinners. Their method of fishing is to pretend to be a floating log until a fish comes near enough to be caught by a sudden sideways jerk of the head.

Many of them also lie in wait for land animals to come to the water to drink. Then, snap! the mighty jaws clamp shut on the beast's leg or muzzle. The crocodile drags its prey into deep water by backward sculling motions of its tail, drowns it and, if it is too large to be swallowed whole, tucks it away in an underwater hole. When time has softened the carcass, the predator dismembers it by seizing some part and jerking it violently or by rolling over and over. When a part tears loose, the animal swallows it whole. Even such an enormously powerful animal as an African rhinoceros has been dragged under water and drowned by a pair of crocodiles that had seized its hindlegs.

This kind of life presents the problem of breathing with one's mouth full of fish. Yet modern crocodiles are so completely conditioned to eating in the water that a baby alligator will often refuse to eat anywhere else.

When one of your authors was an undergraduate, long ago, he

owned a baby alligator named Algernon. Having no intelligence whatever, the creature would walk right off a table top and harm himself unless stopped. He bit his owner once only, however, when he mistook a thumb for an insect. It was a mere pinch, and the alligator let go as soon as he realized his mistake.

Algernon was not a very rewarding pet; but once he did earn his keep. With a pink ribbon tied in a bow around his neck, he went to class in a mailing tube and was slid out on the desk of an English instructor who had a horror of creeping things. With a cry of: "My God, what's that?" the poor man nearly jumped out of the window.

After some months, Algernon came down with some obscure crocodilian disease and died. Meanwhile, his owner had learned the technique of feeding such reptiles. Once a week, one fills the bathtub with water that is at skin temperature and several inches deep. When the beast is well thawed out and swimming briskly in this water, one drops lumps of raw hamburger on its head. After three or four lumps have hit the target, the creature realizes that dinner is served and swims about gobbling it up. Afterwards, it gruesomely picks its teeth with its hind claws.

It is, by the way, deplorable that pet shops sell baby alligators to the public at large. Either the alligators are starved to death by their new owners, who do not know how to feed them; or if they do survive, they soon grow to alarming size and are often flushed down the toilet or otherwise summarily disposed of. As a result of such procedures, a story became current some years ago that the City of New York suffered a plague of alligators in its sewer system, where they throve by eating eels and other fishes until they were all either shot by employees, drowned by the backing up of water in the branches, or swept out to sea by the swift current in the mains. Later, however, the story was branded a mere hoax.

To be a successful crocodile, then, one must be able to hold one's prey in the water and breathe at the same time. This is impractical with a normal reptilian skull, in which the nostrils open directly into the palate and the same passage through the mouth is used for food and for air. The phytosaurs solved the problem by moving the nostrils back, so that their lower opening was at the extreme rear of the mouth. Then the phytosaur could block off its air passage with its tongue and a flap behind its palate and breathe while keeping its grip on its wriggling prey.

The true crocodiles employed another expedient. They developed a long bony tube, extending back from the nostrils in the muzzle and above the palate. This tube opened at the rear of the mouth, as in the phytosaurs, and thus the same goal was gained.

The pseudo-crocodiles and the true crocodiles also paralleled each other in another way: they developed both broad-headed and narrow-headed forms. These head shapes are connected with the way in which the animal makes its living: a narrow snout indicates a pure fish diet; a broad muzzle, a mixed diet of fish and higher vertebrates. For example, among living crocodiles, we find the very broad-headed American alligator, the moderately broad-headed Old World crocodiles, the moderately narrow-headed American crocodile, and the very narrow-headed gavial of India, the last being a pure fish-eater. The broad-headed design, being more powerful, is more effective for preying upon large land animals.

The phytosaurs became extinct at the end of the Triassic, although the true crocodiles had not yet evolved to the point of competing with them. Still, we have found a direct ancestor of the true crocodiles from the uppermost Triassic of Arizona. This is *Protosuchus,* a reptile two or three feet long (Fig. 22). Like the phytosaurs, it had longer

Figure 22. *Protosuchus,* the two-foot ancestor of the crocodiles, from the Late Triassic of North America.

hindlegs than forelegs, showing its descent from early bipedal pseudosuchians. A double row of bony plates down its back provided it with light but serviceable armor. By mid-Jurassic, the descendants of *Protosuchus* had evolved into true crocodiles scarcely different from those of today.

Of all the archosaurs, none fascinate men so much as the dinosaurs. These heroes of the Age of Reptiles are not really one order, but two, which evolved separately from common ancestors—from small, swift, bipedal carnivorous pseudosuchians like *Ornithosuchus*. A British paleontologist, Harry Govier Seeley, first noted in 1887 that the dinosaurs were really two orders, differing anatomically from each other as much as they differed from other archosaurs. It took more than a quarter-century for Seeley's proposal to be generally accepted; it was finally adopted largely as a result of the efforts of an eminent German paleontologist, Friedrich von Huene.

The two orders of dinosaurs are the Saurischia or "lizard-hipped" and the Ornithischia or "bird-hipped." It is easy to remember which kinds of dinosaurs belong to each other. The saurischians include two of the best-known kinds: the long-necked, small-headed, elephantine plant-eaters, like *Brontosaurus* (suborder Sauropoda); the short-necked, big-headed, two-legged flesh-eaters like *Tyrannosaurus* (suborder Theropoda); and the smaller relatives of both kinds. The ornithischians include all the other dinosaurs.

As for the pelvic difference between the two orders, an explanation and a diagram will make it clear. The pelvis of reptiles is made up of six bones—three pairs—solidly fused together. Of the three bones on each side, the uppermost one, which is clamped to the backbone, is called the *ilium*. The bone sloping downward and aft from the ilium is the *ischium*. Forward of the ischium and joined both to the ischium and to the ilium is the *pubis*. Where the three bones on each side come together, a hollow affords a socket for the end of the thighbone.

These bones vary widely in shape among reptiles and mammals. In walking and running reptiles, the pelvic bones provide strong

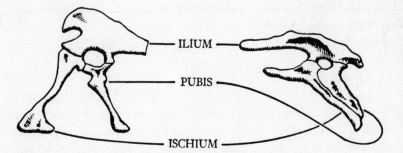

Figure 23. Pelves of saurischian (left) and ornithischian (right) dinosaurs.

attachments for the muscles of the hindlegs and the abdomen. In some swimmers, like the ichthyosaurs and mosasaurs, the pelvis practically disappeared, because the hind flippers were used as guiding vanes and stabilizers only, not as propellers. In sea reptiles that actually rowed with their flippers, like the plesiosaurs, the pelvis was well developed.

In the saurischians, the pubes extend downward and forward, as they do in most reptiles. They are usually joined together to form a single, strong prop or strut to support the reptile's guts. In the ornithischians, on the other hand, the pubes extend down and to the rear, parallel to or joined with the ischia. In many ornithischians, the pubes are forked, with one branch extending forward and one aft; but the rearward prong *always* occurs.

Why are the carnivorous theropods like *Tyrannosaurus* and the herbivorous sauropods like *Brontosaurus*—so different in appearance and way of life—lumped together in the same order? This puzzle is cleared up if we go back to the earliest known dinosaurs, the theropod saurischians called coelurosaurs. The coelurosaurs were not very different from their ancestors, the speedy, bipedal pseudosuchians discussed above.

These early coelurosaurs were even more slender and lightly built than their pseudosuchian ancestors and had teeth in the form of sharp, narrow blades with serrated edges. *Saltopus* from Scotland

15.   Model of a swamp forest at the beginning of the Permian Period, showing a large amphibian, *Eryops* (foreground), a finbacked pelycosaurian reptile, *Dimetrodon* (left background), and the giant dragonfly *Meganeura* (right background). *Photo from the Carnegie Museum.*

16.   *Cotylorhynchus*, an herbivorous pelycosaur from the Lower Permian of North America. *Photo from the Smithsonian Institution.*

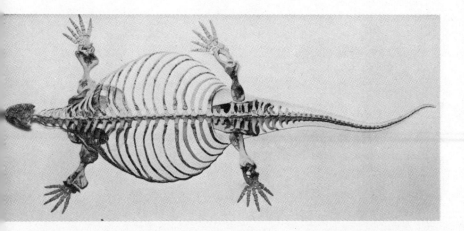

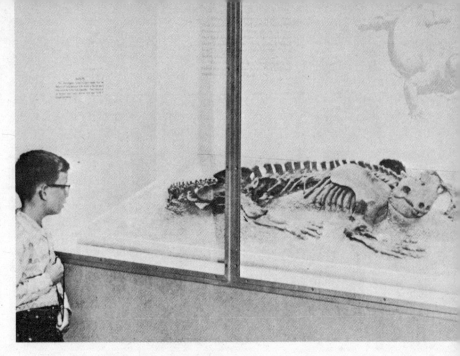

17.   *Diadectus*, a plant-eating cotylosaur from the Early Permian of No[r]
America. *Photo from the Smithsonian Institution.*

18.   Pelycosaurs from the Early Permian of North America. *Dimetrod[e]*
a carnivorous finbacked reptile (right); *Edaphosaurus*, a mollusk-eating [fin]
back (center); *Casea*, a pseudo-lizard (left). *Courtesy of the Chicago N[at]
ural History Museum.*

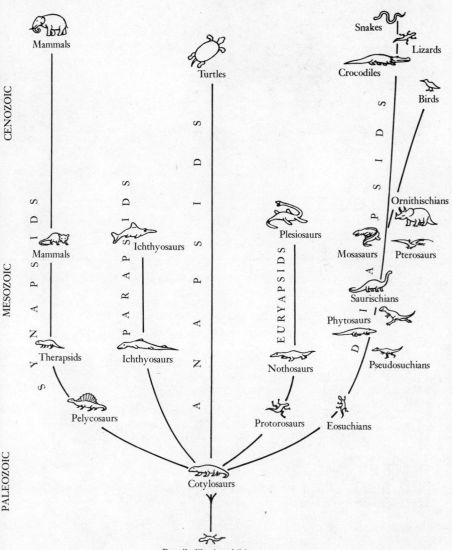

19. Evolution of the reptiles, showing the five main subclasses and the principal groups within each subclass.

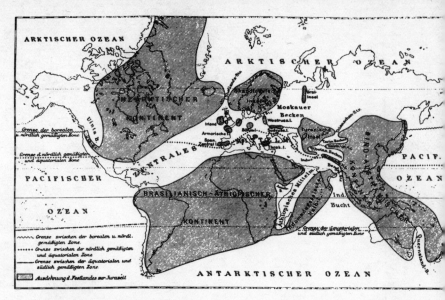

20. Map of the world in Jurassic times, according to Melchior Neumayr's *Erdegeschichte* (1887).

21. The world in the late Paleozoic Era, according to the *Grundlagen und Methoden der Palaeogeographie* (1915) by Edgar Dacqué, a follower of Eduard Suess.

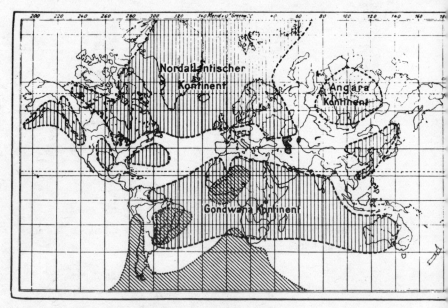

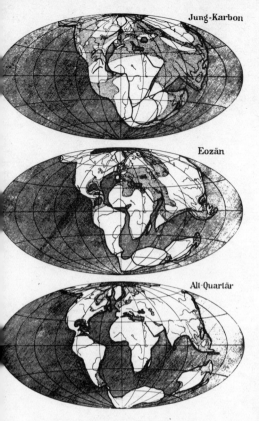

Jung-Karbon

Eozän

Alt-Quartär

22. The world in the Pennsylvanian, Eocene, and Pleistocene Periods, according to the continental-drift theory of Alfred L. Wegener, as set forth in his *The Origin of Continents and Oceans* (1920).

23. *Paracyclotosaurus,* a nine-foot crocamander (amphibian of the order Rhachitomi) from the Australian Triassic. *Courtesy of the British Museum (Natural History).*

A

B

C

D

24. Examples of parallel evolution, showing how a similar environment and way of life brings about similar forms in animals of widely different ancestry. (A) the modern American alligator. (B) *Campsosaurus*, a Cretaceous eosuchian. (C) *Rhytidodon*, a Triassic phytosaur. (D) *Mastodonsaurus*, a Triassic rhachitomian amphibian. (B and C after Osborn.)

25.   Mammal-like reptiles from the Early Triassic of South Africa: *Kannemeyeria*, an herbivorous anomodont, confronted by a pack of *Cynognathus*, a carnivorous therapsid. Painting by Charles R. Knight. *Courtesy of the Chicago Natural History Museum.*

26.   *Ornithosuchus*, a pseudosuchian ancestor of the dinosaurs, from the Late Triassic of Europe. *Courtesy of the British Museum (Natural History).*

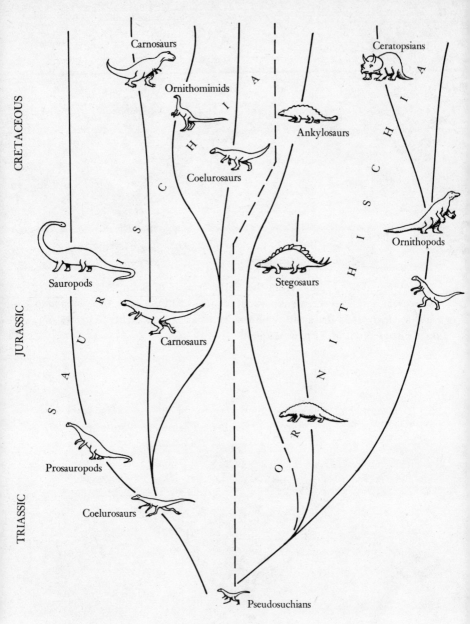

27. The family tree of the dinosaurs. (The animals are not drawn to scale.)

was a mere two feet long; *Podokesaurus* from Connecticut reached a yard in length. Another coelurosaur, *Coelophysis,* found at Ghost Ranch, New Mexico, was a reptile six to eight feet long, weighing forty to fifty pounds, which preyed on smaller game.

Figure 24.   *Coelophysis,* a coelurosaur (small theropod saurischian dinosaur) from the Late Triassic of North America.

Developing as a plant-eating offshoot of the coelurosaurs, the prosauropods—ancestors of the sauropods—appeared in the Triassic. Adaptations to their new diet of vegetation included blunt, peglike teeth, a large paunch to hold a more extensive intestine, and more massive legs to support the added weight.

These reptiles were both bipeds and quadrupeds at the same time. Like a modern kangaroo, they dropped to all fours in order to feed but, when in a hurry, stalked on their hindlegs, balancing themselves by their tails. They ranged from the 5-foot South African *Gyposaurus* to the ponderous European *Plateosaurus,* which reached a length of 20 feet. Like *Coelophysis, Plateosaurus* is well known from several sites where a number of skeletons have been found together. Its descendants grew larger, reverted entirely to a four-footed gait, and turned into full-fledged sauropods. An American prosauropod, the 8-foot *Anchisaurus* (or *Yaleosaurus*), made many of the famous dinosaur tracks of Massachusetts.

Figure 25. *Plateosaurus,* a prosauropod from the Late Triassic of
Europe.

Thus the millennia of the Triassic passed slowly. The land
remained grassless and nearly flowerless. Continental drift broke
Pangaea into northern Laurasia and southern Gondwanaland,
separated by the long ribbon of Tethys Sea, but sometimes in actual
contact, permitting migration back and forth. The foliage of the
lowlands changed with the newer trees. The reptiles that swarmed
upon this low-lying earth went their various ways, evolving more efficient hearts, adapting to various climates, and developing new and
more effective ways of getting food and avoiding being eaten. Reptiles ruled the world.

Then, like the Permian before it, the Triassic Period closed with
a worldwide wave of extinction. On land, whole orders of amphibians
and reptiles disappeared. The victims included the rachitomian croco-
manders, the protorosaurs, the pseudo-crocodilian phytosaurs, and
all the mammal-like therapsids save those that were actually in the
process of turning into mammals. Again, the number of genera of
tetropods shrank to a quarter of its former magnitude. In the sea,
twenty-four of the twenty-five families of ammonites (the nautiloid
mollusks) vanished; although the single surviving family gave rise,
during the Jurassic and Cretaceous periods, to a whole multitude of
different forms.

6

The Reptilian Middle Age

The Triassic Period was followed by the Jurassic, the second of the three Mesozoic periods. In the Jurassic, the dinosaurs attained their full size and splendor, albeit not their greatest variety.

The throw of the geological dice has given us only scanty records of the land life of the Early Jurassic. In the American West, for example, occur abundant beds of Lower Jurassic sandstones; but these were desert sands containing few fossils. The best Lower Jurassic beds are marine deposits, rich in ichthyosaurs and other sea creatures.

From the Upper or Late Jurassic, however, we have several fine fossil deposits. In Jurassic times, the American West was a vast, swampy, tropical river basin and flood plain, like that of the Amazon today. Europe was a far-flung archipelago, with islands, peninsulas, and arms of the sea all intertwined. East Africa lay low: the famous Tendaguru beds were laid down at the gaping mouth of a great river, across which stretched a long sand bar.

Back in Permian times, the land stood high; drouth and cold prevailed; and the world displayed a variety of land forms and climates. Jurassic times were just the opposite. The lands were low. Shallow seas washed over parts of the continental land from time to time, so that the continents shrank to far less than their present area. Nevertheless, the distribution of dinosaurs shows that, at times, land bridges joined the main continents, permitting animals to pass from one continent to another. The climate was warm and moist, with little change between tropics and temperate zones, or between summer and winter.

The more humid parts of these low continents were covered by dense forests, like today's Amazon jungles. These forests consisted mainly of cycads, tree ferns, ginkgoes, araucarias, pines, and sequoias. Except for the dubious blooms on the trunks of the cycads, there were still no flowers; just a monotonous palette of dark greens shading across the broad canvas of the scene.

There were a few mountain lands, too; but these mountains were mostly low and rounded like the old Alleghenies of today. There were also areas of dry scrub forest, open plain, and desert. But we know most about the dank lowlands because here, in these extensive bottomlands, the rocks have kept the most faithful records.

Missing was the landscape of prairie, pampas, steppe, or veld—the great, grass-covered plains that we find in the High Prairies of the Rocky Mountain states, or Argentina, or the Ukraine, or large parts of East and South Africa. These grassy plains occur where rainfall is abundant enough to support a continuous cover of plant life but is not sufficient for a forest—10 to 25 inches of rain a year. In the Jurassic plenty of places enjoyed such a rainfall; but there were no prairies because there was no grass. Such lands probably wore the scrubby, semidesert look of western Texas and New Mexico. The landscape was dotted with herbs and bushes, many of them spiny or leathery; while bare earth, slashed with gullies and ravines, stretched from one clump to the next.

Without grass, we do not know whether, in Jurassic times, the lands that would today be prairie supported teeming herds of herbivores like those of recent times. The fossil-plant record is too fragmentary to tell whether such areas were bare or were covered to a greater or lesser extent by primitive plants, such as the moss of the Alaskan tundra, which sustains herds of caribou. Furthermore, if, as many believe, the herbivorous dinosaurs were cold-blooded, they would not eat so much as warm-blooded beasts of the same size. So a sparser plant cover would support equal numbers.

Dense jungles do not support any such swarms of large animals. In a tropical rain forest, the trees are so tall and thick that they almost completely hide the sun. Low-growing plants are shaded out, so that ground is fairly level. Only where a storm fells some forest giant, or men cut a road through the trees so that sunlight glances in, does undergrowth spring up in impenetrable confusion.

Since dense forests lack a wealth of plant food at ground level, such places also lack great herds of herbivores. Large forest animals travel in small family groups or singly. The swarming life of the tropical forest is not at ground level but in the tops of trees. Here, where the leaves form a dense layer of foliage like a green ocean with fixed waves, live millions of small flying and climbing things, like birds, butterflies, squirrels, sloths, and monkeys.

Similar, we can suppose, were the Jurassic jungles: occasional large animals prowling along the ground; vastly more numerous small ones fluttering or chattering in the trees. The Jurassic had no butterflies, squirrels, sloths, or monkeys. But it did have plenty of insects, flying reptiles, the first birds, and probably small, arboreal reptiles and mammals of many kinds. The earliest animals definitely known to be mammals were found in England in rocks of the Middle Jurassic.

In areas of less rainfall, where trees were fewer and smaller and where sunlight could reach the surface, large ground animals were more common. In Jurassic lakes and swamps, where the sun's rays played around the shallow waters and fostered the growth of vast beds of reeds and other water plants, browsed the sauropod dinosaurs, the largest land animals ever to have lived.

By Jurassic times, the competition between the mammal-like synapsid reptiles and the more lizardlike diapsid reptiles had been decided, for the time being, in favor of the latter. By the Early Jurassic, the only living synapsids were small creatures—some of them reptiles, some reptiles on the verge of becoming mammals, and some real mammals.

Meanwhile, one branch of the diapsids, the dinosaurs, dominated the earth. They took over all the rôles that the environment offered for land dwellers of medium to large size. Similarly, in fresh water, diapsids in the form of true crocodiles ousted most of their pseudo-crocodilian cousins. Still other diapsids took to the air.

We have already said that the animals lumped together under the name "dinosaurs" consist of two distinct orders of reptiles. These orders evolved separately from the pseudosuchians of the Triassic. We have discussed one of these orders, the Saurischia or "lizard-hipped" dinosaurs, and shown that in the Triassic, the saurischians split into two stocks: the theropods, which carried on the meat-eating tradition; and the sauropods, which took to plant-eating. The sauropods reached their climax of size and variation in the Jurassic.

The sauropods are the *big* ones—the dinosaurs *par excellence*—the animals that people first think of when they hear the word "dinosaur." Sauropods were the largest land animals of all time, surpassed only by whales. They were a living answer to the question: How big can a land animal get?

As we have seen, animals had to cope with gravity when they first came out of the water. Now, the bigger a land animal is, the more gravity affects it. The principle behind this fact is the *square-cube law*.

If the dimensions of an animal are all increased while the beast retains the same shape or proportions, the areas of the animal and of its parts increase as the square of the dimensions, while the volumes and hence the weights increase as the cube. In other words, if the length is doubled, the area is increased fourfold and the volume eight-fold. If the length is tripled, the area is multiplied by nine and the volume by twenty-seven.

One consequence of the square-cube law is that, as a beast becomes larger, its legs must be stouter in proportion to its body in order to bear its weight. While its weight increases as the cube of its dimensions, the weight-carrying capacity of its leg bones varies approximately[1] as the area of the cross-section of these bones and hence increases only as the square. If the dimensions are doubled, then, areas are quadrupled while masses are multiplied eight times over. For the legs to have the same power to carry the animal's weight, they must have eight times the cross-sectional area. This in turn means that they must be about 2.83 (the square root of eight) times as thick as before, instead of only twice as thick.

If you look at pictures of a mouse and an elephant drawn so that they appear the same size, you see that the elephant's legs are proportionately much thicker than those of the mouse. Moreover, whereas the mouse carries its legs bent under it, the elephant's legs form straight columns. The mouse, having little weight to cope with, finds this crouching posture no hardship. The elephant, nearing the limits of size, keeps its legs straight so that most of its weight is borne by its massive leg bones, relieving the leg muscles of the load.

The same principle limits the size of flying animals, since their weight, too, goes up as the cube of their dimensions, while the weight-lifting capacity of their wings varies as the area of the wings. Hence the wings of very large flying animals, like the condor and the pterosaur *Pteranodon,* are larger in proportion to their over-all size than those of smaller flying creatures. The limitations of wing area explain why 30 pounds is about the practical limit for any flying animal. Sindbad's roc, which flew off with elephants in its talons, is a physical impossibility.

On the other hand, large size has certain advantages. For one thing, size is by itself a protection. If an animal is large enough, it does not need horns or tusks; it can simply step on any creature that bothers it. It is also less at the mercy of temperature changes than a smaller beast. Even if it lacks the homeothermy (temperature control) of mammals and birds, a large mass takes so long to heat up and cool down that the animal can largely ignore daily changes of temperature.

With an animal the size of a sauropod, even if it is a "cold-blooded reptile," its bodily processes generate enough heat to keep it comfortably warm. In fact, it may have trouble in getting rid of excess heat, since the square-cube law again comes into effect. The amount of heat generated is proportional to the animal's weight, but the rate at which the creature loses heat is proportional to its skin surface. Hence, the bigger it is, the more slowly it loses bodily heat. Some people believe that the great, fanlike ears of the elephant act as heat radiators, to help the beast rid itself of excess body heat.

A typical sauropod, like *Brontosaurus,* was a beast about 60 feet long, standing 15 to 18 feet high at the highest point along its back, over its hips. It weighed something like twenty-five to thirty-five tons.

Compare this with the five to ten tons of a big, full-grown, modern bull African bush elephant, and the two to three tons of most of the cow Indian elephants one sees in zoos and circuses.[2]

The sauropod supported this weight on four massive, pillarlike legs somewhat like the legs of an elephant. The sauropod's hindlegs, which carried most of the load, were especially massive, straight, and pillarlike. The top of the femur fitted into a very large socket in the huge, complex pelvis.

The forelegs, which carried only a fraction of the total weight, were shorter, slenderer, and less straight. *Brontosaurus* and many other sauropods walked with their forelegs slightly bowed, the elbows sticking out from the body.

The feet were typical graviportal (weight-carrying) feet, with short toes arranged in a spreading, conical pattern. Under each foot was a thick elastic pad, to take the shock of footfalls and to give the foot the stretch it needed to keep the animal from getting stuck in soft ground.

An elephant is seldom mired, because its foot expands when the animal puts its weight on it and contracts when the weight is taken off. Hence the elephant has little trouble, even in soft, marshy ground, in drawing its feet out of the holes they make. In riding an elephant around one of the Indian game preserves—say, the Kaziranga Preserve in Assam—it is a little alarming to see the beast plow its way across a bog, where its feet sink in until its belly is almost dragging in the muck; but somehow the feet always come out of their holes. From all we can tell about sauropods, their feet worked in the same way.

Both fore and hind feet of a sauropod had five toes. These toes, however, were buried in the round, stumpy, graviportal foot. Some toes bore claws while others did not. The usual arrangement was three claws on each hind foot and a varying number, from none to three, on each forefoot. Because of the animal's build, these claws would have been useless as weapons. However, they were no doubt useful for swimming in shallow water, where they could be hooked into the bottom, and also for climbing muddy banks.

These four pillar-legs supported a huge, paunchy body. In large animals, especially large plant-eaters, the square-cube law works against the animal in another way. The amount of tissue to be fueled increases as the cube of the dimensions. All this fuel, however, must be absorbed through the lining of the intestines. The inner surface of the intestines is measured in area and therefore increases only as the square of the dimensions. Therefore, as an animal's size increases, its intestines must be proportionately larger if they are to pass enough food products through their walls to keep the machine running. Hence all graviportal animals consist largely of a paunch carried on pillars.

Supporting all this mass was a remarkable backbone. It consisted of about eighty vertebrae: twelve or so in the neck; ten or eleven between shoulder blades and pelvis; four or five sacral vertebrae (that is, fused together in the pelvis), and fifty-odd more in the tail. The vertebrae of the neck, the back, and the forward part of the tail were designed to bear terrific loads with an absolute minimum of weight. They were complicated structures, with long branched spines, deep hollows, and yawning gaps. Every ounce of unnecessary bone was sacrificed for structural efficiency. The sauropod backbone has been compared to the structure of a Gothic cathedral or a cantilever bridge.

To help to support the load of the paunch, the trunk vertebrae were fitted to one another not only by means of the usual main bearing—a cartilaginous pad, which joins each vertebra to the next—but one or more auxiliary bearings as well. To enable the monstrous neck to support its own weight, the spines rising from the top of each neck vertebra were forked or V-shaped. Down the trough made by these Vs ran a huge ligament or tendon, which served to raise and support the neck, much as the lifting cable raises the boom of a crane or derrick.

The sauropod's neck had an almost snakelike flexibility. It could be raised on high, lowered to ground level, or curved around to touch the animal's body on either side. The trunk vertebrae on the other hand were rather stiff, since there would be little occasion for bending the trunk.

The tail was somewhat stiff where it left the body but became more flexible farther aft and ended in a long, tapering whip. This whip was, aside from the animal's size, the sauropod's only weapon.

Moreover, the density of the sauropod's bones varied. While the leg bones were solid and extremely heavy, the bones of the upper parts of its body, such as its vertebrae, were spongy for lightness. This construction helped the animal to stay right side up in the water in which it spent some of its time.

The head, a little bigger than that of a human being, was absurdly small compared to the rest of the beast. The skull was very light, with large fenestrae. The jaws were weak; the teeth, peglike or spoon-shaped. The nostrils were set high, so that in the water the animal could breathe without raising much of its head above the surface—a construction found in the crocodile and the hippopotamus today. The brain was only a few inches long and weighed a few ounces, indicating a simple, mechanical pattern of behavior. But then, the brains of all reptiles are very small in comparison with those of birds and mammals of similar size.

Fossil skin impressions show that the skin of sauropods was covered with small, wartlike tubercles. Sauropods, some students think, had great powers of regenerating lost parts. One specimen from Wyoming is thought to have lost the last quarter of its tail and regrown it, along with twenty-one new tail vertebrae. That is better than a modern lizard can do; for the lizard, in regenerating its tail, grows only a stumpy approximation of the original, without new vertebrae.

Fifty to seventy-five years ago, when sauropods were first becoming known, there was much argument about their posture and habits. Astounded by the weight that the creatures must have carried, some paleontologists thought that they crawled along on their bellies, like the modern Gila monster. Others pointed out that their limb bones were clearly meant to be used in an upright position like those of mammals. Perhaps, they suggested, these animals never left the water at all. They pointed out that the ends of the limb bones were roughened and pitted, showing that in life they were covered by shields of cartilage. Cartilage, it was inferred, was too weak to bear the stresses that the sauropod's weight would put on these joints on land.

Well then, said others, how did the creatures reproduce if they spent all their lives in the water? They must have been viviparous like the ichthyosaurs.

Within the last thirty years, however, sauropod trackways from the Paluxy River in Texas have settled these questions. Some of these dinosaurs were walking on land, since their dragging tails left grooves. In other cases, they were wading up to their bellies. Their weight still drove their feet deep into the mud, but their tails floated behind them. In still another case, a dinosaur was half swimming, with its hindlegs floating clear of the bottom but its forelegs reaching down to pole the animal gently along.

One group of tracks was made by a herd of no less than twenty-three sauropods of all ages. The birdlike tracks of a theropod showed that a flesh-eater had been following or chasing the sauropods. Sometimes the pursuer actually stepped into the tracks of its intended prey, proving that the theropod was indeed following the sauropod. When the sauropod angled off to the left, the theropod did likewise.

From these tracks, we can draw conclusions about the life of sauropods. One is that they were sociable creatures. This is not surprising, since a herding instinct is common among plant-eating mammals, and there is no reason why plant-eating reptiles should not behave similarly. Modern reptiles mislead us because a large majority are flesh-eaters, and flesh-eaters tend to be solitary. They are solitary because it would be too hard for them to make a living if they clustered together. Only a few species like the lion and the wolf, living in lands where prey is abundant, find it feasible to hunt in groups.

Now we think we know what sort of lives the sauropods led. Like the modern hippopotamus, they spent much of their time in the water, either submerged or wading. However, they came out on land whenever they felt like it and, like the hippopotamus, could move around quite briskly. Like elephants, they could probably move quite fast even when they seemed to be loafing along, because they covered so much ground with a single stride.

The gait of a sauropod on land was probably like that of an elephant. This is a walk or amble, in which the feet move in the order: left-rear, left-front, right-rear, right-front. When the elephant wishes to go faster, it speeds up its amble. It cannot trot, canter, or jump, and it always has at least two feet on the ground. So, probably, it was with the sauropods.

It is supposed that sauropods could either swim or, if they wished to feed on underwater plants, walk on the bottom at will. This they could do by taking more air into their lungs when they wished to float and letting some of it out when they wished to sink. The sauropod whose tracks show that he was paddling along the bottom with his forefeet had, no doubt, a lungful of air.

From the skeletons of *Brontosaurus* and *Diplodocus,* it has been inferred that they could rear up on their massive hindlegs. Yet the animals' build suggests that they could do this only when buoyed up by water; for so heavy a creature, the maneuver would be impossible on land. In *Brachiosaurus* the forelegs, like those of a giraffe, are longer than the hind. We may guess that *Brachiosaurus* could not rear; its extra-long neck made up for this lack.

There is some question as to how, standing in water 30 or 40 feet deep, a sauropod could, if it stuck its head out of water to breathe, withstand the pressure of the water on its lungs. A man who tries to breathe through a tube to the surface cannot get down more than a few feet before the water pressure squeezes the air out of his chest. All diving outfits furnish air at a pressure that rises as the diver descends, so that the pressure of the air inside his lungs is kept the same as that of the water outside. It would have taken rib muscles of exceptional power to have kept a sauropod's lungs inflated under such pressure from the outside. But then, perhaps the sauropod was so equipped.

It is not so easy to figure out how sauropods—or, for that matter, other graviportal dinosaurs like *Stegosaurus* and *Triceratops*—went about making little dinosaurs. Consider the build of such creatures, with their sexual organs hidden under those enormous tails, which could not simply be raised out of the way as among four-footed mammals. Nor can one imagine a female *Stegosaurus,* with all those dorsal plates, lying on her back. Evidently, among such ponderous beasts, copulation must have required extraordinary gymnastics. Short of a time machine, however, there is no easy way to settle this question.

Once the female was impregnated, the course of events is fairly plain. Since it is known that dinosaurs of several kinds, including the sauropod *Hypselosaurus,* laid eggs, and that sauropods could walk on dry land, there is no reason to doubt that they proceeded like most smaller reptiles. The female came ashore, probably scooped out a hollow, laid her eggs in it, and covered it over with sand.

The baby sauropods—it is a good guess—looked more like conventional reptiles than their sires, not having yet acquired the monstrous necks and tails and columnar legs of the adult. But these came on soon enough. Since all the sauropod skeletons found so far are those either of adults or of half-grown young, it has been suspected that baby sauropods fed on dry land, where the chances of fossilization were less, and did not take to the water until they had reached a fair size.

We can guess that sauropods were probably slow-growing, long-lived animals. Their life span has been estimated at one or two centuries, like that of large turtles and crocodiles. This may be true. On the other hand, the size of an animal alone is not a very good indicator of how long it takes to grow up. Whales reach their full size in two or three years, while in some species the little cicada spends seventeen years as a larva before it is ready to turn into an adult.

It has sometimes been thought that, like many fishes and reptiles, sauropods kept on growing as long as they lived. There was no such thing as "full growth"; the size they reached depended upon their luck in avoiding fatal diseases and accidents. The cartilaginous ends of their limb bones tend to strengthen this theory, because such bones can keep growing indefinitely where the bone and the cartilage meet.

On the other hand, in modern fishes and reptiles, while growth persists throughout life, the *rate* of growth becomes slower and slower with advancing age. Hence the animal never exceeds a certain size, no matter how long it lives. Since a big sauropod was already as large as is practical for a land animal, growth without any upper limit would in itself have been a fatal disease, since the animal would have become too heavy to move about and get its food. It is likely, therefore, that the growth of dinosaurs, too, slowed down to an imperceptible creep as the animal aged.

The diet of sauropods is obvious from their teeth and general build. They ate soft marsh plants by nipping them off with their blunt teeth. To swallow a mouthful, they probably had to raise their heads and let gravity help their throat muscles. A herd of feeding sauropods must have looked something like a battery of dredges, rhythmically raising and lowering their heads.

After a mouthful of greenery had been ingested, it encountered, either in the main stomach or in an auxiliary stomach like the gizzard of birds, a battery of stones. These stones, ground together by the stomach muscles, reduced the food to soup for easy digestion, thus performing the function of grinding teeth.

It is sometimes asked how such a small head could possibly gather enough food to keep such a vast mass of muscle fueled. There are two answers, which together solve this puzzle. One is that, with such a long neck, the animal was really an efficient food-gatherer; it could reach so far in all directions that it lost little time in moving about. The sauropod's neck performed the same function as the elephant's trunk.

The other answer is that, with its lack of homeothermy and its low rate of metabolism, a reptile consumes only a fraction of the food that a mammal or a bird of the same weight does in the same time. If the reader is familiar with the reptiles at his local zoo, he knows how much time they spend lying still and doing nothing. There is no reason to doubt that Mesozoic reptiles were equally sluggish. Like most modern reptiles, they could move fast when they wanted to, but they seldom wanted to. And, when a reptile does engage in a spurt of violent action, it quickly tires and has to rest.

The behavior of the whole class Reptilia features spurts of action separated by long periods of torpor. Such conduct is required by reptiles' slow metabolism, incomplete separation of venous from arterial blood in the heart, and other primitive characters. A mammal of the same size as a reptile needs more food; but, with its faster metabolism and more efficient circulatory system, it can keep going longer.

An elephant leading an inactive life, as in a zoo, needs about fifty pounds of hay and vegetables per day per ton of elephant, and a grown elephant may weigh from two to ten tons. If active, it needs at least twice as much food. A sauropod, with its greater weight but slower metabolism, would need, roughly, about as much food as an elephant. Therefore, a few hundred pounds of marsh plants a day should have been enough to support a sauropod, which spent much of its time just floating in the water.

For generations, people have held up dinosaurs as examples of moronity, citing the huge ratio between the size of the whole animal and that of its brain. Actually, for a given level of intelligence, the brain need not expand in proportion to the animal's over-all size. If of two beasts of equal intelligence, one is twice as heavy as the other, the brain of the larger will be heavier than that of the smaller but much less than twice as large. So dinosaurian brains were adequate for managing dinosaurian bodies on the reptilian level of behavior. There is no cause to think that they were, on the whole, stupider than modern reptiles.

Compared to mammals, most modern reptiles are simple-minded creatures with a few serviceable instincts to enable them to get through life and to eat without being eaten. Some, especially the crocodilians, show more elaborate behavior, such as familial instincts. They guard their eggs and sometimes protect their newly-hatched young. The Nile crocodile, and perhaps others, helps its young to hatch by sloshing the eggs about in its jaws. Crocodilians can even, with enormous effort, be taught a few simple tricks.

We have mentioned the herdings of sauropods. There is evidence that other plant-eating dinosaurs did likewise, and evidence for pack hunting by some smaller carnivores. The way some ornithischians laid eggs suggests that they cared for their young.

We may guess that carnivores were generally smarter than the herbivores they preyed upon. Herbivores need not be so clever as predators to survive, because their food neither flees, hides, nor fights.

Many genera of sauropods are recognized—Colbert lists thirty-four—but all are built on the same general lines. While the various genera differ in minor matters, such as size, proportions of the fore and hind legs, and position of the nostrils, every sauropod looks like a sauropod and nothing else. Paleontologists divide the sub-order Sauropoda into several families and subfamilies. However, since the differences among these groups are small and the experts do not agree upon this classification, we need not go into the subject.

We shall merely describe a few of the best-known kinds of sauropod dinosaurs. The best-known genera are not necessarily the largest, or those that were most numerous in Mesozoic times. They are those for which the most perfect skeletons have been found and mounted in museums, and this is partly a matter of luck.

Cetiosaurus ("whale lizard") is, next to the fragmentary *Rhoetosaurus* from Australia, the most ancient sauropod known. *Cetiosaurus*, from the Middle and Upper Jurassic of England and North Africa, was a medium-sized sauropod, about 50 feet long. Its bone structure was a little less specialized than that of the later genera, but otherwise it was of conventional sauropodal build.

Brontosaurus ("thunder lizard," otherwise called *Apatosaurus*) is the best-known of all the sauropods, thanks largely to the splendid skeleton in the American Museum of Natural History. When Osborn became head of the Department of Vertebrate Paleontology in this museum in the 1890s, he decided that nothing would attract public interest and support like a good, big dinosaur skeleton. Accordingly, in 1897, he sent Walter Granger to Como Bluff, Wyoming, where earlier, rival fossil-hunting crews had once fought a pitched battle.

Walter Granger (1872–1941) was a tall, mustached Vermonter who went to work for the Museum as a lad of seventeen and remained there all the rest of his life. An amiable extrovert, he worked closely with his colleague, boss, and friend William Diller Matthew, and the pair became known as two of the world's leading paleontologists of their time.

Discovering that the Como quarries had been virtually cleaned out of fossils, Granger explored the neighboring countryside. The next year, a few miles north of Como, he found a shepherd's cabin made entirely of dinosaur bones. Here was another fine quarry.

The Museum men spent the summer of 1899 digging out a nearly complete skeleton of *Brontosaurus*. Excavations continued for three more years, while at the Museum the *Brontosaurus* was cleaned, its missing parts were restored, and the skeleton was mounted. In 1905, it went on exhibition and, for sixty-odd years, has been one of the Museum's leading attractions. This dinosaur measures 65 feet along the backbone and must have weighed around thirty tons in life. As sauropods go, it was a rather massive one, with the usual limb arrangement of long, stout hindlegs and smaller forelegs.

Diplodocus, a contemporary of *Brontosaurus,* was even longer, up to 85 feet along the backbone, but slenderer. Earl Douglass dug in eastern Utah from 1909 to 1922 for dinosaurs to fill Andrew Carnegie's new museum in Pittsburgh. Douglass found a nearly complete *Diplodocus carnegii,* as it was named. The beast had a long, horselike skull, with spoon-shaped teeth ranged in front of the otherwise toothless jaws. The nostril or blowhole was on top of the head, between the eyes. Carnegie was so pleased that he ordered five complete sets of casts of its bones and gave them to foreign museums.

When in 1877 O. C. Marsh found the type specimen of *Brontosaurus,* now in the Carnegie Museum, the original lacked the skull. Marsh assumed that the skull was short and round, like that of the similar but smaller *Camarasaurus.* For a century, incomplete *Brontosaurus* skeletons and statues and pictures of the animals as they presumably appeared in life (as in Plate 30) were given these bullet heads. Then it transpired that *Brontosaurus* actually had a long, narrow skull like that of *Diplodocus.* It will take years to correct this error everywhere.

Brachiosaurus ("arm lizard") is known from East Africa, Europe, and North America. It differed in shape from other sauropods, having a relatively short tail and longer neck, and its forelegs were longer than its hind. Its nostril was atop its head in a dome or crest like a kind of snorkel. The best specimen is the 74-footer in the Museum für Naturkunde in Berlin, but fragmentary remains of an even larger animal of this type, with 20-foot forelimbs, were found in 1979 in Colorado by James A. Jensen and tentatively named *Ultrasaurus.* As far as is now known, this was the heaviest land animal of all time.

Camarasaurus (North America, Jurassic), *Hypselosaurus* (Europe, Cretaceous), and *Dicraeosaurus* (Africa, Jurassic), were all built more or less on the lines of *Brontosaurus.* However, they were smaller, averaging around 40 feet. *Torneria,* from the Jurassic of East Africa, was a middle-sized sauropod, about the size of *Cetiosaurus.* In shape, it was intermediate between *Brachiosaurus* and the rest of the sauropods; its fore and hind legs were of the same length.

Since all the spectacular early finds of sauropods came from Jurassic beds, it was once thought that these animals had all become extinct at the end of the Jurassic. Since then, however, many finds of sauropod bones in Cretaceous beds have shown that the suborder flourished to the end of this later period.

If one could time-travel to the Mesozoic and bring a single animal back to modern times, it would be a sauropod dinosaur. Because of its sluggish, placid nature, it should not be hard to keep in captivity. In fact, it might even be useful. In many countries, the African water hyacinth has become a pest, choking navigable waterways. A sauropod would be the perfect living dredge to clean the stuff out!

As we have seen, the saurischian dinosaurs are divided into two suborders: the Sauropoda ("lizard-footed") and the Theropoda ("beast-footed"), names chosen to describe the arrangements of the foot bones. Actually, it would have been clearer to the average reader had they been called "elephant-footed" and "bird-footed" respectively.

Now let us return to the bird-footed theropods, whom we have met in the form of swift, slender hunters, the coelurosaurs, in the Triassic. The coelurosaurs, not much changed, still flourished in the Jurassic. A European genus, *Compsognathus,* was a little fellow two to two and a half feet long. Knight's painting of birds and flying reptiles (Plate 1) shows a couple of these dinosaurettes on a beach, wondering (if such simple-minded creatures can be said to wonder) whether a stranded crustacean is edible. An American coelurosaur from the same period was *Ornitholestes,* an animal much like the Triassic *Coelophysis.* About six feet long and weighing forty or fifty pounds, *Ornitholestes* had well-developed grasping forelegs, each ending in three large claws.

The big development of the Jurassic was the evolution of another

Figure 26. *Ornitholestes,* a coelurosaur from the North American Jurassic.

group of theropods from the coelurosaurian stock. These were the carnosaurs (the superfamily Carnosauroidea or Megalosauroidea). The best-known member of this group is the famous *Tyrannosaurus,*[4] from the end of the reign of the dinosaurs.

Several carnosaurs, most of them known from fragments only, occur in Upper Triassic beds. These animals seem to have been like their ancestors the coelurosaurs, but larger—around ten feet long—and more robustly built.

By the Late Jurassic, the carnosaurs had evolved into the most formidable beasts of prey the world has ever seen, ranging from 15 to over 50 feet in length. The largest carnosaurs must have weighed eight, ten, or even twelve tons, as much as one of the biggest African bull elephants.

The typical Jurassic carnosaur was between 15 and 35 feet long and weighed from half a ton to four or five tons. Its hindlegs were shaped like those of a colossal bird of prey but, because of the weight they bore, were stouter and more muscular. The feet were birdlike, with three large toes each bearing a huge hooked claw, and a fourth rudimentary toe with a dew-claw like that on a dog's hindleg. Whereas the coelurosaurs had hollow limb bones, for lightness, the limb bones of the carnosaurs were solid, for strength.

The hindlegs were jointed to a huge pelvis, which in turn supported a massive backbone. Although not so elaborate as those of sauropods, the vertebrae were still very stout, strong structures, connected by similar interwoven ligaments and tendons. As in the sauropods, the trunk vertebrae were joined to each other not only at their main joints but by auxiliary joints as well.

The vertebrae of the trunk and tail were decidedly stiff, with little ability to bend. In fact, the smaller tail vertebrae often had interlocking spines to make the tail even stiffer. This rigid body and tail reminds one of the stiff, boxlike body of birds. In birds, this construction was developed to make flight more efficient; in carnosaurs, the purpose was to enable the backbone to support the elephantine weight of the animal on two legs only.

Since a carnosaur could bend its body and tail only in the slightest degree, it follows that many restorations of these reptiles err in showing their tails bent into undulating, serpentine curves. When a carnosaur rested, it could not curl up like a kitten. It folded its hindlegs under it and lay flat on its belly, with its head resting on the chin.

The forelegs, while much smaller than the hindlegs, were still well developed in Jurassic carnosaurs. They ended in three large hooked claws. Although the forelegs were too small for the animal to rest its weight upon, they were doubtless useful in holding prey while the jaws tore it apart.

Further to solidify their deep bodies, carnosaurs were equipped with a set of slender auxiliary ribs, forming a kind of corset over their bellies. These abdominal ribs occur among several widely separated groups of reptiles, such as the modern crocodiles and the tuatara.

Compared to the sauropods, the carnosaurs had short necks, because long, slender necks could not have supported the weight of their huge heads. The neck vertebrae allowed wide freedom of movement.

The head was somewhat birdlike in general shape, being high and narrow, with large eyes; but it was birdlike on a vast scale. In the largest carnosaurs, the head was over 4 feet long. Very large fenestrae, before and behind the eyes, lightened the skull.

In the larger carnosaurs, in fact, the skull was reduced to a hollow framework of rod-shaped bones, almost entirely lacking in the broad, flat expanses of bony plates that we think of in connection with the word "skull." Seeing such a skull in a museum (provided that it has not been filled with plaster, as many fossil skulls are in preparing them for exhibition) one wonders where the animal kept its brain. It seems not to have had any. Actually, the tiny brain was housed in the upper, rear part of the framework, but the cranium forms such a small part of the entire skull that one would never find it if one did not know where to look.

Despite these weight-saving adaptations, the huge jawbones and the masses of muscle that powered them were enormously heavy. In some carnosaurs, notably the American *Allosaurus,* several bones of the skull were only loosely joined together, so that the whole skull had a good deal of give. This feature enabled the beast to gulp down chunks of meat that would have otherwise been too large to swallow. Today the skulls and jaws of snakes have the same loose articulation, for the same purpose.

The jaws of carnosaurs were armed with teeth shaped like double-edged, curved Arabian daggers, up to 6 inches long in the largest genera. The edges of the blade were sometimes saw-toothed, like a steak knife.

Judging by its eye sockets, ear cavities, and nostrils, the carnosaur had keen organs of sense. Although its brain was tiny in proportion to the rest of the animal, such a brain is adequate for a beast that makes its living by a few simple, instinctive responses to the messages from its organs of sense. The shark gets along well with even scantier mental equipment.

Since no man has ever seen a living carnosaur, and since no similar animals exist today, much about their actions and manner of life is uncertain. For one thing, there is the question of their normal standing and walking position. The earlier restorations showed them standing almost erect, like a man. Sometimes their tails dragged on the ground; sometimes they were held just clear of it.

Now it seems likely that their normal pose was less noble-looking. The animal's body was carried almost horizontally, rising forward at most a few degrees. The tail was held out stiffly in back, like the boom of a sloop, with the end of the tail more or less at the same height as the head. Knight's painting of *Tyrannosaurus* advancing upon a horned dinosaur (Plate 47) gives a good idea of this walking position. On the other hand, the carnosaur may have sometimes leaned back and rested its tail on the ground as a prop, like a kangaroo, in order to raise its head to look around.

It seems that the normal carnosaurian gait was a deliberate, ponderous walk, lifting each foot up and planting it firmly again before raising the other. As the creature walked, it swayed its body from side to side to keep its balance. It probably weaved and bobbed its head at the same time, as birds do in walking today. When it wished to go faster, it simply speeded up its walk, but it could not—as some early restorations showed it as doing—leap into the air, because of its enormous weight. It probably moved cautiously on broken or sloping ground, as elephants do, since a fall that would not be serious for a small animal could fatally injure such a monster. That is one of the disadvantages of large size, which have to be accepted along with the advantages.

A walking carnosaur has been compared to a hen, picking its way slowly over the ground, with its head bent down to watch for grubs and other edibles. When we prowl our lawn looking for dandelions, in a similar bent-over attitude, we can't help wondering if carnosaurs, too, ever had aching backs.

There has been some argument as to whether very large carnosaurs, like *Tyrannosaurus,* were really so formidable as they looked, or whether perhaps they were mere carrion-eaters like the modern hyena. It has been said that such large beasts would have been too slow to catch live prey; that the sharpness of their teeth indicates that they ate meat that had become softened by decomposition; and that the shape of their skeletons implies that they spent much time just lying on their bellies doing nothing.

These arguments may be true, but they are not conclusive. The largest carnosaurs moved fast enough if their prey was also slow-moving. Moreover, an animal of that size can look sluggish and still cover ground at an alarming rate. The state of their teeth proves nothing, since reptiles constantly shed and renew their teeth. As for lying torpid, so do most reptiles. Crocodiles, which certainly grab live prey whenever they can, lie in torpor much of the time.

On the other hand, a carnosaur would surely enjoy a good meal of carrion whenever it came across one. A partial skeleton of *Brontosaurus,* found by the diggers of the American Museum of Natural History, showed tooth marks where an *Allosaurus* had torn the flesh from its bones. The tooth scratches fitted the spacing of the teeth in a typical allosaur skull, and there were even a few broken allosaur teeth mixed in with the brontosaur bones. Today the Museum's prize allosaur skeleton is mounted over those brontosaur bones, in the attitude the animal is supposed to have taken in feeding.

We have to guess at the strategy and tactics used by carnosaurs in bringing down their game. Probably their hunting consisted largely of simply stalking about and going for anything that moved. Carnosaurs' tiny brains may have carried instincts elaborate enough to enable them to lurk in ambush, say in a clump of cycads, to rush out upon passers-by. Many invertebrates, none of which is very intellectual, know enough to set up ambuscades.

Once the prey was within reach, it does not seem likely that the carnosaur used any very refined or sophisticated methods of attack. Most likely, it simply clamped its jaws upon the nearest exposed part of the victim and jerked, wrenched, and shook until something gave.

Once the prey was helpless, the predator planted one or both hind feet on it, sank in its teeth, tugged this way and that until a chunk of flesh came loose, and swallowed it whole. Being a reptile, the victim would not die all at once, but little by little. A reptile's severed head can still bite minutes or even hours after it has been cut off. Therefore, parts of the victim would still be wriggling as they were swallowed. After this active repast, the satisfied carnosaur may have picked its teeth with its fore claws.

If the prey were large, the carnosaur could not eat it all at once. After gorging itself, the dinosaur would lie down—probably across the carcass, to make sure its booty was not stolen while it slept— and go into a digestive torpor. It would hang around a large carcass for weeks at a time, alternately eating and dozing, while the cadaver ripened.

It is a plausible guess that carnosaurs, like most modern carnivores, were solitary in their habits, associating with others of their kind only briefly at mating time. It is not unlikely that they had territorial instincts, as do many modern flesh-eaters. That is, each dinosaur recognized a certain territory as its private preserve and did its best to drive off any strangers of its own species that tried to muscle into this terrain.

Fifty years ago, nature-story writers were fond of portraying carnivores as engaged in a constant fang-and-claw struggle, apparently for the sheer fun of fighting. Although this assumption led to the writing of some dramatic tales of gore and mayhem, in real life a carnivore's instincts tell it what prey to hunt in order to obtain its needed food with the least effort and risk. Unless it is very hungry indeed, it does not attack other animals too big or too tough for it. It avoids other carnivores of anything like its own size, as long as they do not trespass on its turf.

Carnivorous dinosaurs probably acted in much the same way. From the form of their feet and tails, we can be sure that they were land-dwellers and can surmise that they attacked any smaller animals that strayed into their territory. Only to protect its own preserve would a self-respecting carnivore do battle with a carnivore of similar size. While smaller herbivores were its daily food, the monstrous sauropods were generally immune from attack. First of all, they spent most of their time in the water, whither carnosaurs did not usually go. Secondly, if a sauropod did venture out on land and was attacked by a large carnivorous dinosaur, it could usually reach water before suffering fatal damage. Finally, the only way a carnivore could kill a sauropod quickly was to bite its head off; and this it could not do as long as the huge beast kept its head two or three stories high in the air.

Similarly, horned or armored dinosaurs were probably safe from the attacks of carnivorous dinosaurs, just as today's elephant and rhinoceros, when full grown, are immune to the attacks of the large cats. On the other hand, the young of all these species of plant-eating dinosaurs were fair game. Indications are that female dinosaurs laid eggs by the dozen or score but that only a fraction of the young reached maturity, the rest going down the gullets of the carnosaurs. Like many modern reptiles, the latter may even have eaten their own young whenever they could catch them.

The chief prey of the carnosaurs was, besides the young of sauropods and armored dinosaurs, the dinosaurs of the next group we shall study: the ornithopods ("bird-feet")—creatures like *Iguanodon* and the American duckbills. There were many kinds of unarmored dinosaurs, roaming in herds about the land or on the margins of the waters. They relied upon wariness to avoid the carnosaurs and a high birthrate to make up their losses.

The largest carnosaurs, like *Tyrannosaurus* and *Allosaurus,* may have found it difficult to catch even these defenseless creatures, because their very weight made it hard to turn quickly in chasing prey and their size made it equally hard to ambush it. Still, such monsters could supplement their diet by robbing smaller carnosaurs of their kills. In fact, stolen carcasses may have been the main source of food for the largest carnivorous dinosaurs. They located these kills by their keen senses of sight and smell and drove the rightful owners away. They probably did not often have to do battle for the prize. If the hijacker were big enough, a little roaring and snapping would make the smaller predator retreat, since its instincts would tell it to avoid a hopeless fight.

Of course, we do not know what vocal noises dinosaurs made. Most modern reptiles have no real voices at all. The best they can do is to hiss.

However, lizards of the gecko family make a loud chirp, and the dinosaurs' cousins the crocodiles have primitive vocal chords. The young crocodile utters a faint, high-pitched sound like *urk, urk.* When one of your authors had a young alligator named Algernon, he kept him in a pan with an inch of water in the bottom and a rock to climb out on. Since it gets pretty cold in Pasadena on winter nights and the houses have only rudimentary heating systems, poor Algernon would often be frozen stiff by morning. To keep him comfortable, his owner rigged up a heating coil of copper tubing, heated by a Bunsen burner and dipping into Algernon's water. The first time the system was tried, it worked all too well. Poor Algernon climbed out on his rock and cried *urk, urk* until he was rescued from being boiled.

In full-grown crocodiles, the vocal sound becomes a "bellow"— actually a kind of sonorous grunt or groan. These reptiles use their voices mainly when the males challenge each other to fight for females during the breeding season. Probably, dinosaurs made similar noises on like occasions.

Incidentally, in connection with carnosaurs, your authors would like to point out that many people have an illogical attitude towards wild life in general and wild carnivores in particular. They judge animals according to human standards. They hold a rabbit to be morally better than a fox because the rabbit eats only plants, while the fox eats rabbits. They speak and write of carnivores, from foxes to tyrannosaurs, in tones of moral disapproval, as if they were guilty of murder or aggressive warfare.

This is a childish way of looking at nature. Morals are a human invention, and no animal is more moral than any other. There are no heroes or villains in nature. The rabbit eats plants, not because it is more virtuous than the fox, but because its instincts tell it to and because its teeth and stomach are designed for such a diet. The fox eats rabbits for a similar reason; if it tried to live on a diet of plants it would die.

All over the world, men have given predators short shrift—farmers and herders because the predators occasionally kill their chickens or sheep; others because they have inherited this traditional hostility to carnivores. One department of the Fish and Wild Life Bureau of the U. S. Government, in fact, devotes itself to "predator control." Its employees occupy themselves over large areas of the West in trapping, shooting, and poisoning coyotes, foxes, and bobcats.

Now, any biota fits together as a living whole. The flow of living matter from plant to herbivore to carnivore and back again is delicately balanced, so that any drastic change in one part of it brings about changes in the other parts. Thus an increase in Arctic hares causes a similar increase in the foxes, lynxes, and owls that live on the hares. If men kill off the predators, the herbivores multiply until they eat themselves out of range and starve.

Moreover, the predators form part of the process of natural selection by which a species is kept up to the evolutionary mark. Predators cull out the weak and sickly animals, and those suffering from defects and deformities. In this way, they counteract the effect of degenerative mutation. Without the predators, the herbivores degenerate.

Even from the point of view of the farmer, predators have value, although it may be hard to convince a countryman who has lost his chickens to a fox of this. When the predators are killed off, the mice and other rodents that form their regular diet multiply without a natural check and become a worse pest than the predators ever were. So this department of the Fish and Wild Life Bureau is not merely useless; it is positively harmful and should be abolished. For people who favor governmental economy but do not know where to begin, this would make a good starting point.

Even well-meant efforts to improve a natural environment often have disastrous results. For instance, before 1907, a herd of 4,000 deer lived on the Kaibab Plateau in Arizona. Pumas, wolves, and coyotes kept the numbers of the deer in check. Men, thinking to help the deer by destroying their "enemies," killed off the predators. Sure enough, the deer increased to 100,000 by 1924.

Then, however, the deer began to destroy their sources of food by overcropping. In two years, more than half the deer starved to death. Ever since, the deer have been declining from starvation while the range has continued to deteriorate, so that it can now support fewer deer than it could before 1907. The Western public, however, is so used to regarding predators as villains—like the characters played by actors with little black mustaches in the silent movies of our youth—that even governmental experts who know the facts dare not publicly talk of re-introducing predators to the area, for fear of being held up to scorn as madmen.

During the Jurassic Period, on any given continent, carnosaurs of several different kinds and sizes lived in the same areas. On the islands of the archipelago that was Europe and North Africa, for instance, lived *Megalosaurus,* an animal 10 to 15 feet long, the bones of which were among the first dinosaurian fossils to be discovered.

In North America dwelt *Ceratosaurus,* of about the same size as *Megalosaurus.* This animal, whose name means "horned lizard," had a feature unique among carnosaurs: a small horn on top of the nose. Nobody knows what use this horn served; for it must have been a negligible weapon compared to the jaws. Perhaps it was an infantile tool which enabled the chick dinosaur to break out of its egg and which in this particular genus survived to adulthood; perhaps it was a secondary sexual characteristic.

At the same time and in the same continent lived the larger *Allosaurus* (or *Antrodemus*), which was 34 feet long, weighed as much as a small elephant, and had a yard-long skull.

Most people think of *Tyrannosaurus* as the largest of the carnosaurs. This idea derives from the beautiful skeleton in the American Museum of Natural History. Actually, there were other carnosaurs as large as or larger than *Tyrannosaurus* both in the Jurassic and in the Cretaceous periods. They are less well known to the public at large because complete skeletons have not been recovered to be mounted in museums in great metropolitan centers.

One such colossus was found by two cowboys, Collins and Tucker, who in 1934 were squatting on their heels watching a grader scrape the dirt on Highway 64, in Oklahoma. Presently the grader blade dug into something and came up with a monstrous rib. Collins shouted; the grader stopped. Collins, who had read about dinosaurs in the newspapers, suggested:

"Let's write Stovall—that bone-digger at the University of Norman."[5]

They did. J. Willis Stovall hastily put an assistant in charge of his classes, jumped into his Ford, and drove out to the Panhandle. Here he found a cache of dinosaur fossils. Most of them were of well-known genera from the Morrison formation of the Upper Jurassic: *Brontosaurus, Ceratosaurus, Camptosaurus,* and *Stegosaurus.*

The prize find, however, was that of two fairly complete, though scattered, skeletons of a colossal carnosaur. This animal resembled a scaled-up allosaur, with well-developed forelegs. Its estimated length was 42 feet, compared to 47 for the famous *Tyrannosaurus.* The new carnosaur, however, was of even more massive build than *Tyrannosaurus* and may have outweighed it. If ever a carnosaur was built, not for catching its own prey, but for hijacking that of others, this reptile was so built. It is doubtful whether it caught live prey very often, because of its weight and lack of agility. On the other hand, such a mountain of muscle and fangs was admirably designed to drive from its kill any smaller carnosaur.

Stovall named the new carnosaur *Saurophagus* ("lizard-eater"), but this name turned out to have been preëmpted. After Stovall died, his colleagues concluded that this reptile was just a very large specimen of *Allosaurus* and did not deserve a separate generic name. Remains of other allosaurs of about the same size as the Oklahoman monster have been found in rocks of the same age in Utah.

The pelvic bones and several lumbar vertebrae of another huge carnosaur were found by British diggers at the famous Tendaguru site in Tanzania, East Africa. Comparing these 8-inch vertebrae with those of *Tyrannosaurus,* and assuming that the animal bore the same proportions as *Tyrannosaurus,* the African carnosaur must have been about 54 feet long, or bigger than either *Allosaurus* or *Tyrannosaurus.*

By no means were all the carnivorous dinosaurs of the Jurassic and Cretaceous periods enormous. There were medium-sized theropods in the Jurassic forests of North America, as well as the lively little 6-foot coelurosaur *Oritholestes,* which we have already met. Such an assortment of carnivores of the same general design but of different sizes is common in every fauna. For instance, through the American tropics today stalk a group of cats ranging in size from the jaguar down through the puma and the ocelot to the margay, which is no bigger than a house cat. Similar series are found in Asia and Africa, with the tiger or the lion at the top of the scale.

In any such group of carnivores, the different species, by virtue of their different sizes, are adapted to hunt different prey. Hence, despite some small overlap in their diets, they do not severely compete with one another. We say that they occupy different ecological niches in the environment. When two species do compete directly —when both are trying to crowd into the same niche—one or the other usually disappears. Thus, when men introduced the dingo into Australia, it out-competed the native marsupial thylacine or "Tasmanian wolf," so that the latter became extinct in Australia, although it survived down to the present century in Tasmania.

As we have said, the dinosaurs were not one order of reptiles but two, the Saurischia (with a lizardlike pelvis) and the Ornithischia (with a birdlike pelvis). So far we have given details only about saurischians, because these are the dinosaurs that we know the most about during the first half of the Age of Reptiles.

Like the saurischians, the ornithischians evolved from pseudosuchian ancestors (you recall the Pseudosuchia from Chapter 5, in the Triassic) in early Triassic times. Until recently nothing, save for some doubtful fossil fragments, was known about the early stages of ornithischian evolution. In 1961–62, however, a British-South African expedition to Basutoland found the remains of a primitive Triassic ornithischian. Its 4-inch skull included, in the lower jaw, a pair of large fanglike teeth, like the canines of a mammal, and a pair of smaller but similar teeth in the upper jaw. Behind these "canines" were flat-topped "molars." This array of teeth of different shapes caused the creature to be classed at first as a therapsid and to be named *Heterodontosaurus* ("different-toothed lizard").

In many ways, the ornithischians developed parallel to the saurischians. Like the latter order, they started out as small reptiles that walked on their hindlegs. Later, some lines went back to a four-footed gait and grew to great size. Others attained large size while keeping their original bipedal pose, while still others remained small bipeds.

A main difference between the two orders is that, whereas the saurischians began as flesh-eaters, some of whom switched to a diet of plants, the ornithischians seem all to have been plant-eaters from an early stage in their evolution. As things worked out, the ornithischians developed more advanced chopping and mashing teeth for coping with vegetable matter. We may suppose that these ornithischians, which were able to chew their food, did not have to rely upon gizzard stones, as did the sauropods.

The ornithischians diverged into four suborders: one horned, two armored, and one neither. The last of these, the Ornithopoda, was the most conservative. The ornithopods kept the original two-legged gait of their forebears and did not develop the horns and the armor of the other three suborders.

Ornithopods varied from small to large, *Iguanodon* being one of the larger kinds. Their general shape was much like that of the carnosaurs; but they were, size for size, of heavier and less agile build. More of their weight had to go into a large paunch to cope with plant food. They had three or four toes on the hind feet and four or five on the fore. Their claws were blunter than those of the carnosaurs and in many later kinds were hooflike.

The forelegs of the ornithopods were never reduced to vestiges as in some carnosaurs. On the contrary, they were large enough so° that the animal could walk either on two legs or on four. Probably, when eating, they walked on all fours and dragged their tails on the ground behind them. When in a hurry, however, they stood up on their hindlegs, hoisted their tails into the air for counterweights, and trotted along at a good speed, swaying their bodies and bobbing their heads.

Their skulls were in many ways more specialized than those of the saurischians. These skulls were of rather solid construction. The fenestrae tended to be smaller, and those in front of the eyes tended to disappear.

The teeth at the front of the jaw were either reduced to rudiments or discarded altogether; and a horny beak, suitable for nipping twigs off plants, took their place. The back teeth developed complex, leaf-like shapes for slicing and grinding plant food. The hinge of the jaw was below the level of the grinding teeth, so that, as the reptile closed its jaws, the upper and lower rows of teeth approached each other obliquely, like the jaws of a pair of channel-lock pliers.

The most primitive ornithopod is not from the Triassic or the Lower Jurassic, where one would expect to find it, but from a later time—the Lower Cretaceous of England. This is *Hypsilophodon,* a slender animal around 5 feet long (see Plate 49). Except for its long hindlegs, *Hypsilophodon* looked quite lizardlike. In its own day, it was a "living fossil," having survived with little change for tens of millions of years because it happened to fit its ecological niche so well that no other form could crowd it out.

Hypsilophodon still retained small teeth at the front of its jaws. Down its back ran a double row of large scales or small plates, like those of the little ancestral crocodile *Protosuchus.* Its toes had some grasping power, leading some paleontologists to believe that it climbed trees. Perhaps, like the house cat, it did not live in trees but could climb when it had to, as when a carnosaur attacked it.

A more progressive type of ornithischian was *Camptosaurus,* from the American Jurassic. *Camptosaurus,* a rather unimpressive-looking reptile, varied from 4 to 17 feet in length, depending upon the species. Skeletons of different sizes have been given several dif-

Figure 27.   *Camptosaurus,* an iguanodont of moderate size from the Late Jurassic and Early Cretaceous of North America.

ferent specific names. In some cases, however, the difference may be merely that of different ages. In *Camptosaurus,* the front teeth had disappeared altogether.

In addition, *Camptosaurus* is known from the Jurassic of Europe, and fragmentary remains of related genera have been found in Europe and Asia. Tendaguru in East Africa yielded abundant remains of an ornithopod, *Dysalatosaurus,* which might be called a small camptosaur or a large hypsilophodont. All these dinosaurs probably roamed in herds. Since their remains are not more common, it is likely that they lived in uplands; for upland faunas are more sparsely represented in the fossil record than those of the lowlands.

The two armored suborders of the Ornithischia used to be lumped together in a single suborder; now, however, they are usually separated. They are separated not only by physical differences but also by time. One suborder appeared in the Early Jurassic, reached its climax in the Late Jurassic, and disappeared completely in the Early Cretaceous. It was the only dinosaurian suborder to become extinct so early. The other suborder appeared in the Early Cretaceous, radiated and flourished, and then disappeared with all the other dinosaurs at the end of that period. Since this chapter concerns Jurassic dinosaurs, we shall ignore the second group of armored dinosaurs for the present.

The armored suborder that flowered in the Jurassic was the Stegosauria ("roof lizards"), of which the American *Stegosaurus* is the best known. However, an earlier and more commonplace stegosaurian, *Scelidosaurus* (bad Greek for "leg lizard") comes from the Lower Jurassic of England. This beast gives a good idea of the ancestral form whence all the later stegosaurs descended.

Scelidosaurus was a stout, four-footed reptile about 12 feet long (Plate 37). As its hindlegs were longer than its fore, its back was arched. It had a small skull (incompletely known) and armor consisting of bony scales or plates with upstanding keels, like the ridges along a crocodile's back. These projections ran in lines along its back and tail, giving it some protection. When *Scelidosaurus* lived, the carnosaurs had not yet reached their full size and might, so this modest armor no doubt served its purpose.

As the Jurassic Period ticked by, however, the carnosaurs grew bigger and bigger. Their jaws became even larger and more powerful; their teeth, longer and sharper. To keep from being eaten up, the stegosaurs also became larger and developed stronger defenses. The process culminated in the American *Stegosaurus,* for whom the family is named.

The appearance of *Stegosaurus* is well known. Twenty to 25 feet long, it possessed a back with an exaggerated arch. The hindlegs were twice as long as the fore, with particularly long femurs. As with most graviportal dinosaurs, the hindlegs were carried nearly straight, while the forelegs bent out at the elbows. The feet were elephantlike, with three nails or hooves on each foot. The head was small, with small, weak teeth.

The most striking features of *Stegosaurus* were its spines and its defensive plates. After O. C. Marsh dug up the first specimen in the 1870s, a fifty-year argument raged as to how these defenses were arranged. Some thought the plates stood on end in a single row down the back; some, in two rows, the plates being paired. Some believed that they were fixed; others, that they were movable. Some even thought that the plates lay flat against the animal's body, like the scutes of a turtle's shell. Some inferred that there were two pairs of tail spines, some three, some four, and some five; some asserted that they sprouted all over the animal's body.

A later specimen hinted that the plates, which averaged about twenty in number, were arranged down the back in a double row; but that they alternated, right-left-right-left, instead of being paired. There is little doubt now that these plates stood on edge and were not movable, being attached to the underside of the skin by broad bases. Presumably they were covered with horn. The largest plates were over the rump, growing smaller to the front and rear. At least, we can be sure the stegosaur did not use its plates to fly with, as one does in Edgar Rice Burroughs's novel *Tarzan at the Earth's Core.*

The last few feet of tail were fitted with two pairs of spikes. For extra protection, numerous pebbly bones were embedded in the stegosaur's thick skin, especially around its throat.

Although it had the weight of an elephant, *Stegosaurus* had a brain the size of a walnut, weighing 2.6 ounces. Such small brains are typical of plant-eating dinosaurs. Because the sacral enlargement of the spinal cord, where it passes through the pelvis, was twenty times the size of the brain, the fable arose that the animal really had two brains, one fore and one aft. This story inspired a columnist for the *Chicago Tribune,* Bert Lester Taylor, to compose the following verse in 1912:

> Behold the mighty dinosaur,
>   Famous in prehistoric lore,
> Not only for his power and strength
>   But for his intellectual length.
> You will observe by these remains
>   The creature had two sets of brains—
> One in his head (the usual place),
>   The other in his spinal base.
> Thus he could reason "A priori"
>   As well as "A posteriori."
> No problem bothered him a bit
>   He made both head and tail of it.
>
> So wise was he, so wise and solemn,
>   Each thought filled just a spinal column.
> If one brain found the pressure strong
>   It passed a few ideas along.
> If something slipped his forward mind
>   'Twas rescued by the one behind.
> And if in error he was caught
>   He had a saving afterthought.
> As he thought twice before he spoke
>   He had no judgment to revoke.
> Thus he could think without congestion
>   Upon both sides of every question.
> Oh, gaze upon this model beast;
>   Defunct ten million years at least.[6]

Alas for poetry! The sacral enlargement was not really another brain. It was just a junction point in the nervous system. The enlargement was merely the place where the many nerves from the legs and viscera entered the spinal cord. It may have had some function as a subordinate control center, to direct automatic movements of the hindlegs, trunk, and tail; but a brain it was not. Such an enlargement occurs in all reptiles, although not usually to the degree of *Stegosaurus*.

Ever since *Stegosaurus'* strange architecture became known, scientists have puzzled over the back plates. The purpose of the tail spikes is obvious. Although the animal's tail was not very flexible, it could probably swing back and forth through an angle of something like 90 degrees, thus making the animal's rear an unhealthy place for predators.

But what earthly good were the plates, stuck up in a double row along the back, leaving the stegosaur's flanks and front undefended? Another theory is that, besides whatever defensive purposes they served, the plates also acted, like the pelycosaurs' dorsal fin, as heat-control mechanisms, absorbing heat from the rising sun and radiating away excess heat at midday.

Our own guess is that the plan of the spines and plates agreed with the simple, instinctive behavior of these dinosaurs and of their carnosaurian foes. The carnosaur, let us suppose, was driven by its instincts, when it sighted anything edible, to march straight towards it, open its jaws wide, and make one great slashing lunge, paying no heed to which way the victim was facing. Then suppose that the stegosaur's instincts told it, when it sighted a carnosaur, to head straight away from its foe as fast as its unequal legs would carry it, swinging its tail from side to side as it went. If the carnosaur did, by accident or design, get around to its opponent's flank or front, the stegosaur turned away again.

Attacked from the rear by random snapping and lunging, the stegosaur was well protected. The attacking carnosaur would not only be gored by the lashing tail spikes but would also gash its jaws on the plates. After it had suffered enough damage in this way, it might give up the pursuit to go after easier prey. Unless they were very hungry, most carnosaurs probably left full-grown stegosaurs alone. They did not circle round to take the stegosaurs from the front or side because they did not have the wit to do so.

Obviously, such a defense was not completely predator-proof. By sheer blundering accident, the attacker sometimes found itself within snapping distance of the stegosaur's side or front, and a stegosaur that had its head bitten off left no more descendants. Maybe carnosaurs even evolved more complex instincts, which taught them to avoid the spikes and plates. This would not take much change with carnosaur brain; and carnosaurs' brains, while still minute, were larger than those of other dinosaurs of the same size. Once the carnosaurs developed such a skill, the stegosaurs' doom was sealed; hence their early disappearance is not surprising. The next time that dinosaurs developed armor, the armor was placed to meet attack from any quarter.

A paleontologist of our acquaintance has another theory: that stegosaurs went in herds and, when attacked, formed a circle, the way musk oxen do when assailed by wolves. However, the stegosaurs faced inward instead of outward. Hence the attacker, wherever he tried to break into the circle, confronted a row of lashing, spiked tails. Although the spectacle would certainly be an arresting one, we are doubtful about the idea on the ground that it calls for a more complex behavior pattern than could be expected in so simple-minded a creature.

Whatever their methods of defense, the stegosaurs were successful in their time. They flourished for millions of years over most of the earth. Europe had *Omosaurus,* a smaller relative of *Stegosaurus,* which seems to have been armored with spikes alone, no plates.

At Tendaguru, the Germans found remains of *Kentrurosaurus,* 16 or 17 feet long and intermediate in armament between *Stegosaurus* and *Omosaurus.* The skeleton in the Museum für Naturkunde in Berlin has fourteen plates, smaller than the plates of *Stegosaurus* and arranged in pairs over the neck, shoulders, and back. Seven pairs of spines protect the after back, pelvic region, and tail, while an additional pair of spikes projects from the sides of the pelvis. This animal, too, is designed to beat off an attack from the rear. Frag-

mentary remains of other members of the family have been found in
Asia, South Africa, and South America.

So we have the Jurassic world, with its vast, steamy lowlands and
great, reedy swamps, its stretches of desert and uplands, its modest
mountains. It is a world of bare earth between trees and shrubs; a
world of great forests of cycads, tree ferns, ginkgoes, and evergreen
conifers.

In the swamps wallow colossal sauropod dinosaurs, endlessly
dredging up mouthfuls of soft plant food and living out their long,
slow, placid, brainless lives. Through the jungles lumber stegosaurs
and camptosaurs. After them stalk great dagger-toothed carnosaurs.
In the open areas, the drier plains and hills, live other, smaller reptiles, such as the coelurosaurs, fast enough to run away from a wandering carnosaur. Always, the herbivores outnumber the carnivores
many times over, and the small animals outnumber the large by even
greater margins.

Over the ground and up the tree trunks scuttle swarms of small
reptiles: lizardlike rhynchocephalians and true lizards. On the
ground, also, live a host of small, shrewlike, mouselike, and ratlike
mammals. These include the plant-eating multituberculates, the
insect-eating pantotheres, and the flesh-eating triconodonts. Through
the air wing pterosaurs and the first true birds. Everywhere swarms a
multitude of creeping, scuttling, buzzing invertebrates.

A set of fossil footprints from the Upper Jurassic of the southwestern United States gives a glimpse of this world of small lives.
There are prints of reptiles of several kinds. One looks like that of a
lizard. Another is a yard-long quadruped with a broad, heavy body;
perhaps a turtle. Several small, slender reptiles—perhaps coelurosaurs—raced about on their hindlegs. There are also tracks of a snail,
a scorpion, worms, and something that might be either a crab or a
large spider.

But now, let us leave the land and look at the reptiles of the sea
and the air.

7

Reptiles of Sea and Air

No sooner had the reptiles become established on land than certain of them invaded the sea again. Like their descendants, the birds and mammals, they have continued this invasion ever since. The mere fact of having to evolve into a land animal had forced upon them certain physical characters, such as a tougher skin, a more efficient heart, and a stronger skeleton, which in turn gave them competitive advantages over the fishes and amphibians that stayed in the water.

In some ways, the reptiles that took to the water reversed their previous evolutionary direction. Their bodies resumed the streamlined form of their fishy ancestors. Their limbs turned again into fins. Their vertebrae lost the elaborate structures needed to stiffen the backbone against the pull of gravity; they became simple disks, like those in the backbone of a fish.

These reptiles did not devolve into true fishes. They did not abandon their lungs for gills, although some fresh-water turtles have developed gill-like structures in their windpipes or their cloacae, by means of which they can supplement the oxygen in their lungs and thus stay under water for days at a time. Neither did they recapture the ability to lay their eggs in water.

These facts imposed certain limitations upon them. Unable to extract oxygen from the water, they had to come to the surface to breathe, just as a whale does today. Not being able to lay their eggs in water, they either had to come out on land for the purpose, as sea turtles do now, or give birth to live young. If they chose the former method, they could not become fully adapted to the water, since their limbs had to be usable as legs as well as flippers. Hence, they could not be quite so swift in the water as an animal that need not concern itself with land travel at all.

Louis Dollo (1857–1931), a Frenchman who took Belgian citizenship and who dug twenty-nine iguanodons out of a Belgian coal mine and mounted them, propounded the principle that came to be known as "Dollo's law," namely: that *evolution is irreversible.* Like a lot of other "laws" of evolution advanced about the same time by other paleontologists, this "law" must be understood as only relatively true. It expresses, not an absolute law, but a general tendency with many exceptions.

For example, the usual direction of evolution is from small to large. For most animals, large size gives more advantages than disadvantages, not only in competing with animals of other species but also in competing with others of its own kind. Large males, for instance, can drive the smaller ones away from the females and thus build up harems, or they can occupy the choicest territories and repel all trespassers.

Sometimes, however, this trend is reversed. If a species lives on an island or in a barren environment where food is short, smaller size gives an advantage. The smaller animal has a better chance of getting through a bad season because it does not eat so much. Moreover, it can get at food growing in places that a larger beast cannot reach. Hence dwarf races arise, like the pygmy elephants and hippopotami that lived in Pleistocene Sicily.

The reptiles that took to the sea did reverse their evolution in some respects, such as shape of body and limbs, but not in others. To understand why they could backtrack in some ways but not in all, we must go into the subject of genetics; and this is material for a later chapter.

The first known reptiles to go back to the water were the mesosaurs (not to be confused with the mosasaurs), found in South Africa and South America from the Late Pennsylvanian and the Early Permian. These were lizardlike reptiles two to three feet long, with flattened tails, large webbed feet, and long slender jaws full of needle-sharp teeth. Their relationships are not certain; they seem

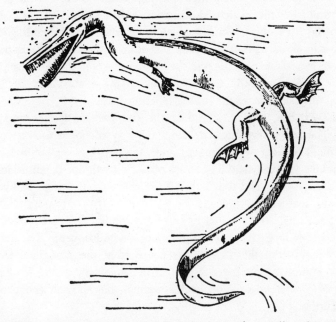

Figure 28. *Mesosaurus,* a small Permian aquatic reptile of uncertain relationships. (After Osborn.)

to have sprung from early cotylosaurs, flourished briefly, and then vanished without leaving descendants. The original skeleton of *Mesosaurus* was discovered about a century ago by a French paleontologist in South Africa, under unusual circumstances. The skeleton was embedded in a slab of rock, which was serving as a lid of a pot in a Hottentot's hut.

Soon after the mesosaurs came the turtles, the only order of the anapsid reptiles to last to our day. The skeleton of an animal 8 or 10 inches long from the Permian of South Africa, named *Eunotosaurus,* gives a good idea of the ancestral turtle, although some paleontologists doubt that this creature is their actual ancestor. *Eunotosaurus* has no shell, but the body is wide. The ribs are flattened to a leaflike shape, forming an almost solid layer of bone under the skin of the back.

Early in the Mesozoic, turtles split into three suborders: the primitive Amphichelydia, which could not pull their necks into their shells at all; the Pleurodira, which pulled in their heads by bending their necks into a horizontal S-curve; and the Cryptodira, which pulled in their heads by bending their necks into a vertical S-curve. The amphichelyds are extinct, and the surviving pleurodires or side-necked turtles all live in the southern hemisphere.

Most existing turtles, including the true sea turtles, are cryptodires. The sea turtles have developed a way of life with little competition. They eat water plants and slow-moving sea animals like sea urchins and jellyfish. They rely on their shells for defense and on their horny beaks and tough throat linings to enable them to live on otherwise scarcely edible fare.

The sea turtles evolved early and have continued with little change save that their shells tend to thin out and disappear. The largest known sea turtle, the 12-foot *Archelon* from the American Cretaceous (Plate 42, showing a related form), had only a sketchy framework of a shell. The modern leatherback has carried the process even further.

The loss of the shell lightened the animal and made it easier for the turtle to float. It also exposed the slow-moving turtle to attack. One of the best specimens of *Archelon,* in the Peabody Museum at Yale, had its right hind flipper bitten off, probably by a shark or a mosasaur. It is something of a wonder how the unarmored leatherback has survived at all.

As we noted in Chapter 5, the euryapsid reptiles (with one pair of holes on top of their heads) began in the Permian with slender, lizardlike protorosaurs like *Araeoscelis*. In the Triassic, their descendants became the nothosaurs, 2 to 10 feet long and semi-aquatic like modern seals and crocodiles. That is, they sought their food in the water but came out on shore to loaf, breed, and lay eggs.

Figures 29 and 30. The ancestors of the plesiosaurs: at the top, the lizardlike, Permian *Araeoscelis;* below, *Lariosaurus,* a primitive Triassic nothosaur. (After Osborn.)

The nothosaurs in turn divided in early Triassic times into two branches, the placodonts and the plesiosaurs.

The placodonts were stout-bodied reptiles, typically around 5 feet long, with blunt heads, short necks, four paddles or flippers, and bodies tapering in the rear to a pointed tail of short to medium length. The peculiar thing about the placodonts was their teeth. Instead of sharp fish-catching spikes, they were equipped with blunt front teeth, which slanted forward almost horizontally. The back teeth were reduced in number, much enlarged, and flat-topped like paving stones. The lower jaw carried a single row on each side; the upper jaw, a double row, the teeth of the inner row being enlarged until they took up most of the palate. Sometimes the rearmost tooth was so large that a single pair of them occupied most of the palate by themselves.

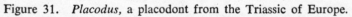

Figure 31. *Placodus,* a placodont from the Triassic of Europe.

Evidently, the placodonts were mollusk-eaters and made their livings much as the walrus does today. They cruised the bottoms of shallow water, tore shellfish loose from the rocks by their front teeth, crushed them in their ponderous dental mills, and swallowed them. In the late Triassic, some placodonts developed armor and became pseudo-turtles. Then they all disappeared.

The other branch sent forth by the nothosaurs were the plesiosaurs. The typical Jurassic plesiosaur has been compared to a snake threaded through the body of a turtle. This is a good simile if we remember that the "turtle" had no shell—just a flattened, streamlined body covered by a rubbery skin. From this body sprang a long, snaky neck, bearing a flattened head armed with many long, sharp teeth; four powerful paddles, with which the animal could not only shoot ahead but also quickly stop, back, or turn; and a short tail, sometimes adorned with a lozenge-shaped fin at the end. It is not certain whether plesiosaurs could shuffle awkwardly about on land, as sea turtles do to lay their eggs, or whether they never came ashore and so must have practiced live birth.

It has been suggested that the medieval notion of a dragon was based on one or more plesiosaur skeletons. This is not impossible, for one can easily see the resemblance to medieval dragon pictures (Plates 81, 82). However, without any definite historical record of such a skeleton's being known in medieval times, this speculation cannot be confirmed.

The plesiosaurs had a strong, basketlike mass of abdominal ribs protecting the nether part of the body. As they evolved, some plesiosaurs increased their number of neck vertebrae and foot bones almost indefinitely. Most land vertebrates have reduced the number of their bones as they became more specialized. Once lost, such bones are almost never regained; and bones are seldom duplicated or increased in number.

Plesiosaurs, however, seem to have had no trouble in multiplying certain bones. Among the more primitive reptiles, for instance, the normal maximum number of phalanges or joint bones in each toe or finger is five. Sometimes this number of bones is reduced, but it is seldom increased. Man, for instance, has four such bones in each finger and toe except that the thumb and the big toe have only three phalanges. In man, one bone of each digit forms part of the main portion of the hand or foot, leaving only the last three (or two in the thumb and big toe) free to move independently.

In plesiosaurs, however, the number of phalanges increased to eight or ten, all buried in an oarlike flipper. Likewise, the neck vertebrae increased from the normal number of six to ten. The longest-necked plesiosaurs acquired the appalling number of seventy-six cervical vertebrae.

Since paleontologists disagree as to how the plesiosaurs should be classified into families, we will merely say that, during the Jurassic, they split into two main branches. In one, the pliosaurs, the head became larger and neck shorter. In the other, which culminated in the Cretaceous elasmosaurs, the neck became longer and longer until, in the 43-foot *Elasmosaurus* itself, the neck was as long as all the rest of the animal.

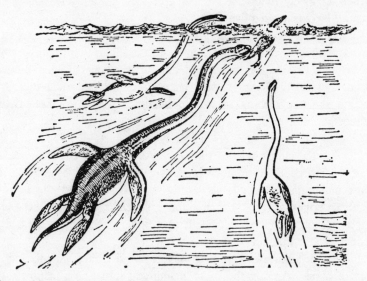

Figure 32. The long-necked Cretaceous plesiosaur *Elasmosaurus,* pursuing the flightless, toothed diving bird *Hesperornis.* (After Osborn.)

Meanwhile the pliosaurs were increasing in size. The champion of this line was *Kronosaurus,* from an Australian Cretaceous bed. In 1931, Harvard's Museum of Comparative Zoology sent an expedition to Queensland. William E. Schevill, the paleontologist of the team, asked a sheep rancher whether he knew of any fossils on his ranch. Why yes, said the rancher, and took Schevill to a place where some bones projected from the earth. The remains turned out to be those of one of the biggest known sea reptiles, *Kronosaurus,* 42 feet long.

To recover the skeleton, six tons of rock were blasted out and shipped to Cambridge, Massachusetts. Preparation was slow be-

Figure 33. *Kronosaurus,* a whale-sized, short-necked plesiosaur from the Cretaceous of Australia.

cause of the size of the job and limitations of time, money, and museum space. The 9-foot skull—the largest known reptilian skull—was placed on display in 1939. In the 1950s, a nonegenarian of Boston named Godfrey Lowell Cabot (1861–1962) gave the money to finish the work. Cabot, who lived to be over 100, was a sea-serpent enthusiast—or, as the Museum more tactfully put it, "a man with a lifelong interest in marine reptiles."[1] The whole 42-foot skeleton went on exhibition in 1958. Nowadays, perhaps in memory of the durable Mr. Cabot and his hobby, a sign reading TO THE SEA SERPENT points the way to the famous skeleton.

There has been some argument over the speed of plesiosaurs in the water. Some paleontologists insist that they moved slowly, on the theory that an animal that swims by rowing itself with flippers, like a sea turtle, is bound to be slower than one that sculls itself along by wagging a tail fin.

Sea lions, which also have flippers, manage to move very fast indeed, as anyone will see who watches a tankful of them at feeding time in the zoo. One of your authors spent a morning at the Philadelphia zoo watching one large male Californian sea lion and four females. When it is in a hurry, the sea lion's main propulsion is by means of the fore flippers, with the hind flippers held stiffly rearward and used only for steering. We suggest that it is not the use of flippers that makes a sea turtle slow but the facts that sea turtles eat slow-moving or stationary food, like sea urchins, and that they depend upon their shells for protection. Plesiosaurs, which like modern sea lions pursued swift prey, flapped along by means of flippers but could doubtless move fast enough to suit anybody save their victims.[2]

The speed of a plesiosaur, the flexibility of its neck, and its method of fishing are all interconnected. The earlier plesiosaurs had moderately long necks, neither very limber nor very stiff. Some paleontologists, who have studied their neck bones, believe that these plesiosaurs could just about bend their necks sideways around in a complete circle. Up and down they could bend them much less—no more than a half circle, if that; they could not assume the graceful swanlike curve shown in some early restorations. It is common among reptiles—snakes, for instance—for the vertebrae to bend more readily in horizontal than in vertical movement.

We may also suppose that the earlier plesiosaurs were fairly fast; not so fast as an ichthyosaur, perhaps, but quite lively. The slower fish they could overtake; the faster ones they could catch by gliding up alongside them and seizing them by a quick sideways jerk of the head. That is how alligators fish today. Undoubtedly, plesiosaurs ate any meat they could catch. The stomach of one fossil plesiosaur contained the remains of a fish, a belemnite (a squidlike cephalopod), and even a piece from a dead pterosaur.

When the plesiosaurs split into pliosaurs and elasmosaurs, the former (we may suppose) specialized in overtaking their victims. To achieve this end, the head became larger, while the neck became shorter and stiffer. This line reached its climax with *Kronosaurus.*

The elasmosaurs, on the other hand, specialized in stealing up on their prey, then shooting their heads out in a sudden snakelike lunge. An elasmosaur's neck was not only longer than that of its plesiosaurian ancestors but also more limber.

The same experts who examined the neck of a Jurassic *Plesiosaurus* also scrutinized that of *Elasmosaurus.* They concluded that

28. Fossil tracks of a sauropod dinosaur, found in a stream bed in Texas. *Photo from the American Museum of Natural History.*

29. *Cetiosaurus*, a medium-sized sauropod from the European Jurassic. *Courtesy of the British Museum (Natural History).*

31. Skeleton of *Diplodocus*, a long, slender sauropod, in the Carnegie Museum, Pittsburgh. *Photo from the Carnegie Museum.*

30. *Brontosaurus* (or *Apatosaurus*), a large sauropod dinosaur from the Late Jurassic of North America. Crocodiles in the left foreground. *Courtesy of the Chicago Natural History Museum.*

32. Restoration of *Diplodocus. Courtesy of the American Museum of Natural History.*

33. *Brachiosaurus*, a gigantic sauropod from the Late Jurassic of Africa, with (right) the stegosaur *Kentrurosaurus*. *Drawn for this book by Roy Krenkel.*

34. Skeleton of *Ceratosaurus*, a horned carnosaur from the Late Jurassic of North America. *Photo from the Smithsonian Institution.*

35.   Model of *Ceratosaurus. Photo from the Smithsonian Institution.*

36.   *Allosaurus* (or *Antrodemus*), a large carnosaur from the Late Jurassic of North America. *Courtesy of the American Museum of Natural History.*

37. *Scelidosaurus*, an ancestral stegosaurian from the Early Jurassic of England. *Courtesy of the British Museum (Natural History).*

38. *Stegosaurus*, a large armored ornithischian dinosaur from the Late Jurassic of North America. By Charles R. Knight, *Courtesy of the Chicago Natural History Museum.*

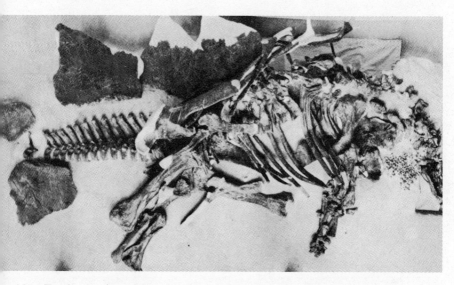

39.   Fossil remains of *Stegosaurus* in their original position, viewed from above. *Photo from the Smithsonian Institution.*

40.   Marine reptiles of the Early Jurassic: *Plesiosaurus* (left) and *Stenopterygius*, an ichthyosaur (right). *Courtesy of the Chicago Natural History Museum.*

41. Fossil ichthyosaurs, as found in England (above) and Germany. *Photo from the Smithsonian Institution.*

42. *Tylosaurus,* a thirty-foot mosasaur from the Late Cretaceous of North America, with the pterosaur *Pteranodon* and the sea turtle *Protostega. Courtesy of the Chicago Natural History Museum.*

43. Shell of a Cretaceous ammonite, showing the marks of the teeth of the mollusk-eating mosasaur *Platycarpus*, in the National Museum of Natural History.

44. *Pterodactylus*, a common type of pterodactyl or short-tailed pterosaur, less than a foot in length, from the Late Jurassic and Early Cretaceous of Europe. *Courtesy of the British Museum (Natural History).*

45.   Pterosaur track, from an Upper Jurassic formation of North America. *Courtesy of the Journal of Paleontology.*

46. Skeleton of *Tyrannosaurus*, a gigantic Late Cretaceous carnosaur, found by Barnum Brown and mounted in the Carnegie Museum. The three-toed forelegs and the bend in the tail are now considered probably incorrect. *Photo from the Carnegie Museum.*

47. *Tyrannosaurus* (right), a gigantic carnosaur from the Late Cretaceous of North America, and (left) *Triceratops*, the largest and last of the horned dinosaurs. *Courtesy of the Chicago Natural History Museum.*

48. *Quetzalcoatlus,* the largest known pterosaur, with a wingspread of over 40 feet, found in the 1970s in Texas. A life-sized model in the National Museum of Natural History. *Courtesy of the Smithsonian Institution and Chip Clark.*

49. *Hypsilophodon*, a small ornithopod dinosaur from the Early Cretaceous of Europe, resembling the common ancestor of all the ornithopods. *Courtesy of the British Museum (Natural History).*

50. *Iguanodont,* a large ornithopod dinosaur from the Early Cretaceous of Europe. *Courtesy of the British Museum (Natural History).*

the animal could bend its neck, in the horizontal plane, in a spiral with two complete turns. It could also curl it upwards or downwards in the vertical plane through more than one complete turn. This means that the animal was probably slower in the water than the other kinds of plesiosaurs. If an animal with such a long, flexible neck swam really fast, it would have trouble in keeping that monstrous neck pointing forward, because of the resistance of the water. It would not do for the beast to paddle along with its neck and head fluttering behind it.

At any rate, one can see that the critical factor in determining the animal's speed is not whether it flaps along with paddles or wags a tail behind it, so much as it is the food it eats and the speed it must attain to get that food.

As we have already learned, the parapsid reptiles had a single pair of holes in the tops of their skulls, as did the euryapsids; but the bones surrounding these fenestrae were differently arranged. The parapsids that returned to live in the sea comprised one single group: the ichthyosaurs. We do not know the lineage of the ichthyosaurs so well as that of their euryapsid relatives, the plesiosaurs and the placodonts. The earliest known ichthyosaurs, from the Triassic, are already adapted to life in the water, albeit not so completely as the later kinds.

Two of the earliest genera of ichthyosaurs come from the Middle Triassic of Europe, North America, Indonesia, and Spitzbergen. One, *Cymbospondylus,* has the flippers and beak of the true ichthyosaur. Its general shape, however, is eel-like, with a straight, flattened tail tapering to a point. Another, *Mixosaurus,* has a slight downward kink in the tail, showing the beginnings of the distinctive ichthyosaurian tail fin. One short-lived side branch developed flat-topped teeth for crushing mollusks, like their contemporaries the placodonts.

The famous ichthyosaurs of the Holzmaden slate in Germany, from the Lower Jurassic, had evolved the full, crescent-shaped tail with the backbone extending into the lower lobe—an arrangement called a "reversed heterocercal" tail. Their limbs were modified even more than those of plesiosaurs. Whereas in the paddles of a plesio-

Figures 34 and 35. The evolution of the ichthyosaurs: at the top, *Cymbospondylus,* from the Triassic; below, *Baptanodon,* from the Cretaceous. (After Osborn.)

saur, the original finger-bones could still be clearly distinguished, in the fins of an ichthyosaur the bony structure had become a mosaic of little bones, in which the original plan can hardly be discerned. We have told you how the plesiosaurs developed extra joints in their digits. The ichthyosaurs went farther than this; they developed extra

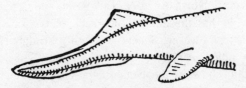

Figure 36. Tail of the Triassic ichthyosaur *Mixosaurus,* intermediate between the eel-like tail of the primitive *Cymbospondylus* and the later kinds with full, crescent-shaped tails.

digits as well. The number of digits in the fin of an ichthyosaur varied from three to eight. Some lines developed short, broad fins; some, long narrow fins. In some, the rear fins shrank until they were hardly more than vestiges. While most ichthyosaurs ranged from 3 to 30 feet in length, one genus, *Leptopterygius,* grew to be more than 40 feet long. Isolated vertebrae indicate specimens of this genus that were even larger—over 50 feet, which puts them in a class with modern whales.

The nostrils of ichthyosaurs were at the base of the long upper jaw, just in front of the eyes. One Early Jurassic genus, *Eurhinosaurus,* combined a long upper jaw with a short lower jaw, less than half the length of the upper, so that its head looked much like that of a modern swordfish. The upper jaw appears to have borne teeth for its whole length, despite the fact that the farther half had no lower jaw for the teeth to bite against. However, the teeth, instead of pointing downward, seem to have been aimed outward horizontally, like the teeth in the beak of a modern sawfish. The teeth suggest that this ichthyosaur was in the habit of darting into a school of small fish and slashing right and left, to kill or cripple as many as it could before the school scattered. Then it snapped up its victims at leisure.

As with many other reptiles, the eyes of ichthyosaurs contained a ring of small, overlapping bony plates, called sclerotic ossicles or sclerotic plates. These plates form part of the mechanism by which the reptile focuses its eyes upon nearby objects.

Ichthyosaurs unquestionably produced live young. In the Holzmaden slate beds some little ichthyosaur embryos were found inside their mother. In one case, the adult female died in the process of giving birth. Among some aquatic mammals, notably the beluga or white whale, the young are born slowly, tail first. In the beluga, the process may take weeks, and the young whale learns to use its flukes before the process is completed. Ichthyosaurs probably were born in the same way.

Besides this mother ichthyosaur, the slate preserved many beautiful specimens, including microscopic particles of skin pigment, showing that ichthyosaurs were, as suspected, dark gray above and pale gray below, like a modern porpoise. Naturally, scientists asked themselves, why were the dead ichthyosaurs not torn apart by scavengers?

One of the several theories is that the slate beds mark the site of an ancient bay floored with black mud. This mud, it is thought, held an unusually high content of sulfur compounds, especially the highly poisonous hydrogen sulfide. Hence no crabs lived on this bottom. Near the surface of the bay, the water was ordinarily pure enough for life. Once in a while, however, a storm roiled the mud, or a pod of ichthyosaurs charged into the bay in pursuit of a school of fish. Then the hydrogen sulfide bubbled up, and the bay became a death trap. Since there were no scavengers to pick them apart, the bodies that settled on the bottom lay there until covered over.

From their stomach contents, we learn that one of the ichthyosaurs' favorite foods consisted of mollusks, which swarmed the Mesozoic seas: belemnites, ancient relatives of the squids, and ammonites, ancient relatives of the pearly nautilus. But the diet of these sea reptiles was not limited to mollusks.

Most ichthyosaurs ate whatever they could catch, which in those days meant practically every small swimmer in the sea. One long-lived genus, *Ophthalmosaurus* ("eye lizard"), which lasted through the entire Jurassic and Cretaceous periods, seems to have specialized in hunting belemnites. *Ophthalmosaurus* was an ichthyosaur of medium length—around 13 feet—but of rather stout build. Its eyes were even huger than those of most ichthyosaurs, while its teeth were very small and were confined to the front of its jaws.

These facts suggest a relationship between the habits of *Ophthalmosaurus* and those of the belemnites it pursued. The huge eyes imply that it hunted its prey at night, while the general build of ichthyosaurs suggests that they were adapted to life near the surface and did not go in for deep diving.

In recent decades, with the development of echo-sounding apparatus, it has been learned that there is a reflecting layer in the sea, which moves up and down according to the time of day. In the daytime it sinks to a depth of 700 to 2,400 feet, often separating into two or three distinct layers; while at night it comes close to the surface. These "scattering layers" are mainly composed of, first, millions of small crustaceans, like the more familiar shrimps and water fleas, which rise at night to "graze" on the single-celled plants that drift near the surface; next, a multitude of small fishes, many having luminous spots, which eat the crustaceans; and finally, squids and larger fish, which eat the smaller fish. It is not unlikely that belemnites had habits like those of modern squids; that is, they sank during the day but at night followed their prey to the surface to hunt and to be, in turn, hunted by ichthyosaurs.

Ichthyosaurs lived on, far into the Cretaceous. In this period, their remains are scarcer and mostly fragmentary. Hence, it is often supposed that they dwindled and disappeared before the other great reptiles did. However, this scarcity may be to some extent an illusion, begotten by the fact that nobody has found a death trap like Holzmaden Bay from the Cretaceous Period. It has been suggested that the ichthyosaurs could not stand the competition of the large sharks, similar to the modern white shark but even larger, which appeared during the Cretaceous. Be that as it may, the last of the fish-lizards comes from the Benton Formation at the beginning of the Upper Cretaceous. Ichthyosaurs evidently lost out in competition with sharks, plesiosaurs, and mosasaurs; but just exactly how and why we do not know and probably never shall.

Two other groups of Mesozoic reptiles, both diapsids, went into the sea-serpent business. One was a branch of the true crocodiles, inappropriately named geosaurs ("earth lizards"). Modern crocodiles are mainly fresh-water animals; and so, presumably, were most ancient crocodiles. But one modern species, the salt-water crocodile *Crocodilus porosus,* ranges far and wide from southeast Asia through the Indonesian and Melanesian islands. It crosses freely from one island to another and is often found swimming far out at sea. This is the largest living reptile; specimens reach thirty and even possibly forty feet in length.

In contrast to this salt-water crocodile, which comes out on land like other modern crocodilians, the Jurassic geosaurs took to the water altogether and became as fully aquatic as ichthyosaurs and plesiosaurs. The geosaurs, of moderate 6- to 8-foot length, had a long, eel-like shape, long pointed jaws, and paddles for limbs.

Figure 37. *Geosaurus,* a small, marine, Jurassic crocodile. (After Osborn.)

Two features of their construction are worth noting. The long tail ended in a reversed heterocercal tail fin, just like that of the ichthyosaurs. And, while the forelimbs were small, short, broad paddles, useful only for steering and balancing, the hind flippers were long and narrow, like the flippers of a plesiosaur, and seem to have been muscled for rowing the animal. Since geosaurs probably could not crawl out on land, they presumably produced their young alive, like the ichthyosaurs. The experiment does not seem to have been a great success; for, while they first appeared in the Middle Jurassic, the geosaurs flourished only during the Late Jurassic and disappeared in the Early Cretaceous.

The next diapsid family to take to the sea did better. This was a branch of the varanid lizards, the monitors. They appeared in the Early Cretaceous as a group of smallish, semi-aquatic lizards, the aigialosaurs, with short necks and powerful tails flattened for swimming. (One aigialosaur, the rare, foot-long Bornean lizard *Lantha-notus,* survives to this day.) By the Late Cretaceous, these animals had evolved into the mosasaurs. Mosasaur skeletons range up to 30 feet in length; fragments indicate that some species reached lengths of around 45 feet. It is thought that they were covered with small scales.

Like the ichthyosaurs and the geosaurs, the mosasaurs were unable to move on land. Yet, from the fact that their skeletons are sometimes found with those of land reptiles, some paleontologists think that, like salmon, mosasaurs swam up rivers to breed.

The typical mosasaur was shaped like a moray or salt-water eel, with the addition of four broad paddles, built for steering rather than for rowing. The flattened tail by which the creature swam occupied half the animal's entire length, while a fringe or crest decorated the back.

The large head tapered to a point in front, with nostrils opening a short distance in front of the eyes. The mosasaurs had large, sharp teeth in both jaws and some teeth growing from the palate for good measure. The lower jaw was remarkable. Instead of being fused together into a rigid mass, the jaw had three hinges, one at the tip and one on each side. These hinges enabled the creature to bend its lower jawbones outward, and at the same time to draw the front of its jaw —and any prey gripped in it—back towards its throat. Naturally, this made it easier to swallow a large, wriggling fish.

Not all mosasaurs, however, were fish-eaters. For example, *Plate-carpus* ("broad wrist") had a short muzzle and teeth with blunt, peglike points. From the structure of its ears, some paleontologists think that *Platecarpus* and its kind, unlike most mosasaurs, were designed for deep diving. We know that they ate ammonites. Many ammonite shells have been found with holes the size of a dime punched in them. Finally, one shell turned up with two rows of such holes, forming a pattern that perfectly fitted the teeth of *Platecarpus*. This very shell is now on display in the National Museum of Natural History in Washington. Other mosasaurs were adapted to a diet of mollusks; one such was *Globidens* ("globe teeth") with round-topped teeth for crushing shellfish.

Then came the end of the Cretaceous; and all the mosasaurs—deep-water and shallow-water, fish-eaters and shellfish-eaters alike—vanished from the seas of the earth.

Some archosaurs, not satisfied to dominate the land as dinosaurs, the fresh waters as crocodiles and phytosaurs, and the high seas as geosaurs, took to the air. Two separate lines of archosaurs became airborne. One evolved into the pterosaurs or flying reptiles; the other, into the birds. These lines evolved independently; the pterosaurs were not the ancestors of the birds but their cousins. At the end of the Cretaceous, the pterosaurs became extinct along with most of the Mesozoic reptiles; but the birds lived on.

We may suppose that, like the dinosaurs, the pterosaurs, and the birds evolved in the Triassic from small, lizardlike pseudosuchians. However, the oldest known pterosaurs and birds are already complete fliers. Nobody has yet found the remains of any intermediate gliding forms—animals that were not fully airborne. This is not surprising when we consider what sort of creatures these intermediates must have been: very small, light, and fragile, like modern flying squirrels. Such animals are rarely fossilized, but perhaps these links will be found someday. Any paleontologist would rather find one such fragile missing link than the hugest sauropod dinosaur.

The nearest thing to a flying reptile living today is the "flying dragon" (*Draco volans*) of southeast Asia and Indonesia. This is not a very impressive dragon, being a dainty little lizard about 8 inches long, including 5 inches of tail. Moreover, it does not really fly. It glides, like a flying squirrel. Instead of the flying squirrel's web of skin connecting its fore and hind limbs, the flying dragon has a set of false ribs—about six on each side—which can be spread fanwise. A thin membrane of skin joins these ribs, making a pair of supporting planes. By means of this apparatus, the flying dragon can leap from a tree and glide a long distance to the ground.

In 1961, a trio of high-school students in New Jersey found a similar gliding reptile of Triassic age. Headed by Alfred Siefker and inspired by a passion for paleontology, these young men had haunted an abandoned shale quarry in North Bergen, collecting remains of coelacanth fishes and other fossils. When they found the rock containing this little glider, they started to clean the overlying stone

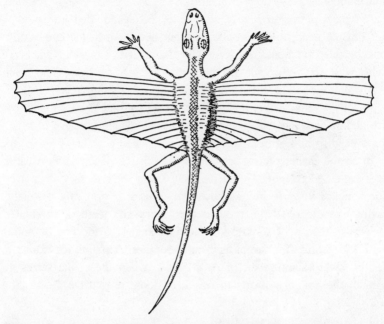

Figure 38.   Triassic gliding reptile found in fossil form in New Jersey by Alfred Siefker and friends.

away but then, realizing the importance of their find, brought the specimen, rock and all, to the American Museum of Natural History. Here, three months' work exposed the skeleton. A similar form, *Kuehneosaurus,* comes from the English Triassic.

However, these gliding reptiles could not be the ancestors of the pterosaurs. The wings of pterosaurs were carried by the forelegs, as in birds and bats, and not by the ribs.

The pterosaurs flourished through the Jurassic and Cretaceous periods, right down to the end of the reign of the reptiles. They ranged in size from a sparrow to a condor. Most were small, like today's insect-eating bats and birds. Although a fair number of skeletons are known, these probably represent only a small fraction of the different kinds that flew. Because the remains of flying animals are so perishable, the fraction fossilized is even smaller than with land animals.

A typical pterosaur had a large head, a long, toothed jaw, a short but flexible neck, and a small, compact body. As in ichthyosaurs, a ring of sclerotic bones protected the large eye. The skull was very light, with sizable openings before and behind the eyes. The brain was rather large for a reptile, not because the animals were intelligent, but because—like birds—they needed a highly developed coördination between the eyes and the flying mechanism. As in birds, the eyesight was keen but the sense of smell had practically vanished.

In all the earlier pterosaurs, the jaws were full of long, sharp teeth. In the later Cretaceous, some pterosaurs lost their teeth and evolved horny beaks instead, just as birds did. This was probably a weight-saving expedient. In the toothed pterosaurs, the teeth often slanted forwards, instead of standing up at right angles to the jaw or pointing back towards the throat as in most reptiles. A snake, for example, has backward-slanting teeth. As a result, when the snake seizes an animal, the animal's efforts to tear itself loose only drive the sloping teeth deeper into its body.

The forward-sloping teeth of certain pterosaurs present a puzzle. Perhaps they are an adaptation to seizing large, soft-bodied insect prey in flight. If the pterosaur were flying at a high speed relative to its prey, the slant of its teeth would drive them deep into the body of its victim, whereas backward-sloping teeth would strike the prey at right angles and might even be broken by the impact. Pterosaurs of other kinds had teeth of different shapes or no teeth—and presumably different habits to match.

The wing structure of the pterosaurs differed from those of birds and of bats. In a bird, the three digits of its forefoot are more or less welded into one. The limb is covered with long feathers, which furnish the lifting surface. In a bat, the thumb is free but the remaining four fingers are elongated, and the wing is a web of skin stretched unbrellawise between them and the flank and leg.

In a pterosaur, the thumb was missing, the next three fingers were normal and armed with claws, and the fifth or "little" finger was vastly enlarged. The wing was a web of skin stretched from the fifth finger to the body and hindleg. As in bats, there was also an auxiliary web between the hindlegs and the tail. In place of the thumb, a thin sliver of bone extended from the wrist back towards the neck to stiffen the leading edge of the wing membrane.

The upper arm bones were attached to the body by a strong system of bones. Each shoulder blade was joined to the breastbone or sternum by a coracoid bone, which performed much the same function that our collar bones do for us. In back, each shoulder blade was joined by another special bone to the backbone. The sternum had a structure like a breastplate in front, rising to a kind of keel, for the attachment of the strong muscles needed to bring the wings downward in flying.

In birds, this keel is even more strongly developed, as anybody knows who has carved the breast of a chicken or turkey. To judge by birds, the pterosaurs that had the most keel flew by flapping their wings, while those who had the least keel depended on gliding.

It is probably wrong to say that, because pterosaurs had smaller keels on the average than birds, they were therefore feeble fliers. Bats lack breastbone keels altogether but are nonetheless excellent fliers. The smallness of the breastbone keels probably means that pterosaurs relied upon other means, such as the strong bracing of the shoulder blades, for making themselves efficient in the air.

Although small in proportion to the rest of the animal, the bodies of some pterosaurs found room for a pouch or crop, in which food snapped up on the wing could be stored until the little flier could roost and digest its dinner in peace.

The slender legs were directed backwards, like those of a bat. In this position, they helped to spread the wing membranes. To some extent, depending on the species, the leg could be brought forward under the animal's body, so that the pterosaur could walk on its hind feet and on the claws of the free fingers at the leading edge of its wings. In the walking position, the wings were folded so that their farther ends stuck up and to the rear.

Figure 39. *Dimorphodon,* a large, long-tailed Early Jurassic pterosaur.

The bones of pterosaurs were extremely light. The long limb bones were not only hollow, like those of birds, but often hardly thicker than stiff paper. Although modern birds are on the whole more robustly muscled than pterosaurs of the same size, pterosaurs made up the difference by reducing weight even further. The extreme flimsiness of their construction reminds one of a model airplane, made of balsa wood and plastic film and driven by a rubber-band motor. One can crush such a model with one hand, but in its proper element it does very well.

The order Pterosauria is divided into two suborders. One, with the ponderous name of Rhamphorynchoidea, had long tails; the other, the Pterodactyloidea, had short tails. The rhamphorynchids were the older and more primitive of the two. The oldest pterosaurs, from the Lower Jurassic of Europe, are all of this kind.

The oldest of all are *Dimorphodon* and its relatives. *Dimorphodon* was a good-sized flier, with a wingspan of 3 or 4 feet; in other words, as big as a large modern hawk. Many smaller rhamphorynchids are known from the Late Jurassic, mostly sparrow-sized to pigeon-sized. *Rhamphorynchus* itself had, on the end of its long tail, a small, lozenge-shaped vertical rudder.

Although the rhamphorynchids became extinct at the end of the

Jurassic, the short-tailed pterosaurs or pterodactyls, which abounded in the Late Jurassic, continued on through the Cretaceous. They developed some peculiar forms. *Ctenochasma,* a 6-inch Jurassic pterodactyl, had jaws armed with scores of fine, bristle-like teeth.

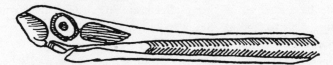

Figure 40. Skull of *Ctenochasma,* the bristle-toothed pterosaur, from the Late Jurassic of Europe.

We can only guess at the purpose of this strange dental apparatus. It reminds one of a baleen whale's whalebone, a kind of internal mustache through which the whale strains its dinner of small sea animals, such as sardines and shrimps. As the whale closes its mouth, the water it has taken in is squirted out through this sieve while the prey stays inside and is swallowed. One wonders if *Ctenochasma* did something similar, as it soared over still waters and dipped its lower jaw into the water to scoop up water fleas and other pinhead-sized prey.

Other pterodactyls tended to lose their teeth. In some, there were teeth only at the front of the jaw; in others there were no teeth at all. *Nyctosaurus,* from the Upper Cretaceous of North America, had a body as big as a pigeon, a wingspread of 6 or 7 feet, and a long toothless beak.

Pteranodon, from the same time and place, carried the same principles of design to an extreme. A latecomer on the scene, it was one of the largest of the pterosaurs (although fragments of an even larger kind have been found in the Cretaceous of Jordan). With a body the size of a goose, its wings spanned nearly 30 feet. This is a wider wingspread than that of today's condor, although the condor might have outweighed *Pteranodon.* The enormous head carried not only a long, pointed, toothless beak but also an equally long crest projecting rearward. This crest balanced the beak and, no doubt, served as a rudder.

Since *Pteranodon's* sternum keel is small, we may suppose that the animal made little use of wing-flapping in flight. It was almost a pure glider, depending upon rising air currents to help it to gain altitude. Of all animals, it was the one most purely adapted to life in the air. Some paleontologists believe that its wing structure was too rigid to be folded up, as the smaller pterosaurs furled their wings in walking. Able to fold its forelimbs only partway, it would have been very awkward on land.

Pteranodon is the best-known of all the pterosaurs, partly because of its size and partly because many good speciments have been recovered from the Niobrara Chalk of Kansas. The animal lived around the borders of the shallow Kansas Sea. It probably spent its days soaring endlessly over this sea, skimming just above the waves and snapping up the small sea creatures—fish, belemnites, or crustaceans—that chance brought to the surface. Fossils have been found a hundred miles or more from what was then the nearest shore. Between flights, *Pteranodon* probably roosted on sea cliffs, whence it launched itself in a long glide.

This would seem a precarious sort of life. If an accident or a miscalculation forced a landing either on water or on level land, it is hard to see how *Pteranodon,* with its vast, flimsy wings and feeble powers of walking or swimming, could ever take off again. On the other hand, the animal cannot have been badly designed, since it throve in swarms for millions of years. It must either have had means of launching itself from the surface that are not evident to us, or its control in the air must have been so perfect that forced landings almost never happened. Of course it might, during one of its water-skimming flights, be snapped up by a mosasaur or an elasmosaur, if the sea reptile were hungry enough to go for such a mass of skin and bone. But that is the kind of hazard that all wild animals, save the largest and most powerfully armed, face every day of their lives.

The fact that *Pteranodon* is so well-known sometimes misleads people into thinking of all Cretaceous pterosaurs as pteranodons. Actually, it was only one of many different kinds. The accidents of preservation happen to have made it famous. All through the Juras-

sic and Cretaceous periods, pterosaurs of all sorts swarmed on all
the continents much as birds do today. In the 1970s, scattered
remains were found in Texas of an even larger pterosaur, *Quetzalcoatlus,* with a 40-foot wingspread.

The smallest pterosaurs ate insects. The larger ones ate fish; some,
perhaps, ate small mammals and reptiles, including smaller pterosaurs, as well. They could not eat fruit, as some birds and bats do
nowadays, because, until the Late Cretaceous, fruit did not exist.
It has been suggested that some ate seeds, which is not impossible;
but the great majority were carnivores of one kind or another.

Any Late Mesozoic twilight was full of pterosaurs, soaring and
swooping in a never-ending hunt for food. At first glance, one might
mistake them for swallows or bats. They were probably slower than
swallows and less agile than bats; but then, their prey was probably
slower on the wing than modern insects are.

There has been much argument about the daily lives of pterosaurs; how well they could walk, fly, and take off; how they reared
their young; whether they were warm-blooded. It seems likely that
they did have some sort of homeothermy like that of mammals and
birds, because without it they would have had a hard time keeping
up the fast metabolism that a flying animal needs.

In fact, although restorations usually show pterosaurs as covered
with naked, leathery skin, there is a suspicion that they had hair,
or at least that some did over some of their surface. A European
paleontologist, Broili, in 1927 described a specimen of *Rhamphorhynchus* in which impressions of the skin were preserved. These
impressions, he said, showed traces not only of fur but also, at the
bases of the hairs, of the sebaceous glands, which among mammals
furnish each hair with its protective coating of oil.

Such a pelt is plausible. If pterosaurs were warm-blooded, then
even in the mild Mesozoic climates they needed better insulation
than that of naked skin. With fur or feathers, a small, warm-blooded
animal loses less body heat to the cool night air than it would if
naked and, therefore, needs less food to keep itself fueled.

Figure 41. *Pterodactylus* (or *Cycnorhamphus*), a short-tailed pterosaur from the Late Jurassic of Europe, in the walking posture.

As for their ability to walk, some say that pterosaurs were practically helpless on a flat surface and could only hang head-down, like bats, from the branches of trees or from ledges on cliffs. Others say they could walk on all fours.

A trackway from the Upper Jurassic of Arizona proves that at least some pterosaurs could walk quite competently. The tracks were those of a fair-sized animal, with a 14-inch step. Moreover,

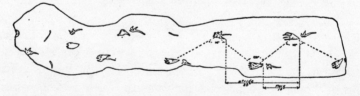

Figure 42. Pterosaur trackway from the Upper Jurassic of Arizona. Courtesy of the *Journal of Paleontology*.

the fossil footprints were not formed near any cliffs, but in the middle of a broad, half-desert river plain, where trees grew only along the streams. The pterosaur may have lived in these trees, making long, soaring flights and, when forced down, scuttling to the nearest tree to climb up by means of its wing claws in order to take off again. If a tree was wanting, perhaps a boulder or the crest of a sand dune would serve. Or, perhaps, it had enough spring in its legs so that a hop into the wind would make it airborne.

As for the gait of grounded pterosaurs, they probably varied widely in this respect, just as they did in size, shape, and habits, in order to fill different niches in the environment. Probably, some walked better than others; some hopped about on branches like modern birds, while others hung upside down below them. We may compare them to modern bats, some of which cannot really walk at all because their legs are permanently directed aft and their feet are turned backwards. They must flop along on their bellies, hooking themselves forward with their wing-claws. Others, like the vampires, furl their wings and walk on all fours quite briskly.

There is no reason to doubt that pterosaurs, like most reptiles, laid eggs. The sea reptiles took to live birth because they had become completely aquatic and never came out on land. But a flying animal, no matter how perfectly adapted to the air, must come to earth from time to time.

The small bodies of pterosaurs, with narrow pelves, imply that their eggs were also small. The newly hatched pterosaurs must have been half-formed little creatures with rudimentary wings, since full-sized wings would not have fitted inside the eggs. Hence, they must have been, at hatching time, incapable of getting their own food, as a newly hatched snake or crocodile does. In the early years of this century, the learned Othenio Abel inferred that pterosaurs, like birds but unlike other reptiles, must have had some sort of nesting instinct and familial organization. If the young could not feed themselves, one or both parents must have fed them. Such details of pterosaurian family life, however, we can only surmise.

At the end of the Cretaceous Period, the pterosaurs, like the mosasaurs and the dinosaurs, became extinct. Even if they had escaped the general doom that overtook the ruling reptiles, it is doubtful if they could long have survived the competition of the birds. Although the pterosaurs were marvels of aerodynamic efficiency, at least as effective in their way as birds, they had a couple of built-in shortcomings. These structural features probably gave the birds an advantage that could not be overcome.

One was that, since the pterosaur's wings were attached to its legs, the usefulness of these legs in walking was impaired. In birds, on the other hand, the legs remain free. Therefore most birds, even though they are flying animals, can still run on the ground with a speed that compares with that of a mammal or a reptile of the same size.

The other shortcoming was inherent in a wing made of a thin membrane of skin. Any slight accident that tore the membrane would ground the pterosaur and doom it to death by starvation or predation. Whereas a bird can lose several quills from a wing without being much handicapped, the pterosaur had no means of defense while waiting for its wing to mend. Moreover, even the bone structure of the wing was flimsy. Since its wing was spread by a single strut only, the pterosaur was more vulnerable to damage than even a bat. Bats, which have evolutionary limitations somewhat like those of pterosaurs, have been unable to oust the birds from command of the air. They have survived only by adopting a few specialized ways of life, wherein they do not severely compete with birds. In these ecological niches, however, they have become extremely numerous and successful.

During the Mesozoic Era, true birds were also developing. From the Jurassic comes the famous long-tailed, toothed, claw-winged *Archaeopteryx,* of which we have three more or less complete skeletons and one isolated feather, all from Germany. At Tendaguru, the Germans also found a single bird's wrist-bone. Some students thought that this bone resembled that of *Archaeopteryx* and indicated that similar birds lived on the African continent in Jurassic times.

Archaeopteryx is such a fine case of a link between birds and reptiles that paleontologists argue whether it is "really" a bird or a reptile. If we had only the skeleton of *Archaeopteryx* and no feathers, it would be natural to class it as a small, lizardlike, pseudosuchian reptile; but the feathers show it to be a bird.

Although we think of *Archaeopteryx* as a flying creature, it can hardly have been a very powerful flier. Its wings were small for its size; it had hardly had any keel to its sternum and so could not have had powerful wing muscles. With neither large wings nor the strong flying muscles to make small wings effective, *Archaeopteryx* could only leap from a tree and glide, flapping, for a considerable distance. Whether it could maintain altitude, let alone gain it, remains an unanswerable question.

Paleontologists would love to find a fossil of *Archaeopteryx's* Triassic ancestor. They have theorized about the build of such a creature and have already picked a name for it: *Proavis.* Some hold that this ancestor was a climbing, lizardlike reptile with feathers, and that feathers formed a fringe on the fore and hind legs, which enabled the animal to make leaping glides.

It is believed that the feathers evolved from scales, not originally for flight but as a means of keeping warm. In time, the longer feathers came to be concentrated on the forelimbs, which thus evolved into wings. If this is correct, then the stages of the bird's evolution were: first, the development of homeothermy or "warm-bloodedness"; second, a coating of feathers to reduce the loss of body heat; third, the conversion of these feathers into means of gliding; fourth, the growth of wing power until the little beast could not only glide but also fly; and finally the loss of teeth, the development of a beak, and the enlargement of the breast keel. Thus did reptiles evolve into the birds familiar to all of us.

Remains of Cretaceous birds are a little more abundant than those of Jurassic birds but still scanty. The best-known genus of Cretaceous birds is *Hesperornis,* "western bird," a specialized diving bird from the western United States, with rudimentary wings and a long beak armed with many small, sharp teeth. *Hesperornis* looked rather like a large loon, with legs thrust out sideways like oars and a small, movable tail for a horizontal rudder. Some species reached a length of 6 feet. Since these oarlike legs must have made *Hesperornis* very awkward on land, it must have been even more aquatic than a modern penguin.

Fragmentary remains of Cretaceous birds of several other kinds have been found. In all but one case, however, the fossil did not include any jaws well enough preserved to settle the question of whether

Figure 43. *Hesperornis,* the large, flightless, toothed diving bird from the North American Cretaceous.

the bird had teeth. The one exception is a toothless jaw from the Cretaceous of western Canada, four times the size of a chicken's jawbone. This fossil, called *Caenagnathus,* indicates either a large bird—perhaps a flightless running bird—or even a small, beaked dinosaur.

After the end of the Cretaceous Period, rudimentary teeth persisted in two families of large, flightless birds, found in Lower Eocene deposits of North America and of Europe. If any toothed birds lived in later periods, their remains have not been found.

Whatever the limitations of *Archaeopteryx* and other Mesozoic birds, compared with the more finished products of our own times, in their day they were effective. They were adaptable enough to outcompete the pterosaurs, survive the Great Death at the end of the Cretaceous, and give rise to all the vast variety of birds that live today.

8

The Doom of the Dragons

No sharp break marks the end of the Jurassic Period and the beginning of the Cretaceous. Across the continents still spread vast, low-lying plains, dotted with lakes and swamps in which sauropods lazed and snorted, and sluggish rivers where crocodiles lurked and snapped. Dense, dark jungles clothed much of the land. Through these forests, carnosaurs ponderously stalked their prey and hopefully sniffed the air for the taint of carrion.

True, the earth's crust twitched a little here and there. A few minor mountain ranges rose; the ridges of Nevada's Great Basin are relics of this movement. Broad seas overspread wide stretches of the land, shrinking the land masses to the smallest area that they are ever known to have reached. In these shallow seas, the single-celled animals called Foraminifera, whose compacted skeletons make chalk, lived and died by the billions, leaving many beds of chalk among the Cretaceous deposits.

A present opinion as to how the map looked at the beginning of the Cretaceous is as follows: The northern supercontinent, Laurasia, was still intact; but a rift, extending northward from the south, had begun to split North America from Asia. The southern supercontinent, Gondwanaland, had already fragmented into three parts: South America-Africa, Antarctica-Australia, and India. During the Cretaceous, all the major continents of today parted company, except that Antarctica and Australia were still attached. This pair separated during the following Cenozoic Era or Age of Mammals, while India became part of Asia.

Meanwhile, a revolution in the plant kingdom was in the making. The Early Cretaceous started with the typical Mesozoic flora. Ferns, cycads, ginkgoes, and conifers still formed the forests. All of these plants have left survivors, but some of them nearly failed to survive to modern times.

For instance, when Westerners discovered the ginkgo, it grew only in scattered, cultivated spots in China and Japan, where it was found in temple courtyards or in places where human dwellings were reputed to have once stood. How long it had been planted by the hand of man we do not know; nor can we tell whether any completely wild ginkgoes grow anywhere today.

The ginkgo itself is a fairly large tree, with fan-shaped leaves that are cleft in the middle. A ginkgo leaf betrays the primitive plan of the species. The veins, instead of dividing and subdividing to form

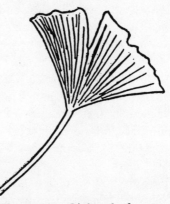

Figure 44.   Ginkgo leaf.

a close network, as do the leaves of most trees, radiate out from the base of the leaf like the ribs of a fan.

The tree has a main stem and many stout branches. But, instead of forking again and again to form a solid mass of greenery, each main branch gives rise to numerous small, short twigs, on the ends of which grow the leaves. This lack of branches of intermediate size gives the ginkgo a distinctive, tentacled appearance. Once having seen it, one can easily recognize it at a distance.

The first Westerner to describe the ginkgo was Engelbrecht Kaempfer, a German physician who traveled widely in Asia and spent the years 1690–92 in the Dutch trading post at Nagasaki, Japan. A few decades later, ginkgoes were brought from Japan to Europe, where they proved hardy. In more recent times, many have been planted in the United States. The tree tolerates a variety of climates (except for the Arctic winters of the Great Lakes region) and stoutly resists the attacks of insects and fungus diseases. Thus it is no longer in danger of extinction.

The cycads form a more numerous group of surviving trees, with nine genera and eighty-seven species. Most of them look like palms and are called by such names as "sago palm," "nut palm," and "fern palm." They occur in three groups: one in Africa, one in Australia and southeast Asia, and the third centering in Central America. Mexico is especially rich in cycads.

Of the conifers, the pines, larches, cedars, spruces, hemlocks, firs, cypresses, junipers, yews, and araucarias thrive in vast numbers. Certain interesting trees of the cypress family, however, almost suffered the doom that threatened the ginkgo. These are the redwoods of California and China, the largest living things on earth.

The redwoods were long supposed to be the oldest things as well. The largest tree-ring count of a fallen redwood gave an age 3,126 years, and the famous General Sherman tree is conservatively estimated to be a little under 4,000 years old. It was a sapling when Khammurabi codified the laws of Babylon, a giant when Solomon reigned in Jerusalem, and immemorially ancient when Alexander burned Persepolis and Brutus slew Caesar.

A few years ago, scientists at the University of Arizona made a surprising discovery. By boring a small hole through the boles of bristlecone pines and counting the rings with a special device bearing a light and a mirror, they learned that some of these pines were older than the oldest sequoias. Three of these pines were over 4,000 years old. The bristlecone pine, which grows on the windy crests of the Sierras, is not a handsome tree. A mature example looks like a gnarled old stump, at least half dead, with patches of live bark and a few twigs with needles here and there. But, then, how many of us would look hale at that age?

At any rate, the redwoods are the largest living things. The coast redwood, *Sequoia,* is the taller, with heights ranging up to 364 feet. The Sierra redwood, *Sequoiadendron,* is the more massive; several trees measure more than thirty feet in diameter at the base. One has an automobile road running through its trunk.

A generation ago, Chinese botanists discovered a third genus, the Chinese or dawn redwood, *Metasequoia,* already known from fossils. About a thousand dawn redwoods grow in the Valley of the Tiger in the west-central part of the country, not far from the Second World War capital of Chungking.

Since the local peasantry, like most farmers, are entirely concerned with their own immediate needs, they cut down these trees for timber whenever they wish. To save the species, Chinese and American botanists arranged to send a number of seeds, seedlings, and cuttings to the United States, where they now are growing.

Metasequoia looks much like the American bald cypress, to which it is, indeed, related. Unlike the American redwoods, it sheds its needles in winter. None of the existing dawn redwoods approaches the American redwoods in size; the largest are around 100 feet tall. But nobody knows how big the tree would grow if protected from the ax for thousands of years.

In the past century, all three species of redwood have been planted in many parts of the world; therefore none is now likely to become extinct. In Mesozoic and earlier Cenozoic times, the redwood family was much more widespread. At that time, the world provided the peculiar climates the redwoods needed over far wider areas than it now does. As the climate changed, the ancient redwood forests moved with the changes of climate until most of them, driven up against mountains, deserts, or oceans, perished.

The ginkgoes, cycads, and conifers all belong to the first of the two groups of higher plants: the gymnosperms or "naked seeds" and the angiosperms or "covered seeds." An angiosperm has a sophisticated apparatus for the fertilization of its seeds. Each seed is inclosed in an ovary with a sticky-ended projection called a stigma. When a pollen grain touches the stigma, it sticks fast and grows a shoot down into the ovary to fertilize the seed. Gymnosperms use several methods of reproduction, but their systems are generally simpler and more primitive.

Generally speaking, angiosperms are flowering plants and gymnosperms are not. Likewise, angiosperms bear fruit, nuts, or berries, while gymnosperms do not. These distinctions, however, are not absolute. Some fossil cycads, which were gymnosperms, bore flowers or at least flower-shaped structures, while ginkgoes bear fruit of a sort. Yews inclose their seeds in berries. Fruit and berries are merely some of the many methods used by plants to spread their seeds. The seed in a fruit travels in an animal's stomach, the seed in a burr travels in an animal's fur, while the winged seed of a maple is borne by the wind.

The big botanical change of the Cretaceous Period was the rise of the angiosperms. Up to the end of the Jurassic, there are only scanty records of angiosperms, except for some trees, related to the cycads, which might be transitional to the angiosperms. One of these is *Williamsonia,* which had a palmlike trunk. From this trunk sprang a few stumpy branches, curving upward like the arms of the giant saguaro cactus. Bunches of feathery fronds grew from the ends of the main and auxiliary trunks.

A Lower Cretaceous deposit in Greenland yielded not only the usual assortment of ferns, ginkgoes, and other Mesozoic plants, but also an array of modern-looking planes, magnolias, oaks, and other broad-leaved trees. Little by little, these and other angiosperms spread over the earth. By the end of the Cretaceous, modern-looking forests of poplar, beech, plane, willow, dogwood, magnolia, palm, laurel, elm, oak, and countless other angiosperms clothed the plains and mountains of the earth's more humid climes.

Figure 45. *Williamsonia,* a Jurassic plant related to the cycads and transitional between the gymnosperms and the angiosperms, from North America.

Towards the end of the Cretaceous—or a few million years later—an even more striking change began to take place in the earth's more arid reaches. From the angiosperms arose a family of small but prolific plants, the Gramineae or grasses, which conquered half the earth. Strictly speaking, only plants belonging to this family, which includes wheat, rye, rice, maize, sugar cane, and bamboo, are grasses in the botanical sense. In common speech, however, many plants, only distantly related to these but of similar form, are also called grasses. Now, over vast areas that had hitherto presented only the browns and grays of sand and rock, speckled at most with isolated shrubs and herbs, spread a soft green carpet of grass.

As with the Jurassic Period, fossil records of land animals are scanty for the early part of the Cretaceous Period. The best so far found is the Wealden formation of England. In contrast, the Late Cretaceous deposits are extraordinarily rich in land animals.

Among Early Cretaceous land animals, the dinosaurs still ruled. Two sets of tracks from South Dakota, of Early Cretaceous age, give us a glimpse of this world in action. On one crowded slab of sandstone appear the tracks of seven to nine individuals of a single carnivorous species of modest size. A nearby exposure shows not only the footprint of a larger flesh-eater with a foot 18 inches long, bearing sharp claws, but also that of a heavy plant-eater with a waddling gait, another herbivorous dinosaur with a foot 16 inches long and a two-and-a-half foot stride, and a web-footed animal whose foot was 5 inches long and five and a half inches wide.

Among the saurischian dinosaurs, the sauropods continued their wading, reed-gulping lives. New genera and families took the place of Jurassic sauropods, but they all looked much like their predecessors.

Sauropods are rather rare in North American Cretaceous. This may mean either that the animals were really scarce, or that the Cretaceous beds of North America do not happen to include the swamps in which the sauropods lived. Sauropods are found in Texas but not in the rich dinosaur beds of Wyoming, Montana, and western Canada. Perhaps the climate in these northern regions was a little too cold for sauropods, even if dinosaurs of other kinds throve in it. On the other hand, sauropods continued to be common in South America, Africa, southern Europe, and Asia. In many of these places, they survived right up to the end of the Cretaceous.

Of the theropods, the carnosaur *Megalosaurus* and light, fast coelurosaurs of several kinds still haunted Europe. Africa harbored a huge carnosaur, bigger than *Tyrannosaurus*.

Huge carnosaurs throve in North America, too. In 1940, J. Willis Stovall, who had recovered colossal allosaurs from the Oklahoma Panhandle in 1934, heard of more large fossils in the southeastern part of the state. With Wann Langston as his assistant, he dug up another pair of Early Cretaceous carnosaurs, although these specimens were fragmentary and badly damaged by tree roots.

These skeletons proved to be of animals about the size of *Allo-saurus,* 30 to 40 feet long but of somewhat different build. As the spines of the vertebrae were long, forming a foot-high ridge or frill along the animal's back, Stovall named this carnosaur *Acrocantho-saurus,* "high-spined lizard."

Figure 46.   *Spinosaurus,* a finbacked carnosaur from the Late Cretaceous of Egypt.

This spiny tendency was carried even further in a carnosaur from the Upper Cretaceous of Egypt. This was *Spinosaurus,* whose back spines reached a length of 6 feet. If the back fin was a heat-control organ in the pelycosaurs, it presumably served the same purpose in *Spinosaurus.*

As the Cretaceous advanced, the great Jurassic family of carno-saurs, the megalosaurids, faded out in most parts of the world, al-though some survived into the Late Cretaceous of Asia and Africa. Elsewhere a new family, the deinodonts or tyrannosaurids, took the place of the megalosaurids. The three best-known genera of the dei-nodonts in North America are *Gorgosaurus,* 20 to 25 feet long; *Deinodon,*[1] around 30 feet long; and lastly the famous *Tyrannosau-rus,* 45 to 50 feet in length. Their remains occur in different beds, with the smallest reptiles earliest and the largest last. Since they are much alike in their bony structures, some think that they represent a single line of descent.

However, these are only the three best-known of seven or eight different genera from the Upper Cretaceous of North America. The other genera may have been quite as important in their day. At each stage, probably, there were several kinds of carnosaur existing at the same time, preying on herbivorous reptiles of different sizes. The largest carnosaur of all, we suspect, made most of its living by robbing the smaller ones of their kills.

The deinodonts ("terrible teeth") differed in several ways from the megalosaurids. Their skulls were more rigid, without the give of the earlier kinds. They bore a strong cuirass of abdominal ribs. The upper bones of their hind feet were fused together to give a stronger support. Finally, their forelegs had dwindled away to mere vestiges, so small that it is doubtful if they were even useful for picking the creatures' teeth after a gorge.

Barnum Brown, one of the leading fossil-hunters of the American Museum of Natural History, dug up two specimens of *Tyrannosaurus* whose skeletons were unusually complete—except for the abdominal ribs and the forelegs. When these skeletons were first mounted, one in the American Museum of Natural History and one in the Carnegie Museum, they were fitted with three-clawed forelegs like those of *Allosaurus*. Later, several skeletons of *Gorgosaurus* and *Deinodon* proved to have two-clawed forelegs. Since *Tyrannosaurus* is closely related to these and may even be directly descended from them, *Tyrannosaurus* is now usually taken to have had two claws only on each diminutive foreleg. The American Museum's skeleton has been altered to agree with this new knowledge.

It is not known why the carnosaurs of this family practically discarded their forelegs. Perhaps their heads, and especially their jaws, had developed to such an enormous extent that their forelegs were no longer of practical use in fighting or eating. So the evolutionary force of rudimentation shrank them down.

Tyrannosaurus was the climax of the deinodont line and close in size to the largest carnosaur that ever lived. It inhabited Mongolia as well as North America, while a similar carnosaur lived in Russia.

If not quite the "ten tons of ravening ferocity" that journalists have made of it—being, perhaps, more of a robber and carrion-eater than an active predator—*Tyrannosaurus* would have been glad enough to snap you up if it had had a chance. We do not know how fast a tyrannosaur could move. An African elephant of similar bulk can hit 20 miles an hour for a distance of 50 or 100 yards but then gets winded and has to slow down. Given a reasonable head start, an athlete in good running condition, lightly clad and on smooth ground such as a golf course, can outrun an elephant. The Victorian big-game hunter Samuel W. Baker once escaped from a charging elephant by sheer fleetness of foot. It is a good guess that a tyrannosaur's performance would be similar.

The trouble is that elephants do not usually chase people on golf courses, but in bush and forest, where the advantage lies with the pursuer. The same applies to the tyrannosaur. So, if you journey back through time and encounter one of these monsters, be sure to stay at least several hundred yards away.

Tyrannosaurus was one of the last of the dinosaurs. After the last of the plant-eaters died, a few tyrannosaurs may have been left wandering about the land until they died of starvation. Deprived of their normal prey, they were not agile enough to catch small mammals, birds, or lizards.

While the megalosaurids and deinodonts evolved monstrous, lumbering forms, the other branch of the theropod dinosaurs, the swift coelurosaurs, continued on into the Cretaceous. *Elaphrosaurus,* known from scattered remains in the Lower Cretaceous of Africa, was much like the American *Ornitholestes,* but twice as big—in other words, about 12 feet long. Fragments of similar animals come from Lower Cretaceous beds in many parts of the world, including Australia.

In the Late Cretaceous, the coelurosaurs evolved a specialized family, the Ornithomimidae ("bird-mimics"). As the name implies, these were even more birdlike than other dinosaurs. A reptile of the best-known genus, *Ornithomimus,*[2] looked rather like an ostrich from which a passing tornado had stripped all the feathers. As one

Figure 47.   *Ornithomimus,* a long-necked, toothless, omnivorous coeluro-saur from the Late Cretaceous of North America.

looks closer, one sees differences: the long reptilian tail and the well-developed forelegs, ending in three long, slightly curved claws. The hindlegs were elongated and slender, indicating that the animal owed its long geological life to its fleetness of foot. The head was small and light, with a toothless, birdlike beak.

Paleontologists have wondered what *Ornithomimus* ate. Fruit? Hardly any fruit existed. Did it pull down branches with its forelegs to eat the leaves? Unlikely, because that long neck enabled it to reach much higher with its beak than with its foreclaws. Ants? Those fore-limbs seem well adapted to tearing open the nests of ants and ter-mites; but, if *Ornithomimus* had a long, sticky tongue, it has left no trace in the skeleton. The eggs of other dinosaurs? Very likely, but not exclusively, since caches of eggs were probably not easy enough to find to support a large population of ornithomimids. Like modern reptiles, dinosaurs probably buried their eggs.

The best answer seems to be that *Ornithomimus* was an omnivore, eating practically everything small and digestible: eggs, lizards, snails, insects, worms, seeds, buds, and tubers. Those fore-claws would serve to turn over stones to see what sort of scuttlers and wrigglers had taken refuge beneath them.

Although the saurischian dinosaurs held their own through most of the Cretaceous, the age really belongs to the ornithischians, who now achieved their greatest variety. Although no ornithischian ever surpassed the sauropods in size, they far exceeded them in range of shapes.

Of the ornithischians, the conservative ornithopods continued their sober way. They retained the two-legged gait of their forebears. To be more exact, they kept a combination of two-legged and four-legged gait, the latter for feeding and the former for running. In general shape, they resembled the carnivorous theropods. But the ornithischians were of more massive build than theropods of the same general size, since they had to carry a bigger paunch to digest plant food. At the front of their jaws, they had beaks instead of teeth, but to the rear of these jaws, they developed efficient grinding teeth.

In the early Cretaceous, Europe and North America each harbored an assortment of ornithopods of different sizes. The other continents will probably be found to have done so, too, when their fossil-bearing beds have been more thoroughly explored. Europe had the 34-foot *Iguanodon* and the 5-foot *Hypsilophodon*. In North America, several species of *Camptosaurus,* ranging from 4 to 17 feet in length, lived on from the Jurassic into the Early Cretaceous. With it lived relatives of *Hypsilophodon,* from the 6-foot *Laosaurus* at the beginning of the age to the 11-foot *Thescelosaurus* at the end of it.

In the Late Cretaceous, the largest known iguanodont of all dwelt in North America. Although no bones of this reptile have been found, in 1934 Barnum Brown recovered a pair of footprints from the roof of a coal mine in Colorado. Each footprint is 34 inches long and wide, and the distance from one to the other—heel to heel or toe to toe—is 15 feet 2 inches, as long as a generous modern room.

Some have thought that these prints were made by a *Tyrannosaurus.* However, there are several arguments against this. For one thing, there is no sign in these footprints of the mighty claws that carnosaurs bore on their feet. For another, this stride is about half again as long as that of a tyrannosaur. For still another, the pattern of the foot pads seemed typical of iguanodons.

So the unknown strider was probably an iguanodont—but an iguanodont 60 feet or more in length! A few isolated, similar, but slightly larger prints have been found in other mines of the same formation. One of these prints measures 32 inches wide by 44 long. Whatever the shape of these animals, they were surely the largest bipeds that ever bestrode the earth.

During the Cretaceous, the ornithopods produced two specialized families, the pachycephalosaurs ("thick-headed reptiles") and the hadrosaurs ("stout reptiles"). It is easier to call them boneheads and duckbills.

The boneheads were small dinosaurs, about the size and shape of one of the earlier camptosaurs. In the smaller and earlier genus, the 6-foot *Stegoceras,* the top of the reptile's head bulged up to form a dome. If this gave the dinosaur an intellectual air, the look was deceptive, since the dome was of solid bone.

The later and larger form was *Pachycephalosaurus,* whose skull (the only part known so far) measured 26 inches in length. This is thrice the length of *Stegoceras'* skull. *Pachycephalosaurus* has not only a dome of bone on top of its head but also a number of small spikes around the front, sides, and back of the head. Nobody knows the purpose of these spiked domes, but it is possible that the male boneheads butted each other in fighting for territory and females, as mountain sheep butt with their horns today.

The other family, the hadrosaurs or duckbills, ranged in herds over North America and Asia throughout the Late Cretaceous. They were large dinosaurs, growing up to 40 feet long in *Edmontosaurus.* The hadrosaurs retained the general shape of the other ornithopods: long hindlegs, forelegs short but usable for walking, long heavy tail to balance the body when the animal walked on its hindlegs, and the whole covered with an unarmored, warty skin. The feet were often webbed for swimming, since these dinosaurs seem to have fed on the margins of lakes and rivers and to have plunged into the water to escape from carnosaurs. Their tails are flattened as if for swimming by a side-to-side sculling motion.

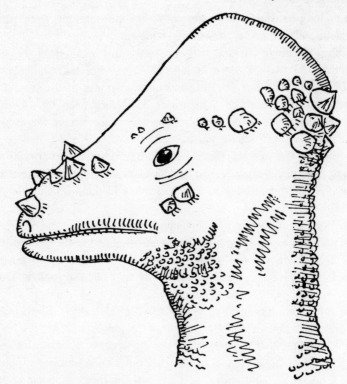

Figure 48.   Head of *Pachycephalosaurus,* a bone-headed ornithopod dinosaur from the Late Cretaceous of North America.

There is some doubt, however, as to whether the tail was really
thus used. For one thing, some fossils show that the tendons that
strengthened the vertebrae, including the vertebrae of much of the
tail, were ossified. This implies a tail too stiff to be wagged in this
eelish fashion.

Moreover, if the tail were limber enough to flutter in this way, it
is hard to see how it would, at the same time, be stiff enough to be
held up as a counterpoise when the animal walked bipedally. And
tracks of dinosaurs of this kind show that they did walk thus. Perhaps
they swam entirely by froglike kicks of their webfooted legs.

In any case, the main specializations of the duckbills were in their heads. The forward ends of their jaws had spreading, ducklike, tooth-less bills. The after part of their jaws, however, bore efficient batteries of small grinding teeth. These teeth were packed together in ranks and files, in a mosaic pattern, so that in some species there might be as many as 2,000 teeth in the jaws at one time.

Each tooth began its life in the bottom of a groove in the reptile's jaw, in an oblique position. As a lower tooth moved upwards, wear against the upper teeth ground it down to a beveled end. By the time there was hardly anything left of it, it was shed. The beveled ends of several rows of teeth were in action at once, while more teeth con-tinually sprouted at the bottom of the groove to take the place of those that wore out.

Such a tooth structure suggests that the duckbills ate calamites—that is, horsetails and scouring rushes. The latter contain much silica. That is why our ancestors scoured pots with scouring rushes, much as we use steel wool today. Such abrasive food would soon wear down ordinary teeth; hence these durable dental batteries.

Of the several subfamilies of duckbills, one retained the simple duckbilled skull to the end of the Age of Reptiles. The others, how-ever, developed peculiar crests and other excrescences on their skulls. Thus *Kritosaurus* had a high-bridged muzzle, while in *Saurolophus* the nasal bones extended back from the top of the skull in a short, sharp spike. *Corythosaurus* had a kind of cockscomb or half-disk on top of its head; *Lambeosaurus,* a crest shaped like the blade of a hatchet, combined with a backward-projecting spike; *Parasaurolo-phus,* a long backward projection that reminds one of the crest of *Pteranodon.* Other genera had heads of other shapes.

Of the crested duckbills, *Kritosaurus* and *Saurolophus* had skull ornaments of solid bone. In the other three genera, the nasal passages ran up into the crest and were somewhat coiled or zigzagged before they turned down to the windpipe.

Men have long disputed the purpose of these structures. Once it was thought that the long spine of *Parasaurolophus,* for instance, might serve as a snorkel to enable the feeding dinosaur to breathe with its head under water. But more complete skulls show that the crest did not open to the outer air.

Another suggestion is that the crest served as a trap to keep water out of the lungs when the animal's head was submerged. This is unlikely. First, it would not be effective, since a slight increase in water pressure would compress the air and force the water past the trap. Secondly, it would probably be unnecessary, since practically all air-breathing animals that spend much time in the water have sphincter muscles for closing their nostrils.

The idea of a sand trap for desert life is hardly more plausible. Nor is the suggestion convincing that the hollow spaces in the crests were resonators, so that the dinosaurs could bellow more loudly. The idea that the crests provided a reserve of air for the lungs, when the animal was diving, falls down on the fact that this "reservoir" would add a small fraction only to the duckbills' total lung capacity. Moreover, there would be no way to get the air from the crest down into the lungs when the animal was under water, since the reservoir was in a rigid skull.

The general opinion now seems to be that the crests provided space for extra-large mucous membranes, to which ran the olfactory nerves. Thus they were part of a hypersensitive smelling apparatus, to enable the duckbill to detect the rank odor of an oncoming carnosaur a long way off and flee. The crests of the solid-crested duckbills, however, are still a puzzle.

Having been brought up on the story of David and Goliath, many people are prejudiced in favor of speed and agility as opposed to weight and armor. When they learn that some massive armored animal became extinct, they mutter that it served such a slow, clumsy creature right.

Such feelings, however, have no place in science. Armor is but one of many adaptations whereby an animal preserves itself in a world of enemies. It is not the least effective adaptation, either. The turtles are armored, yet they have proved to be one of the most successful vertebrate orders. True, the armored dinosaurs perished at the end of the Cretaceous; but then, so did the far more numerous small, swift, unarmored dinosaurs.

In any case, the first dinosaurian essay with armor, that of the

stegosaurs, failed. Perhaps the carnosaurs learned to attack stegosaurs from the side or front instead of from the rear. Whatever the
cause, the stegosaurs dwindled early in the Cretaceous. Fragmentary
remains of a few genera are known from the Lower Cretaceous of
North America, Europe, and Africa, but the suborder did not long
abide.

However, that was not the end of armor. Into the stegosaurs' footprints soon stepped the ankylosaurs.[3] The ankylosaurs bore as much
armor as had the stegosaurs, but the armor was better designed. It
was placed to meet attack from any direction.

The first ankylosaurs come from the Lower Cretaceous, just when
the stegosaurs were passing away. Of the several ankylosaurian genera
that lived at this time, the 13-foot *Acanthopholis* from England is
the most primitive, although it survived into the Late Cretaceous. As
you can see from Parker's drawing (Plate 55), the animal looked
rather like *Scelidosaurus,* the ancestral stegosaur. This restoration is
uncertain, because the main specimen, discovered in 1867 and described by Thomas Huxley, consists only of a part of a skull and a
few scattered bones and scales. The most likely arrangement of its
meager armor is that shown in the picture, with spines over the neck
and shoulders and keeled plates over the rest of the back and the tail.
The reptile's weak jaw and small teeth imply a diet of soft plants.
Gideon Mantell's *Hylaeosaurus* seems to have been closely related.

Since a primitive ankylosaur looks somewhat like a primitive stegosaur, scientists have naturally wondered if the two suborders were
not really one, which split apart late in its history. That may be so.
Now, however, the general belief seems to be that the split took place
much sooner—say, in the earliest Jurassic—if indeed the two suborders
did not evolve separately from primitive ornithischian stock. It will
take many more fossils to settle this question.

From the Lower Cretaceous of Mongolia comes a more specialized
ankylosaur, *Syrmosaurus.* This animal, 12 to 15 feet long, was
plainly evolving into one of the animated tanks of the Late Cretaceous. Its legs were stumpier than those of *Acanthopholis,* its back
was more arched, and its armor was more effective. This armor consisted of many knobbed plates scattered over its back and sides. It

Figure 49.   *Syrmosaurus,* an ankylosaur from the Early Cretaceous of Mongolia.

also bore a weapon at the end of its long tail. This was a bony disk, like a crude double-bitted ax lying flat. The after part of its tail was fused into a solid mass to serve as a helve for this battle ax. In life, probably, the blade and the bony knobs were covered with horn.

A more advanced ankylosaur from the same age was the English *Polacanthus,* whose startling array of spines and plates is shown in Plate 56. The head and feet are missing from the fossil on which the restoration is based, but it is not likely that the artist went far astray in those respects. Like *Acanthopholis* and *Syrmosaurus,* this dinosaur was about 14 feet long. Note that it reversed the arrangement of armor of the stegosaurs: it had its spines in front and its sharp-edged plates in back. Over its hip region, between the spines and the plates, *Polacanthus* bore a massive, rigid shield. The American *Hoplitosaurus,* from the same age in South Dakota, seems to have borne a similar panoply.

In the Late Cretaceous, the ankylosaurs flourished. Ten genera are known from North America alone and smaller numbers from Europe, Asia, and South America. In their fully developed form, these dinosaurs looked something like turtles and something like gigantic horned toads. Their armor of keeled, spined, or knobbed plates was thickly set all over their backs, not quite in a solid mass like a turtle's shell but still not very flexible. Sometimes the tail bore spikes; sometimes it ended in a solid club of bone.

Three typical American Late Cretaceous ankylosaurs are shown in the pictures: *Edmontonia,* the American equivalent of *Syrmosaurus,* with a heavy knob on the end of its tail; *Scolosaurus,* with armor arranged in bands as on an armadillo, and blunt spikes on its neck, shoulders, forelimbs, and tail; and *Palaeoscincus,* with spines along its sides. The last bore a club at the end of its tail. For millions of

Figure 50. *Scolosaurus,* an ankylosaur from the Late Cretaceous of North America.

years these animals and others like them plodded peacefully from plant to plant, nibbling and munching, and then lying still for hours or days to digest their food.

Once an ankylosaur had attained its full growth, nothing much could bother it. It has been suggested that a tyrannosaur could turn an ankylosaur over on its back in order to tear open its soft underbelly. We doubt that a tyrannosaur had that much wit. Besides, a big ankylosaur weighed a ton or more, and a tyrannosaur would hardly find it easy to balance on one foot while it turned its victim over with the other.

Most likely, the ankylosaur simply squatted down when attacked, or tried to wheel around to bring its attacker within range of its tail. A crack on the shins with that club would discourage even the hungriest carnosaur, if it did not break a leg. True, an ankylosaur might sometimes lose its footing on a steep slope, accidentally roll over, and be unable to right itself before an enemy arrived. But that would be another story.

The last group of dinosaurs to appear was the suborder Ceratopsia ("horned faces"). The ceratopsians came to light in 1887, when a couple of geologists, working in the West, sent O. C. Marsh a pair of fossil horn cores, which one of them had found near Denver. Marsh glanced at the horns and pronounced them the remains of a fossil bison.

The next year, however, a whole skull turned up. Cowboys rounding up cattle on the ranch of Charles A. Guernsey, in Montana, discovered a fossil skull protruding from the side of a ravine, "with horns as long as a hoe handle and eye holes as big as your hat."[4] Informed of this find, Guernsey and his foreman went to the spot and tried to dig the fossil out. When it came loose, Guernsey and the skull slid with a roar to the bottom of the gulch, where the fossil shattered into several pieces.

The battered Guernsey picked up the horn cores and the jaw and took them back to his ranch house. There John Bell Hatcher, prospecting the Judith River Valley for Marsh, saw them. Hatcher realized that he was looking at the remains of a member of a whole new group of dinosaurs. He informed Marsh, who named the new dinosaur *Triceratops* ("three-horned face").

Triceratops proved one of the largest ceratopsians and also one of the last of the dinosaurs. At the very end of the Age of Reptiles, it roamed the uplands of North America in herds. Its fossils are very common; one collector said he counted 500 skulls or parts of skulls in seven seasons of collecting in Montana. However, *Triceratops* was only one of twelve to twenty genera of ceratopsians.

The typical ceratopsian was a kind of reptilian rhinoceros, 20 to 25 feet long and standing 6 or 8 feet high. Four massive, graviportal legs supported a paunchy body. The legs, however, were less straight and pillarlike than those of a sauropod dinosaur, since the weight to be carried was less. A medium-sized ceratopsian may have weighed two or three tons, like the cow Indian elephants one sees in zoos and circuses. The ceratopsian's forelegs bowed out at the elbows. The toes of the short, elephantlike feet ended in blunt, hooflike nails.

The distinctive part of a ceratopsian, however, was the head. The skull was very large in proportion to the whole animal, reaching a length of 7 or 8 feet. About half of this length consisted of a bony frill, which not only protected the neck from the bites of carnosaurs but also provided attachments for the powerful muscles that supported and moved the head and worked the jaws.

In some genera, the bone of the frill contained large fenestrae or openings. This does not mean that the living animal had holes in its frill, because the entire frill was probably covered by horn or leathery skin. In some kinds, the after edge of the frill was ornamented by spikes or hooks.

In front, the skull ended in a toothless, hooked beak. The hinder parts of the jaws were armed with multiple rows of grinding teeth, arranged somewhat like those of the duckbill dinosaurs.

The horns of a ceratopsian arose from above the beak and the eyes. Different genera developed their horns to different degrees. In some like *Monoclonius* ("one-sprouter") the nose horn was large, while the eyebrow horns were mere knobs. In some like *Torosaurus* ("bull lizard") the eyebrow horns were everything and the nose horn practically nothing. *Triceratops* has all three well developed, while *Pachyrhinosaurus* ("thick-nosed lizard") had no horns at all—just a thick, bony bulge on top of the head, like that of a bonehead.

The ceratopsians were more limited in range than most dinosaurs. Their main theater of life was in North America. Several kinds also ranged eastern Asia, and one doubtful set of fragments comes from South America.

The most primitive members of the suborder lived in Mongolia. Here, in Lower Cretaceous beds, have been found remains of a small dinosaur called *Psittacosaurus* ("parrot lizard"). This is a slender biped 4 or 5 feet long. It is much like the British *Hypsilophodon,* or one of the smallest ornithopods, except for its high, narrow skull and parrotlike beak.

Some paleontologists like Edwin H. Colbert are sure that this animal, although not the true ancestor of the ceratopsians, is close to the main line of descent. It could not be the true ancestor, they say, because it shows certain specializations that the later ceratopsians lack. For instance, *Psittacosaurus* has only three functional fingers and a rudiment of a fourth, whereas the later ceratopsians possess all five. As we shall see, an animal that has lost an organ cannot usually re-evolve it.

The next step on the evolutionary ladder is represented by an American form, *Leptoceratops*. This reptile was a little larger than *Psittacosaurus,* with slightly larger forelimbs. Most significant is the fact that it had the beginnings of a frill over its neck. Like *Psittaco-*

saurus, Leptoceratops cannot be in the direct line of ancestry. The reason is that it lived late in the history of the group, when much larger and more specialized types had already evolved. Evidently it was, in its day, another "living fossil," which had preserved a primitive bodily form and survived beside its more specialized relatives.

Protoceratops, the Mongolian egg-layer that gave such fame to the Third Asiatic Expedition, was further along the evolutionary road. It had even more of a neck frill and had gone back to a four-footed gait. It comes from an Upper Cretaceous deposit, but a comparatively early one.

After *Protoceratops* come a multitude of horned and frilled American ceratopsians. The stock split into two main lines: those with a short frill and those with a long frill.

Figure 51. *Styracosaurus,* a ceratopsian from the Late Cretaceous of North America.

The short-frilled ceratopsians included *Monoclonius,* with a nasal horn only, and *Styracosaurus.* The latter had a single nasal horn and, in addition, six or eight horns or spines around the edge of the frill. These projections made *Styracosaurus* one of the most ornamental of all the ceratopsians. *Triceratops,* with three well-grown horns, is the culmination of this line. It reached a length of 25 to 30 feet, a height of 8 to 10 feet, and perhaps a weight of seven to ten tons.

The long-frilled ceratopsians, for their part, gave rise to the modest-sized *Chasmosaurus,* whose name refers to the large holes in its frill. A later member of the group was *Pentaceratops,* which also occurred in Asia. Its name ("five-horned face") refers to two bony spikes that stick out from the cheek region, one on each side, making a total of five such projections. Finally, the long-frilled ceratopsians culminated in *Torosaurus,* a contemporary of *Triceratops.* This creature's two-horned skull reached a length of eight and a half feet, making it the longest known skull of any land animal.

The purpose of the ceratopsians' horns is obvious. If a carnosaur rushed upon a ceratopsian in its usual headlong, blundering fashion, the horned dinosaur had only to face its foe squarely and make a short charge. Even at the lumbering gait of such an animal, its momentum would drive the horns up to the hilt in its enemy's belly.

Even if the carnosaur had the intelligence to circle round to attack from the rear, the bowed forelegs of the ceratopsian, if less efficient at supporting its weight without muscular effort, gave the beast a fair degree of agility. Therefore, it should have had little trouble in wheeling to face its foe. Perhaps ceratopsians moved in herds and, like the musk ox, formed circles when attacked. Probably, the only ceratopsians really in danger from carnosaurs like *Tyrannosaurus* were either the young and tender or the old and weak.

Judging by their teeth, ceratopsians were plainly plant-eaters. Their beaks and their flexible, powerfully muscled necks fitted them for biting off the tops of cycads and similar plants with a quick twist of the neck. Their batteries of grinding teeth were designed for chewing this food to pulp without the need for gizzard stones.

For many millions of years, the ceratopsians throve. Scarred frills and broken horns suggest that they fought not only the carnosaurs but also others of their own species, to defend their territories or their harems. So endowed by nature, one would have expected them to go on forever. But, by the end of the Cretaceous, they had all disappeared. Why? We shall soon discuss that crucial question.

By Late Cretaceous time, the many kinds of pseudo-lizards and pseudo-crocodiles, which swarmed the lands and shallows of earlier times, had nearly all disappeared; only a few lingered on. The champsosaurs, pseudo-crocodiles of the order Eosuchia, still flourished in the Cretaceous and lasted into the Paleocene and Eocene; then they, too, took their departure. Pseudo-lizards of the order Rhynchocephalia have persisted right down to the present in the form of the tuatara of New Zealand.

The true crocodiles throve in the Cretaceous as never before. They spread over a much wider area of the earth than they now do, showing that climates were still mild and benign in the high latitudes. A large, fresh-water air-breather cannot live where the water freezes over in winter, since it is too big to bury itself in the mud and hibernate.

Cretaceous crocodiles produced one monstrous form, *Phobosuchus* ("fearful crocodile"), with a 6-foot skull and a total length of 40 to 50 feet. Presumably, *Phobosuchus* lurked in waters where dinosaurs came to drink, in hope of snapping its jaws on one of the smaller ones and dragging it under water, as in Mr. Ferguson's picture (Plate 62). We can imagine that the duckbill dinosaurs, which fed on the margins of lakes and rivers, must have led a hectic life. They had to be prepared to leap into the water at the approach of a carnosaur and to leap out again when *Phobosuchus* appeared.

During the Cretaceous, also, the crocodiles put out a branch in South America, the sebecosuchians. These had skulls that were high and narrow instead of low and broad as in most crocodiles. They ended with the Eocene genus *Sebecus,* named after the ancient Egyptian crocodile god.

The true lizards flourished too, producing forms like today's monitors and iguanas. The snakes now branched off from the lizards; the oldest known true snake, *Pachyophis,* comes from a Lower Cretaceous bed in the Balkans. The early snakes resembled today's boas, pythons, and other constrictors. These, the most primitive of living snakes, even retain vestiges of leg bones.

The most specialized snakes are the venomous kinds, which have converted their salivary glands into poison sacs. Some fossil snakes from the Upper Cretaceous may be early vipers and cobras. However, the pedigree of snakes is poorly known, because snakes have lightened their skulls to such an extent that these fragile structures are seldom preserved. Nevertheless, snakes not only survived the great extinction at the end of the Cretaceous but went on to thrive and radiate throughout the Age of Mammals. They evolved into such formidable creatures as a 60-foot constrictor from the Egyptian Eocene and a venomous serpent from the South American Pleistocene with fangs two and a half inches long.

During the Cretaceous, the mammals continued much as they had before. They were still a host of small creatures, looking much like today's shrews, mice, rats, and woodchucks. They climbed, burrowed, kept out of the way of the reptilian overlords, and ate flesh, plants, or insects according to their kind.

By the Late Cretaceous, the triconodonts of earlier times had vanished. The multituberculates still throve, but not for much longer. The pantotheres had evolved into two types that still exist: the marsupials or metatheres, and the placental mammals or eutheres. The marsupials included opossums much like today's. The placental mammals consisted of insect-eating animals somewhat like today's shrews and hedgehogs.

Now came the Great Death. At the end of the Cretaceous, most of the Mesozoic reptiles disappeared, along with animals of certain other kinds, such as the ammonites. Wherever sedimentary rocks that cover this transition period are found, the effect is the same. Below a certain level, we find dinosaurs, mosasaurs, and other dragons; above that level we do not. That is all. There is no evidence of a catastrophe—the fossils of the great reptiles simply cease.

Of fifty families of reptiles known to have lived in the Late Cretaceous, only fifteen survived into the Paleocene, and five of these vanished by the end of the Eocene. Since that time, radiation of snakes and lizards has to some extent restored variety to the class Reptilia. In fact, today there are more living species of reptiles known than there are of mammals.

Some readers may jump to the conclusion that there is an element of circular reasoning here. We assume that the dinosaurs died out everywhere at once. Then we infer that the latest beds in which dinosaurs occur are of the same age everywhere. And, since no dinosaurs are found above these beds, we infer that they all died out at once.

But geologists are not so naïve. They judge the age of these sedimentary rocks not only by the presence or absence of dinosaurs but also by the presence or absence of fossils of other kinds. These other fossils are consistent with the idea that the Great Death occurred, if not exactly at the same time everywhere, at least, speaking in geological terms, at approximately the same time. If dinosaurs survived in a few out-of-the-way places for one or two million years longer, this does not mean much in comparison with the seventy million years that have elapsed since the departure of the dinosaurs.

Had there been any big discrepancy in the dates of the disappearance of dinosaurs on different continents, or among dinosaurs of different kinds, then we should have expected some of them to have survived well into the Paleocene, where their remains would be mixed with those of mammals of that time. If they had lived side by side with these mammals, fossil-bearing formations that have preserved fragile little mammal skeletons would surely have preserved the missing reptiles, too.

But no dinosaur remains have ever been found with Paleocene and Eocene mammals. Only a few kinds of distinctly Mesozoic animals—certain families of lizards, turtles, crocodiles, and toothed birds, for instance—survived the Great Death, only to die out soon thereafter.

At the time of the Great Death, the world of the giant reptiles had undergone some marked changes. Among the dinosaurs, the stegosaurs had long since become extinct. The sauropods had dwindled from their palmier days, although several families continued to exist. Although the remaining suborders of dinosaurs—the thero-pods, the ornithopods, the ankylosaurs, and the ceratopsians—flour-ished, there had been an ominous reduction in the number of species some time before the actual number of individual animals declined.

The most common land dinosaurs of the time, in point of numbers, were probably the small ornithopods of the hypsilophodont, campto-saur, and bonehead groups, and the swift, slender, omnivorous orni-thomimids. The larger duckbills and the ceratopsians, too, probably formed sizable herds. The flesh-eaters, as usual, were in a small minority.

In the seas, the geosaurs had long since vanished, and the ichthyo-saurs became extinct well before the main catastrophe. On the other hand, the mosasaurs and plesiosaurs throve as never before.

In the air, the pterosaurs were still active, although yielding to the toothless birds, which were also supplanting their toothed rela-tives.

Then all the dinosaurs, mosasaurs, plesiosaurs, and pterosaurs disappeared. At the same time, the ammonites vanished from the seas, while the belemnites were reduced to a small remnant. Another group to disappear were the mollusks called Rudista, which were bivalves with very asymmetrical shells. Certain common kinds of foraminifers went also. Why?

There are many theories to account for the Great Death, but all have objections; for any theory must take into account the oddities of this extinction. All the dinosaurs became extinct—large and small, plant-eating and flesh-eating, swamp-dwelling and upland forms alike. But the crocodiles, the lizards, the snakes, the turtles, and the small primitive mammals did not become extinct. In fact, they seem not to have been affected at all. Likewise, the flying reptiles disappeared but the birds did not. The most spectacular sea reptiles—the mosa-saurs and plesiosaurs—also disappeared, but the sea turtles lived on.

Now, animals and plants are always becoming extinct and being replaced by others. At least a hundred species have perished in the last century, and many others are in a precarious state.

The causes of the recent extinctions, however, are obvious. The culprits are the hunter with his gun and traps, the stockman with his flocks and herds, and the farmer with his plow and pesticides. These kill off wild animals—sometimes for gain, sometimes to protect their crops and livestock, and sometimes for the sadistic pleasure of killing. They also take the wild animals' land away from them to convert it to human uses.

Even before there were men, the causes of some extinctions are plain enough. For the first half of the Age of Mammals, South America was isolated from all other continents. The predators of the continent were, first, large flightless birds (the largest of them eight feet tall) and, second, carnivorous marsupials. By parallel evolution, the latter developed into animals much like the weasels, badgers, dogs, bears, and cats (including a marsupial saber-tooth) of other continents.

Then the Isthmus of Panama was raised above the waters. The placental carnivores—the ancestors of today's jaguar, puma, ocelot, bush dog, kinkajou, tayra, and the rest—swarmed across this land bridge. The flightless birds of prey and the carnivorous marsupials, unable to compete with the more efficient invaders, all died out.

Besides these understandable extinctions, however, there have been worldwide waves of extinction for which no obvious causes are known. The most striking of these occurred in the Permian, at the end of the Cretaceous, and at the end of the Pleistocene. The most lethal of all was that of the end of the Cretaceous.

Now, when a species becomes extinct because it cannot compete with some other species, the victor lives on. In these general extinctions, however, there were no victors. Whole orders of animals perished without leaving any survivors or competitors. After the Cretaceous extinction, the earth was almost barren of large animals for millions of years, until the little mammals expanded into the ecological niches that the dinosaurs had left vacant by their passing.

So far, no logical way has been found to connect the known causes of the extinction of individual species with these worldwide Great Deaths. Some other cause, operating on a worldwide basis, would seem to be called for. It is asking too much of coincidence,

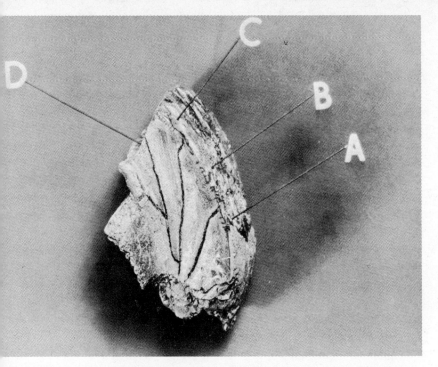

51. Section of the jaw of a hadrosaur, showing the wear and replacement of the teeth. A is a new tooth, just coming up; D a worn-out tooth about to be shed. *Photo from the Smithsonian Institution.*

52. Hindlimbs and tail of *Corythosaurus*, from the Late Cretaceous of Alberta, showing the skin impressions and the ossified tendons. *Photo from the Smithsonian Institution.*

53. *Corythosaurus*, a crested ornithopod from the Late Cretaceous of North America. In the background, left to right: pterosaurs; crested ornithopods *Psaurolophus*; a large carnosaur, *Gorgosaurus* or *Deinodon*; a crocodile. *Courtesy of the Academy of Natural Sciences, Philadelphia.*

54. Dinosaurs of the Late Cretaceous of North America: the large duckbilled ornithopod *Edmontosaurus* (right), the armored *Palaeoscincus* (center, front), the ostrich-like *Ornithomimus* (center, rear), and at the left two kinds of crested ornithopod: *Corythosaurus* (front) and *Parasaurolophus* (rear). *Courtesy of the Chicago Natural History Museum.*

55. *Acanthopholis*, a primitive ankylosaur from the Early Cretaceous of England. *Courtesy of the British Museum (Natural History).*

56. *Polacanthus*, an ankylosaur from the Early Cretaceous of England. *Courtesy of the British Museum (Natural History).*

57. Model of *Edmontonia*, a Late Cretaceous North American ankylosaur. *Photo from the Smithsonian Institution.*

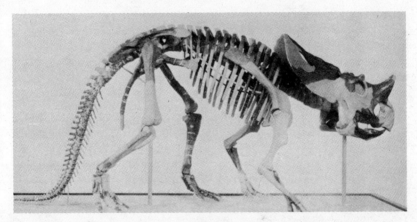

58. Skeleton of *Monoclonius,* a ceratopsian dinosaur from the Late Cretaceous of North America. *Photo from the Smithsonian Institution.*

59. Model of *Monoclonius*, a one-horned ceratopsian. *Photo from the Smithsonian Institution.*

60. *Protoceratops*, the ancestral ceratopsian from the Late Cretaceous of Mongolia. *Courtesy of the Chicago Natural History Museum.*

61. *Torosaurus*, a two-horned ceratopsian with the longest skull of any known land animal. *Photo from the Academy of Natural Sciences, Philadelphia.*

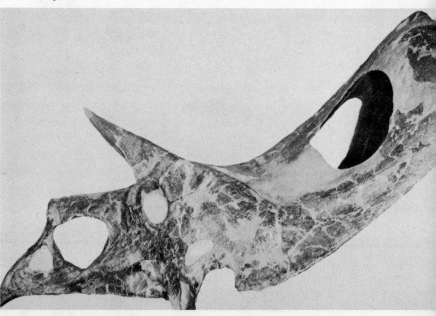

62. *Phobosuchus*, a giant crocodile from the Late Cretaceous of North America, trying to seize a young ceratopsian of the genus *Chasmosaurus*. *Courtesy of the American Museum of Natural History.*

63. Joseph Leidy (1823–91), the founder of American vertebrate paleontology. *Photo from the American Museum of Natural History.*

64. Part of the slab with dinosaur tracks collected by Prof. Edward Hitchcock in 1836. *Photo from the Pratt Museum, Amherst College.*

65. Fossil footprint of a large carnosaur. *Photo from the Pratt Museum, Amherst College.*

that scores of genera, dozens of families, and several whole orders should all perish at once by sheer happenstance.

Paleontologists have racked their brains over this question for a century, but it cannot be said that they have yet found the answer. Some, puzzled by the fact that the dragons of the land and the sea died out at the same time, suggest that we should allow for at least two separate causes, one operating on land and the other in the sea.

Of the single causes proposed for the doom of the dragons, some can be quickly disposed of. One is the theory of "internecine warfare": that the carnosaurs ate all the other dinosaurs and then starved to death. Objection: This does not account for the reptiles of the sea and the air. Moreover, a certain amount of predation is not only good for a species but actually necessary, to cull defectives and to keep the species from increasing to the point where it eats itself out of house and home. Predation is normally kept within bounds by the predators themselves, who claim certain territories and drive rivals away from them.

Another theory is that of a plague, which wiped out the dinosaurs. But real diseases of this sort do not affect more than one or a very few species at a time. No known disease, for instance, attacks *all* mammals or *all* birds, although some like distemper and foot-and-mouth disease attack several different species within a single order.

Moreover, rarely is a species completely destroyed by a disease. It may be reduced in numbers. But, when the survivors become thinly scattered, the disease can no longer spread rapidly among them. Then the parasite and the host adjust to each other. The more fatal varieties of the disease tend to die out because, every time they kill a host animal, the parasites also die. Likewise, the strains of the host species that are more resistant to the disease increase at the expense of the others, until immune strains evolve.

There was once a lot of talk about "racial senescence." It was thought that a group of animals went through processes of youth, maturity, and old age like those of an individual. When a genus or family attained great size or grotesque form, or otherwise became "overspecialized," it was thought to be senile and ready for extinction.

This, however, is reasoning by analogy. There is absolutely no reason to think that a species evolves in such a way. "Overspecialization" is a relative matter. Thus the opossum is a very primitive, generalized mammal; but, if one considers it as a reptile (as one logically may) one sees that it is a very specialized reptile indeed.

Size is also relative. All the larger mammals of today are gigantic by comparison with the mammals of the Paleocene. Gravity limits the absolute size of land animals, but the only land animals that ever pushed hard against this barrier were the sauropod dinosaurs. And the great extinction involved not only these but all the scurrying hosts of little dinosaurs as well. In certain cases, large size or heavy armor might be a poor adaptation and lead to extinction; but, under other circumtances, so might small size or lack of armor. And "grotesqueness" is a subjective idea. To an intelligent stegosaur, a human being might seem quite as grotesque as this creature seems to us.

According to a group of related theories, gigantic size, or prominent horns, tusks, armor, and other excrescences, indicate that something is wrong with an animal's glands. As Swinton and others suggested in the 1930s, the dinosaurs' pituitary glands put out too much growth hormone, causing excessive size and lumpishness.

More recently, Schatz has argued that the rise of the angiosperms increased the concentration of oxygen in the atmosphere, and this caused pituitary troubles and other malfunctions among the dinosaurs. However, the dinosaurs continued to flourish for many millions of years after the rise of the angiosperms. Moreover, they existed in huge numbers, without the slightest indication that the supposed rise in atmospheric oxygen was causing them any trouble.

These hormonal theories go back to the early decades of this century, when hormones had just been discovered but when the mechanism of heredity was not so well understood as it now is. Now we have learned that organs like horns, tusks, or armor are produced only in response to a strong, consistent, selective pressure on the species. They exist, not because the animal's glands have run wild, but because they are useful to the species. If such organs cease to be useful and selective pressure in favor of them relaxes, they soon disappear by rudimentation.

Furthermore, even if these hormonal theories accounted for the extinction of big, specialized dinosaurs like the sauropods, ceratopsians, and ankylosaurs, they would not explain the fact that all the small, swift, unspecialized dinosaurs like *Thescelosaurus* and *Leptoceratops,* without horns or armor, disappeared at the same time.

Another theory blames the death of the dinosaurs, not on a rise, but on a fall in the atmosphere's oxygen. Before life began on earth—say, about three billion years ago—the air contained only traces of oxygen. Since there was practically no free oxygen, there was no layer of ozone (O_3) in the upper atmosphere—roughly between twenty and thirty miles up—as there is now.

Ultraviolet radiations from the sun turn ordinary molecular oxygen, O_2, into ozone. However, ozone is opaque to most of the radiations in the ultraviolet range. Hence, when the ozone layer has formed in the upper atmosphere, it acts as an awning over the entire earth as far as those radiations are concerned. The actual amount of ozone is only a small fraction of the atmosphere, even in the ozone layer; but it suffices. The process of ozone-making reaches equilibrium, because the oxygen in the lower atmosphere is shaded from the sun's ultraviolet, and ozone gradually disintegrates back into ordinary O_2. If the ozone layer disappeared, most land life on earth would soon perish of aggravated sunburn.

It is thought that the first organisms were synthesized in shallow water—say, thirty-odd feet below the surface—by the action of ultraviolet radiations on simple organic compounds, which formed a soupy solution in primitive seas. Nearer the surface, the ultraviolet was strong enough to destroy the life it had created, and farther down it did not penetrate strongly enough to affect organic molecules.

When single-celled plants evolved, they broke down carbon dioxide and released free oxygen, just as they do today. Hence the percentage of oxygen in the atmosphere rose and the ozone layer took form.

Life, now shielded from the life-giving but life-destroying radiations, could invade the surface waters and finally the land.

According to the oxygen-drop theory, this process carried the amount of oxygen in the air past the point of equilibrium. This excess of oxygen caused a reaction, so that the percentage of oxygen fell sharply before it began to rise again. These declines, it is supposed, caused the great extinctions at the end of the Permian, Cretaceous, and Pleistocene periods. The obvious weakness of this theory is that the drop in oxygen would have much the same effect as moving to a higher altitude—say, that of Denver or Mexico City. Most land organisms can adapt themselves to such a change—if not in one lifetime, then in a few generations.

Consider next some theories of changes in climate and geography. First is the obvious suggestion, which has perhaps occurred to you already: Was there an ice age at the end of the Cretaceous? No, there was not. In fact, there is no sign of any sharp change in climate.

Through the later Cretaceous and the Paleocene, continental uplift and mountain-building took place in North America and probably in other continents as well. The Rocky Mountains were born at this time. This is called the Laramide Revolution, although "revolution" seems a questionable word for such a long-drawn-out process. This was not a catastrophic change. The climatic zones of former times shifted around the map a bit but did not suddenly disappear. Therefore the zones where dinosaurs could thrive moved slowly enough for the dinosaurs to keep pace with them.

Well, if cold will not account for the extinction, how about heat? A rise in temperature, it has been said, might kill the dinosaurs' sex cells and thus make them sterile.

Various causes have been proposed for a cold snap or a heat wave. These include a change in the sun's radiation; a change in volcanic activity, altering the amount of carbon dioxide in the air; the opening or closing of land bridges, causing a change in the flow of oceanic currents.

However, there is no evidence for any sharp rise in temperature at the end of the Cretaceous. A gradual rise, like a gradual fall, would merely move the climatic zones about the map.

Another theory combines heat and dryness. The result, it is supposed, was a loss of shade, either in the form of a cloud cover or the shade of trees in the widespread jungles of earlier times. This loss of shade, it is supposed, killed off the dinosaurs by sunstroke or sunburn. Small reptiles, lacking sweat glands and other built-in cooling mechanisms, are notoriously sensitive to solar heat. A snake or a lizard, caught in the open in the middle of a really hot, sunny day, succumbs in a matter of seconds.

But there is no sign of any marked change in vegetation at the end of the Cretaceous. Moreover, some of the dinosaurs seem to have been adapted to life in open country; but these perished with the rest. Nor do any of these climatic theories account for the quietus of the sea and air reptiles.

A more subtle variant of the climatic theories, which might even have the germ of truth in it, combines the effect of heat and cold. It supposes that the geographical changes of the late Cretaceous brought about, not a general worldwide change in average temperature, but the spread of "continental" climates, with hot summers and cold winters, instead of the milder "oceanic" climes of earlier times. This theory is usually combined with the idea of a worldwide spasm of orogeny. This mountain building, it is supposed, involved a rise of the land, an opening of land bridges, and a cutting off of the worldwide circulation of oceanic currents.

Objection: This theory still does not account for the extinction of the marine reptiles, because the temperature of the oceans is not much affected by such changes. In fact, it does not even account, by itself, for the extinction of the land reptiles, because of the persistence of mild climates over parts of the earth. Even today, when extreme continental climates are much more widespread than in the Cretaceous, there are large areas in South America, Africa, and Southeast Asia where we can imagine dinosaurs as living quite happily, if there were no men or other large mammals to bother them.

A variant of the mountain-building theory blames the disappearance of the dinosaurs on the drainage of the inland seas in the

Laramide Revolution. It is said that most dinosaurs were shore dwellers, and this drainage too greatly restricted their habitat. But this is assuming too much from the disappearance of one such sea, the Kansas Sea. It is not known that the same sort of thing happened to an equal degree on other continents. Furthermore, only some of the dinosaurs were shore dwellers; others lived in forests or on uplands.

Then there are various theories that, in combination with one or more of the foregoing, tie the end of the dinosaurs to changes in animal or plant life around them. It has often been suggested, for instance, that Cretaceous mammals ate dinosaurs' eggs. Well, no doubt they did. The dinosaurs, for that matter, probably ate each other's eggs when chance offered.

But this kind of predation goes on all the time. In fact, reptiles lay so many eggs that most of them can be eaten without decreasing the number of adults. Furthermore, the eggs of large dinosaurs, such as the sauropods, were so big and tough as to present a hungry little mammal with a formidable problem.

Then there is the possibility of direct competition between reptiles and the emerging mammals. Some argue[5] that the spread of continental climates restricted the dinosaurs to the tropics; that the mammals, who had evolved in climates too cold for the reptiles, took over the temperate zones vacated by the dinosaurs and there evolved into forms that could compete directly with the dinosaurs; and that at last they invaded the dinosaurs' sanctuaries and out-competed them. They account for the survival of the existing reptiles by noting that they did not compete with these mammals. And they account for the disappearance of the sea reptiles by the appearance during the later Cretaceous of large, fast sharks of the modern type, with which the mosasaurs and plesiosaurs could not compete.

Well, maybe. But we have yet to find a fossil-bearing bed, in the tropics or elsewhere, containing both large mammals and dinosaurs. The largest mammals of the Paleocene were no bigger than a large dog or a small bear and so could not very effectively have competed with a ceratopsian. Unless the mammals and the reptiles occupied the same territory at the same time, they cannot very well have been in competition. Moreover, the evidence seems to be that, after the dinosaurs had gone, the mammals required millions of years to take advantage of the empty world they had inherited and to evolve into large and varied forms.

A variant of this competition theory has to do with changes in plant life, notably the rise of the angiosperms. The trouble here is that this change was very gradual and, moreover, had largely taken place long before the end of the Cretaceous. The dinosaurs of the Late Cretaceous flourished for millions of years amid vegetation of much the modern type. If anything, the spread of broadleaved angiosperms would seem to have offered the plant-eating dinosaurs more abundant supplies of food than ever before, while the radiation of the ray-finned fishes did the same for sea reptiles.

One form of this theory says that the spread of the grasses may have done the dinosaurs in, since their teeth and stomachs were not fitted for such rugged fodder. However, there is no evidence that the spread of grass caused the extinction of any widespread species of plants that dinosaurs ate. Rather, it seems as though grass, when it came, spread mainly over areas which were too dry to support a forest growth, and which up to then had been largely bare earth.

Some scientists have suggested that a sudden burst of penetrating radiation, from a solar flare or from a nearby star that became a supernova, sterilized the dinosaurs or, at least, damaged their genes severely enough to destroy the race. Such a catastrophe should even more have affected small creatures like amphibians, lizards, snakes, and the Cretaceous mammals. But it did not. It should have affected the small dinosaurs more than the large, but all alike perished.

Another theory considers changes in the percentage of poisonous trace elements in the sea as a cause for marine extinctions. Such elements are copper, mercury, silver, and zinc. One paleontologist has calculated that a slight increase in marine copper salts could account for the disappearance of a number of marine animals in the Permian extinction.[6] Such a change might also have caused the marine extinctions at the end of the Cretaceous. It might, that is, if one assumes that the extinctions in the sea and on the land had different causes.

Some more subtle modern theories, still under development, have to do with such things as the breakdown of food chains and the ratios of different age groups in a species. It is, for instance, pointed out that if some species—a marsh plant, for instance—disappears, a whole fauna of animals that depend upon it may disappear, too. The animals that eat the plant go, and then the animals that eat the animals that eat the plant go, and so on.

But such a wave of extinction would mainly affect animals with a very narrow range of diet. Such animals do exist. Anteaters would perish if ants and termites disappeared. The koala eats only the leaves of certain species of eucalyptus and is poisoned by anything else. And there is a mold that has been found only in felt beer-mug coasters.

Most animals, however, are less finicky about their food. A big meat-eater like a carnosaur will gobble up any animal smaller than itself. While they may be restricted either to grazing or to browsing, most large herbivores eat a variety of greenery within these limitations. Rabbits have had no difficulty in living on the strange plants of Australia and New Zealand since certain foolish men brought them to those lands. Moreover, even if *Tyrannosaurus* would have starved without duckbills and boneheads to prey upon, the small coelurosaurs could have gone on living on insects and lizards, as they had been doing all along.

All the foregoing theories are often combined with some statement about the dinosaurs' lack of adaptability. How often have you read that "when an animal becomes overspecialized and fails to adapt itself in changing circumstances, it becomes extinct"? This statement is not very enlightening; it is like saying that a man died because his heart stopped beating. We want to know *what* sudden change called for such quick adaptation that the dinosaurs could not keep up with it. As far as the geological record goes, the changes in geography, climate, and vegetation at the end of the Cretaceous were mild and slow. Furthermore, some of the dinosaurs, such as the ceratopsians, had certainly evolved rapidly during the Late Cretaceous, showing that they could respond to selective pressure when the occasion demanded.

Assuming that some violent change did take place, whether in climate, topography, vegetation, atmosphere, or cosmic radiation, the size of the dinosaurs might have something to do with their lack of adaptability. In general, the bigger an animal is, the longer is its life cycle from egg to egg-laying adult. Hence a small form is likely to pass through many generations while a large form is undergoing only one. Because of the frequency of its generations, the small organism can evolve that much farther in a given time. It can therefore adjust itself more rapidly to the change, or it can shake off the effects of harmful radiations on its genes.

Yet this factor does not seem to have worked in the case of the Cretaceous extinction. The Great Death took not only the larger and more specialized dinosaurs, like *Tyrannosaurus, Triceratops,* and *Ankylosaurus,* but also the small, unspecialized dinosaurs, like the coelurosaurs and the hypsilophodonts, as well.

Such are the theories. Considered singly, there are serious, if not fatal, objections to every one of them. However, we need not consider them singly. Some combination of them could—in fact, probably did—bring about the fall of the dinosaurs and the other ruling reptiles. We do not yet know *what* combination of factors caused their fall, nor whether there were other factors at work that we do not yet know about at all. This puzzle will continue to wrinkle the brows of paleontologists for many years to come.

There is always something sad about the end of any great institution, be it the battleship, the Roman Empire, or the Age of Reptiles. No matter what its faults, we regret the passing of so splendid a spectacle. We wish that at least a sample could have remained for us to admire.

As to the dinosaurs, however, we had better be glad that they went when they did. If they had not, the mammals might never have been able to evolve beyond the shrew-and-opossum stage. In that case we, their descendants, should still be cowering in hidey-holes as the earth above us shook to the ponderous tramp of the dragons.

9

The Great Fossil Feud

The dragon-slayer of legend was a noble knight in well-polished armor, armed with a sword and a lance of the finest quality. The real dragon-hunters—the men who unearthed the dinosaurs—were not quite so picturesque. They were men in dusty work clothes, armed with picks, shovels, and smaller tools. They traveled afoot, on horseback, by wagon, and later by truck and automobile across endless leagues of wasteland. They crawled deep into the galleries of mines; they inched their way up the cliffs of the Rockies; they shivered in the cold, dusty winds of the Mongolian desert. Sometimes they dodged the bullets of bandits or hostile tribesmen. They underwent all these pains and perils to provide the people of today with the true story of life on earth, from its beginning down to the present.

It takes a great many fossils to give a clear picture of life's family tree. In fact, this tree has so many twigs and tendrils that thousands of fossil species must be identified before we gain even a rough idea of the various lines of descent. Now, most of Europe is well-watered and therefore covered with grass, trees, and crops. Such ground is unsuited to fossil-hunting, because the fossils are hidden by humus or destroyed by phosphorus-hunting rootlets. Most European fossils, therefore, have come to light in the course of mining, quarrying, and making cuts for roads and railroads. The first-known of all the Mesozoic reptiles, the mosasaur, came from a Dutch quarry.

The ideal fossil-hunting ground is desert—land where extensive erosion by a few heavy rains each year lays fossils bare. Such a land was the great American desert—an enormous area stretching from Central Mexico to Canadian Alberta—which proved a vast fossil treasure chest waiting to be opened.

Almost as soon as white men set foot upon the American continents, fossils were brought to their attention, although they did not know at the time what these objects really were. In 1519, when Cortés's indomitable band of marauders were in Mexico, the Tlascalan Indians showed them the bones of "giants." Cortés sent back to Spain one huge thigh-bone of a mammoth or a mastodon. Like other monarchs of the time, King Carlos (later Emperor Charles V) harassed his explorers with constant demands for gold, *gold,* GOLD! It would be interesting to know what the king said when, instead of hoped-for tons of gold, he received a colossal bone instead.

The first man who knowingly collected American fossils was the Baron de Longueuil, a French Canadian who, in 1739, led a French force down the Ohio and Mississippi Rivers in a campaign against the Chickasaw Indians. Somewhere along the Ohio, Longueuil gathered three teeth, a tusk, and a femur of the American mastodon, which he later took to France to show to the savants of the Jardin du Roi.

During the next hundred years, a number of Americans, including Thomas Jefferson and the famous artist Charles Willson Peale, collected fossils. Most of these, like Longueuil's find, turned out to be remains of the American mastodon, which roamed the continent in great numbers during the Pleistocene Period.

The first evidence of dinosaurs in North America consisted of fossil footprints from the Triassic Period, discovered in 1802 in a flagstone quarry near Turner's Falls, Massachusetts, by a farm boy, Pliny Moody. Other such tracks turned up near Boonton, New Jersey. The reptiles that made these tracks were relatively small and, like all Triassic dinosaurs, walked on their hindlegs.

Professor Edward Hitchcock of Amherst College, who found similar tracks in Massachusetts in 1836, thought that they were the tracks of birds. Hitchcock's largest slab with these imprinted footsteps is still in the Amherst College Museum. On it can be seen the tracks of several dinosaurs of different sizes, crisscrossing the slab. Most of the tracks show the three-toed hind feet only. But one dinosaur must have gotten tired and sat down; for there are impressions of his five-toed forefeet, his lower legs, his rump, and his tail.

The man who did more than any other to promote the new science of paleontology in America was Joseph Leidy (1823–91). Leidy was a mild, gentle Philadelphian who practiced medicine for several years and took a great interest in the Academy of Natural Sciences of Philadelphia. Deciding on a career in pure science, he traveled abroad in 1848 to meet other leading biologists and soon thereafter was appointed professor of anatomy at the University of Pennsylvania, a post which he held for the rest of his life. Although he wrote several books on microscopic animals, it is as a vertebrate paleontologist that Leidy won his chief fame. Before his time, there were but a few scattered papers on the subject of paleontology in all of America; and the discovery of new fossil deposits in the western states gave him an excellent opportunity to put his knowledge of anatomy to use.

Leidy's first dinosaur came to light when men were quarrying a bed of marl near Haddonfield, New Jersey, across the Delaware River from Philadelphia. In the 1850s, when the skeleton was first discovered, workmen and neighboring busybodies began to cart off bones to put on mantelpieces or use for doorstops.

Then, in 1858, W. Parker Foulke of Philadelphia, an amateur naturalist, heard of the find. He dug further into the excavation, unearthed more of the skeleton, and sent it to the Academy of Natural Sciences. Leidy recovered many of the bones seized by the souvenir-hunters, studied the assembled fossil, and named the creature *Hadrosaurus,* "thick lizard." Because this dinosaur, related to the European iguanodon, had a broad beak, it is often called a duck-billed dinosaur.

Leidy performed the Herculean task that had to be done before the science of paleontology could become established in North America: he collected all the fossils he could, sorted out the bones of individuals, classified the animals, and then saw what interpretations they would bear. Scientists whose work took them to the West sent Leidy fossils; Joseph Henry, secretary of the Smithsonian Institution, made Smithsonian money available so that Leidy could publish descriptions of his finds.

Then, in the early 1870s, Joseph Leidy found his sources of fossils drying up. Two younger paleontologists, both rich, had begun to offer large sums of money for fossils, which people had been sending Leidy free.

To make the situation more painful, one of the young competitors for the fossils was Leidy's former student Edward Drinker Cope (1840–97). Cope was a handsome man with a musketeer's mustache and imperial and a swashbuckling manner. Quakers are supposed to be modest, peaceable folk; and rich Philadelphians are supposed to be quietly respectable to the point of stuffiness. But this rich Philadelphian Quaker was neither peaceable, nor modest, nor quiet. In fact, he was one of the most aggressive, belligerent scientists who ever lived.

For instance, at a meeting of the American Philosophical Society, Cope got into an argument with his lifelong friend Persifor Frazer. The argument became so heated that they stepped out into the hall to settle it with fists. The next morning, young Henry Fairfield Osborn (later a famous fossil-hunter himself) saw Cope with a black eye. Cope barked:

"Osborn, don't look at my eye. If you think my eye is black, you ought to see Frazer this morning!"[1]

Cope began probing the West for fossils in 1868. In 1871–73, the Cheyennes went on the warpath and killed many whites in the region covered by Cope. But Cope, who as a Quaker refused to carry a gun, had no trouble with the Indians. In fact, one time he charmed some visiting Crow chiefs by taking out his false teeth.

Cope had far more trouble with the white hired help, who quit whenever the going got tough, even though they had been paid in advance. Sometimes, they not only deserted in the midst of an expedition but also stole the mules and supplies, leaving Cope stranded.

He also suffered from nightmares in which the monsters dug up the day before pursued and trampled him. Still, Cope throve on outdoor life. He would arrive from the East weary and wan and, after a month of the severest physical hardships, find himself in fine fettle.

Cope was always mixed up in some fantastic situation. He never yielded the smallest point to an opponent and did not mind biting in the clinches. His theft of a whale is a case in point.

A dead whale washed ashore on Cape Cod at a time when few whales had been studied by scientists. One of the scientific centers nearest to Cape Cod was the Museum of Comparative Zoology at Harvard University. This museum, sometimes called the "Agassiz Museum" after the Swiss-American scientist who discovered the Pleistocene Ice Age, was then directed by Louis Agassiz's son Alexander. Alexander Agassiz, who made a fortune by investments in copper mining and who then retired to devote his life to science, heard about the carcass on Cape Cod. Thinking that the skeleton of a whale was just what his museum needed, he sent a crew of students from Harvard to fetch it.

Cope also heard of the whale and thought a whale's skeleton would be just the thing for the Academy of Natural Sciences in Philadelphia. He, too, set out for Cape Cod.

Now, cutting the skeleton out of a very dead whale is no job for the squeamish. Although the Harvard boys were far from professional whalers, they stuck grimly to their task. All day long, they hacked and sawed, wading in guts and blubber. Out of the decomposing mass came bone after bone. And bone after bone, with strips of muscle and tendon dangling from it, was hauled to the nearest railroad spur and piled on a flatcar. The pile grew and grew.

And where was Cope all this time? He was lurking in a nearby farmhouse, peering at the operation from behind drawn curtains.

The sun at last went down, and the job was done. The pile of bones on the flatcar was covered with canvas and lashed down. Staggering with weariness, the students washed off as much of the rancid blubber as they could and stumbled aboard a train for Cambridge.

As soon as the Harvard boys had gone, Cope strolled over to the station and found the station agent. Money passed. Mysteriously, the address on the waybill of the flatcar changed from "Cambridge, Mass." to "Philadelphia, Penn." Then Cope, too, set out for home.

At the Agassiz Museum, Alexander Agassiz waited impatiently for his whale. The days lengthened into weeks, the weeks into months; but no whale appeared. Inquiries to railroad officials brought only puzzled frowns. The great sea mammal had vanished.

One day, Cope published a scientific paper containing a technical description of the skeleton of a whale. Then Agassiz knew what had become of his specimen: it was safely housed at the Academy of Natural Sciences in Philadelphia. There it stayed for three-quarters of a century, until lack of space compelled the Academy to give it away. At the Agassiz Museum, Cope was known as "the biggest thief in the world," because he had stolen the largest piece of loot in recorded history.

After studying under Leidy at the University of Pennsylvania, Cope traveled abroad to avoid the draft in the Civil War. At the end of hostilities, he accepted a professorship at Haverford College. Soon he resigned and moved to Haddonfield, New Jersey, to be near the fossil-bearing formation from which Leidy's hadrosaur had come. On one trip to these beds, in 1868, Cope was accompanied by a slightly older paleontologist, O. C. Marsh.

Othniel Charles Marsh (1831–99) was another colorful character. After a slothful, unpromising boyhood in upstate New York, Marsh graduated from Yale with a brilliant record. He decided to study paleontology and accordingly wrote to his uncle, George Peabody, who had risen from grocery clerk to banker and who went to Great Britain to live in 1837. Marsh told his uncle that he would like to devote his life to science. Peabody wrote back:

> It has always been my intention to consult the wishes and act liberally towards all those who are in a pecuniary point of view, comparatively dependent upon me, and who show by their character and exertions that they are worthy of my confidence. From my own observations and from the report of others I place you on the list.[2]

Peabody accordingly enclosed a check for $2,200 to finance his nephew's graduate studies. Marsh planned his career with the shrewdness of a tycoon. He studied diligently in Europe and America, sent papers to learned societies, and persuaded Peabody, a man of good works as well as of means, to settle $150,000 on Yale to build and maintain a museum of natural history. Marsh became a professor of paleontology at Yale—the first professor of paleontology in America. But, to retain his independence, he declined any salary until 1896, shortly before his death, when most of his fortune had been spent on science and high living.

In some ways, O. C. Marsh resembled the evil scientist of fiction. Many colleagues detested his egotism, selfishness, and unscrupulous duplicity. For example, in 1875, Marsh heard that Professor Arnold Guyot, a kindly Swiss geologist at Princeton, had bought a fine mastodon skeleton from a farmer near Otisville, New York. Marsh dashed up from New York City, bribed the conductor to stop the train at Otisville, found the farmer, outbid his rival, and sent the skeleton rattling off to Yale before poor Guyot knew what had happened.

In spite of his heartless scheming and unbending manner, Marsh had solid virtues as well. He was a first-class outdoorsman: independent, self-reliant, and devoted to the glory of Yale. A lifelong bachelor, he had many firm friends and admirers with whom he could be a delightful raconteur when he chose. The famous Teton Sioux chieftain Red Cloud said that Marsh was the only white man who ever kept his word to him. Marsh shook up the management of American Indian affairs and routed a ring of grafters who, under President Grant, had been robbing the Indians.

In 1870, Marsh began taking parties of students on Western fossil hunts. A chunky man with a short, red beard and an expression of ingrained suspicion, he was a competent and energetic expedition leader. To vary the monotony, the fossil-seekers hunted bison with Buffalo Bill Cody and other Army scouts. Once Marsh rode into a herd to shoot a young cow for supper. The buffalo stampeded. Marsh found himself in the midst of a galloping herd of 50,000 animals, twelve miles wide. To avoid being trampled, he had to gallop his terrified horse among the frightened buffalo, up and down the sides of ravines and over rough ground, until he found refuge behind a butte.

Marsh made many spectacular fossil finds. In the Kansas Chalk, a marine formation of Cretaceous Age, he found the largest flying creature ever known to have lived: the toothless pterosaur *Pteranodon*.

Marsh also found true birds contemporary with *Pteranodon*. These birds played a part in the controversies over evolution. If evolution were true, nineteenth-century scientists reasoned, there must have once existed creatures intermediate between groups of life forms now widely separated. For instance, if birds descended from reptiles, the rocks ought to yield a series of birdlike reptiles, reptilian birds, and true birds. Likewise with mammals. Still, reasoning is not the same as finding the actual missing links.

In 1860, the German paleontologist Hermann von Meyer announced that he had found the mold of an unmistakable bird's feather in the lithographic limestone quarries of the Solnhofen region. His report aroused skepticism, because up to then no birds were known from Jurassic rocks. Nevertheless, Meyer named his feather *Archaeopteryx*, "ancient wing."

Later in the same year, an almost complete, crow-sized bird turned up in the same formation, vindicating Meyer. An elderly physician, Ernst Häberlein, bought the fossil as a financial speculation. This fossil, so perfect as to include casts of the feathers, had one remarkably reptilian feature. In modern birds, the tail is a mere pointed end to a stiff, boxlike body, with a fan of feathers for an empennage. In the Solnhofen fossil, on the other hand, the tail was a long, vertebrate structure like that of a lizard, with a row of feathers down each side.

There were also claws on the ends of the wing bones, like those of he young hoatzin, a modern bird from the American tropics, which ests in trees overhanging rivers. When threatened, the baby hoatzin ıs the singular habit of diving out of its nest into the river below.

Then it swims briskly ashore and climbs back up its tree and into its nest by means of the claws on its wings.

Alas! the Solnhofen fossil did not seem to have a head. True, there were fragments of skull and a piece of jaw with teeth. But, since everybody knew that birds did not have teeth, the jaw, it was thought, must be that of a fish or a reptile accidentally buried with the skeleton.

Scientists came to see Häberlein's fossil; an official of the British Museum offered £500 for it. Häberlein held out for £750—no mean sum in those days—for his whole collection. After a prolonged haggle, the deal was closed. Häberlein's fossils were bundled off to the British Museum, while the old doctor used the £750 for his daughter's dowry.

Then, in the early 1870s, Marsh found Cretaceous birds with teeth, exactly as evolutionary theory had predicted. He found several specimens of the six-foot, loonlike, oar-legged, flightless diving bird *Hesperornis,* with its long beak full of sharp, fish-seizing teeth. He also found a specimen of another bird, which he named *Ichthyornis.* This was a smaller bird, much like a modern gull. The skull was fragmentary, but with the remains was a long, toothful jawbone, which was assumed to belong to the bird. So Marsh announced that he had found toothed birds of two genera.

In recent years, paleontologists have reëxamined the *Ichthyornis* jaw and concluded that it is actually the jawbone of a small or baby mosasaur, accidentally buried with the bird. So we do not know whether *Ichthyornis* had teeth or not. But there is no question about the teeth of *Hesperornis.*

In any case, Marsh's toothed birds caused a sensation. They indicated that the toothed jaw found with the first *Archaeopteryx* belonged to the skeleton of that bird-reptile after all. Moreover, they supplied additional proof of the evolutionary process. Charles Darwin wrote to Marsh:

> Your work on these old birds and on the many fossil mammals of N. America has afforded the best support to the theory of evolution, which has appeared within the last 20 years.[3]

This, however, is not the end of the story. In 1877, while Marsh was still digging up his own toothed birds, a smaller but better-preserved *Archaeopteryx*[4] turned up in Germany a few miles from the site of the first. Marsh cabled a colleague in Germany to try to buy the specimen from the owner. This was Dr. Ernst Häberlein *der Jüngere,* son of the old doctor who had bought the first *Archaeopteryx.* Knowing a good thing when he saw it, the younger Häberlein asked two and a half times the price of the first fossil bird.

While he and Marsh haggled, nationalistic feeling arose in Germany against letting the second *Archaeopteryx* out of the Fatherland. Eventually Ernst Werner von Siemens, the great electrical inventor and industrialist, bought the specimen for 20,000 marks ($4,750) and resold it at cost to the University of Berlin. A third specimen, less well-preserved than either of the first two, came to light in 1956 and ended up at Erlangen University.

Marsh made the name "dinosaur" a household word in the United States because of his finds of these dramatic reptiles. In fact, his discoveries of dinosaurs so aroused public interest in the science of paleontology that Americans began voluntarily to support museums and expeditions and thus to aid in the discovery of more prehistoric animals. In this indirect way, dinosaurs helped to prove evolution a fact and to speed up public acceptance of the scientific point of view that has so revolutionized man's thinking in the past century.

Marsh and his collectors discovered the well-known sauropod dinosaurs *Brontosaurus* and *Diplodocus,* the armored dinosaur *Stegosaurus,* and the climactic horned dinosaur *Triceratops.* He found one of the biggest of the flesh-eating carnosaurs, which he named *Allosaurus fragilis,* although we cannot imagine what possessed him to describe such a monster as "fragile." Since Leidy had previously given similar but fragmentary remains the name of *Antrodemus valens,* there is a question as to which is the rightful name for this very unfragile beast.

Sensational as these finds were, Marsh's most enduring work was not in the field of dinosaurs; it was the disclosure of the evolution of the horse. He collected the remains of thirty-odd species from the horse's family tree. By arranging his ancestral equines in order, he showed how the modern horse had evolved from an Eocene beast the size of a fox terrier, with four toes on each forefoot and three on each hind.

Charles Darwin had foretold this sort of continuing change. But now, for the first time, scientists had enough fossil remains of animals of one single family to arrange them in sequence and to see just how evolution had taken place. It is not too much of an exaggeration to say that Marsh was the man who proved Darwin's evolutionary theory; and he proved it by means of these horses.

Thomas Huxley, the famous biologist and educator, came over from England in 1876 to lecture and to see Marsh's horses. He spent two excited days watching the American produce box after box of fossil horse material. At last, he exclaimed: "I believe you are a magician. Whatever I want, you conjure it up!"[5]

Although Huxley arrived thinking that the horse had evolved in the Old World, Marsh convinced him that North America was the home of the horse. And so it proved. Horses developed in America, spread to other continents, and then, during the Pleistocene Period, became extinct in their homeland. From that time on, there were no more American horses until the Spanish *conquistadores* reintroduced them into the land from which they had sprung.

Thus did Marsh become famous. He built a baroque mansion in New Haven and jammed it with bric-a-brac, such as the heads of beasts he had shot and the peace pipe Red Cloud had given him.

Although Leidy, Cope, and Marsh were the leading American paleontologists of their day, they were men of very different character. Whereas Leidy was cautious, patient, persistent, modest, and self-effacing, the two younger men were much more aggressive. Cope was ebullient, charming, brilliant, daring, and pugnacious. Marsh was coldly shrewd, crafty, grasping, wily, and pompous. Both had splendid physical courage and fortitude, colossal egotism, a talent for scheming, and bulldog tenacity; therefore, when both decided that they wanted all the fossils in the whole wide West, a storm was bound to arise.

For a year or two after their joint fossil-hunt in New Jersey, Marsh and Cope remained on friendly terms. But all too soon, between the two supreme egotists, suspicion and jealousy arose. The impetuous Cope sometimes made ludicrous mistakes in describing fossils but resented the patronizing way in which Marsh pointed out these blunders. The possessive Marsh, for his part, was always complaining that some specimen described by Cope was rightfully his to describe. He accused Cope of borrowing fossils from their owners without permission, or of borrowing fossils that had previously been promised to him.

The feud burst into full bloom in 1872–73, when Cope dug in the Bridger Formation of the Middle Eocene of southwestern Wyoming. Marsh deemed these beds his private domain and put every obstacle in the way of his rival fossil-hunter. Although each tried to corner the market, there were enough fossils in the area to keep dozens of paleontologists busy for centuries. Still, they worked frantically, hiring other men to help with the digging, so that they gathered fossils faster than they could study or describe them. While Cope spent months in the field, Marsh decided to save time by staying in New Haven and, save for quick inspection trips, supervising his work crews from afar.

One day an amateur fossil-hunter, Arthur Lakes, found some sauropod bones in Colorado. He offered them to Marsh and sent him a ton as a sample. When Marsh did not answer quickly enough, Lakes sent some more bones to Cope. Meaning to buy them, Cope wrote a description for publication and spoke of his find at a meeting of the American Philosophical Society.

Hearing of this, Marsh sent one of his men to outbid Cope. He himself sent Lakes a telegram, saying that Cope had decided not to buy any fossils. This, of course, was a lie. The next thing Cope knew, he got a wire from Lakes ordering him to turn his new bones over to Marsh, who had bought them.

After that, it was war. Cope and Marsh tried to outdo each other in being the first to describe extinct animals, ignoring prior publications by each other and by Leidy. Years later, Henry Fairfield Osborn wrote:

> Every new animal that was discovered was given a new scientific name by each of them. *Notharctus* Leidy, for example, is exactly the same animal as *Tomitherium* Cope and *Limnotherium* Marsh. Thus arose a trinomial system—three names for each of the Eocene and Oligocene mammals—the original Leidy name and the Cope and Marsh name. It has been the painful duty of Professor Scott and myself to devote thirty of the best years of our lives trying to straighten out this nomenclatural chaos.[6]

If Marsh found a primitive little horse, *Orohippus,* Cope found a smaller and more primitive one, *Eohippus.*[7] If Marsh found the gigantic *Brontosaurus,* Cope came up with an almost equally big sauropod, *Camarasaurus.* People had been sending Leidy fossils free; but, when Cope and Marsh began jousting against each other, armed with their inherited fortunes, the price of fossils went beyond poor Leidy's reach. Because of this, and because he hated bickering, Leidy withdrew from paleontology.

In 1872, Cope found some fossils in the Washakie Basin and, trying to establish priority over Marsh, sent to the Secretary of the American Philosophical Society one of the strangest telegrams on record:

> I HAVE DISCOVERED IN SOUTHERN WYOMING THE FOLLOWING SPECIES COLON LOXOLOPHODON COPE STOP INCISOR ONE TUSK CANINE NONE SEMICOLON PREMOLARS FOUR COMMA WITH ONE CRESCENT AND INNER TUBERCLE SEMICOLON MOLARS TWO SEMICOLON SIZE GIGANTIC STOP DASH DICORNUTUS SEMICOLON HORNS TRIPEDRAL CYLINDRIC SEMICOLON NASALS WITH SHORT CONVEX LOBES STOP DASH BIFURCATUS COMMA NASALS WITH LONG SPATULATE LOBES STOP DASH EXPRESSICORNIS COMMA HORNS COMPRESSED AND ACUMINATE[8]

Not surprisingly, the telegraph operator got "Loxolophodon" wrong as "Lefalophodon," and this mistake had to be corrected in several later works on paleontology.

The war kept up for years. Marsh accused Cope of pre-dating his finds and stirred up a quarrel between Cope and the officers of the American Philosophical Society. Cope carried on a whispering campaign of slander against Marsh's candidacy for reëlection to the presidency of the National Academy of Sciences in 1889.

The feud caught up friends of the pugnacious pair. At Como in Wyoming, workers, digging in the same beds for the two scientists, fought a pitched battle with fists. Another time, Marsh's men, knowing that Cope was spying on them, deliberately mixed the skull of one creature with teeth from another and left them for Cope to find and describe as a new species.

Then, there was a contest over the job of director of the Geological Survey. The candidates were two noted geologists: Ferdinand Hayden, the father of Yellowstone National Park, and Major John Wesley Powell, the one-armed conqueror of the Colorado. As a friend of Hayden, Cope helped to write a long, anonymous attack on Powell for secret distribution to Congressmen. Naturally, the peppery Powell found this out. When he got the Survey job in 1881, he made Marsh his official vertebrate paleontologist.

Cope had no business sense. In order to raise his income, he put his fortune into mining stock, which gave a fine return until the mines ran out. From 1886 to 1889, when he got a professorship at the University of Pennsylvania, Cope was poor. A few years later, to recoup his position somewhat, he sold his fossils of North American mammals to the American Museum of Natural History for $32,149.89.

In 1889, the feud reached its climax. His enemies Marsh and Powell succeeded in putting Cope in an impossible situation. John W. Noble, the Secretary of the Interior, assuming that Cope's fossils were government property, ordered Cope to turn his specimens over to the National Museum. True, Cope had collected many of his fossils on the Hayden Survey; but since he had spent $75,000 of his own money in doing so, he deemed the fossils his.

During an interview with a New York *Herald* reporter, Cope poured out the fullness of his wrath. To protect the paper from possible libel suits, the reporter showed the story to Marsh, who wrote a reply to Cope's statement. The interview and the first part of the reply appeared in the *Herald* on January 12, 1890, under the headlines:

SCIENTISTS WAGE BITTER WARFARE, PROF. COPE OF THE UNIVERSITY OF PENNSYLVANIA, BRINGS SERIOUS CHARGES AGAINST DIRECTOR POWELL AND PROF. MARSH, OF THE GEOLOGICAL SURVEY—CORROBORATION IN PLENTY—LEARNED MEN COME TO THE PENNSYLVANIAN'S SUPPORT WITH ALLEGATIONS OF IGNORANCE, PLAGIARISM AND INCOMPETENCE. . . .

Cope accused Marsh, among other things, of stealing government-owned fossils and of telling his collectors to break up any fossils they could not carry away in order to keep them from his rivals—an act that dedicated scientists would consider worse than murder. Then came the reply:

MARSH HURLS AZOIC FACTS AT COPE—YALE PROFESSOR PICKS UP THE GAUNTLET OF THE PENNSYLVANIA PALEONTOLOGIST. . . .

With an air of wounded dignity, Marsh said that Cope had mistaken the tail of the plesiosaur *Elasmosaurus* for its neck and so mounted it. Cope retorted that Marsh had supposed the skull of a horned dinosaur to be that of a bison. Marsh accused Cope of stealing some of Marsh's fossils out of their crates in Kansas, while they were awaiting shipment to the East. In truth, Cope had returned the fossils to Marsh—but only after he had preëmpted the glory of describing them.

The war of articles and pamphlets went on for weeks, and a fine time was had by all. Marsh got the support of his colleagues in the government, the National Academy of Sciences, and Yale. Cope had the help of many paleontologists who hated Marsh. Among them were some of Marsh's former assistants who had turned against their one-time employer because of his stinginess in giving credit to those who collected fossils for him.

As the years passed, the feud died down. Cope joined the Texas

Geological Survey and resumed his fossil hunts. In 1892, he worked on the Sioux reservation. Here he had to move warily; for the Sioux, angered by the constant theft of their livestock by white rustlers, were likely to kill a white stranger out of hand. Nevertheless, Cope made friends with them, so that he suffered no worse risk than a ride with an Indian wagon driver who drove down a steep hill on the rude roads at full gallop.

One of Cope's main achievements was the description of the first American fossils from the Paleocene Period, the first subdivision of the Cenozoic Era or Age of Mammals. How the man found time also to write voluminously on such subjects as sea serpents, sex, and philosophy we shall never know.

In 1897, Cope fell ill. His ailment, though serious, was operable; but this brave and impetuous man so feared an operation that he put it off until too late. He died in April of that year, in a house piled ceiling-high with bones and papers.

Two years later, his old foe Marsh, who had likewise come down in the world, also died. Marsh had been fired from his governmental post in 1892, when anticonservationist Western Congressmen, attacking the Geological Survey, used Marsh's famous "birds with teeth" as an example of official waste and so stopped his appropriation.

Today most of Marsh's fossils rest either in the Peabody Museum at Yale or in the National Museum in Washington, while most of Cope's are in the American Museum of Natural History in New York.

The great fossil feud is over, and history has had an opportunity to pass judgment on the two proud contestants. With Leidy, they are unquestionably the outstanding American paleontologists of the late nineteenth century. To the lives of all three of these great men, Osborn wrote the epitaph. This is his evaluation of the scientific contributions of Leidy, Cope, and Marsh:

> Whereas in Leidy we had a man of the exact observer type, Cope was a man who loved speculation. If Leidy was the natural successor of Cuvier, Cope was the natural successor of Lamarck. Leidy in his

contributions to the Academy, covered the whole world of nature, from the Protozoa and infusoria to man, and he lived as the last great naturalist in the world of the old type who was able by both capacity and training to cover the whole field of nature. Cope, in contrast, mastered —and this mastery itself was a wonderful achievement—the entire domain of vertebrates from the fishes up. Marsh, with less breadth and ability, nevertheless was a paleontologist of a very high order and had a genius for appreciating what might be called the most important thing in science. He always knew where to explore, where to seek the transition stages, and never lost an opportunity to point out at the earliest possible moment the most significant fact to be discovered and disseminated.[9]

10

Diggers and Dinosaurs

In the late nineteenth century, vertebrate paleontology became a peculiarly American science. It was not that American scientists were more brilliant than those of Europe, but that local conditions made it easier to practice the science in North America than in Europe. Among the mountains and deserts of the American West lay scientific treasure beyond the wildest dreams of the pioneer paleontologists.

Of the scientists who rushed in to exploit this hoard, Cope and Marsh were the best known. They were, however, only two of many. Much valuable fossil-hunting was done by the men who had worked with them as collectors and who continued in the field after Cope and Marsh had passed from the scene.

One protégé of Marsh, for instance, was John Bell Hatcher, a Yale graduate with a genius for finding fossils. He collected for Princeton University, led celebrated fossil-hunts to South America, worked for the Carnegie Museum in Pittsburgh, and died at a comparatively early age in 1904. Hatcher financed some of his expeditions by the unusual method of playing poker on his way to the field. With this additional source of revenue, he was able to extend his Patagonian expedition far beyond the time originally planned.

Early in the great American dinosaur hunt, a hundred years ago, the regular method of collecting a fossil bone was to thrust a pick or a crowbar under it and simply pry it out of the ground. Often, the brittle bone shattered into many pieces. These the digger collected with a rake, dumped into a bag, and left for the museum staff to struggle with, as with a three-dimensional jigsaw puzzle.

In the 1870s, as a result of the work of Cope, Marsh, and their assistants, the techniques of fossil-gathering were vastly improved. The methods used today are refinements of those worked out at that time.

For one thing, nobody nowadays digs into virgin soil at random, hoping to find a fossil. The searcher always hunts for some surface indication of the fossil, such as a bone or a few teeth laid bare by erosion. To recognize such fragments—which often look almost exactly like the soil and stones around them—is an art that requires both natural aptitude and experience.

Once the fossil has been located, the rock or soil that conceals the skeleton is cautiously removed. If the bone is imbedded in rock, tools like the geologist's hammer are used; if it lies in loose sand or soil, the overburden is brushed away with whisk brooms.

When most or all of a bone has been exposed, the surfaces are painted with a cementing material, such as a solution of gum arabic or shellac. Instead of a natural cementing material like shellac, modern paleontologists often use a synthetic chemical dissolved in acetone.

Then a surface coating of thin paper—tissue or rice paper—is glued to the bone by shellac. A bandage of burlap strips soaked in plaster is laid down over the paper. Some paleontologists prefer flour paste to plaster, because it is lighter; but, unfortunately, mice are also fond of the paste. Long bones are further strengthened with wooden splints.

When a lot of small bones or a complete skeleton of modest size occurs in one solid mass, the paleontologist usually chisels out the whole block and sends it back to the laboratory, where the individual bones can be picked out at leisure. The maximum size of this block, called the matrix, is governed by the available means of transportation. Pieces weighing tons can be taken out intact if the deposit lies in the open, where power machinery can be employed and where large trucks are available.

During the past half-century, the greatest change in collecting methods was brought about by the internal-combustion engine. Until this type of engine was developed, even such rich and well-known fossil fields as the Ischigualasto Valley in Argentina lay untouched. Driving an airplane, such engines help scientists to map fossil-bearing beds and to plan the season's work. Powering jeeps and trucks, they carry fossil-hunters to grassless mountains and desert lands where horses and mules could not go for lack of food and water. Finally, in the form of a winch on a truck, modern engines make it possible to snake out solid masses of fossil-bearing rock much heavier than could be managed by manpower alone.

Because it takes a specialist to give proper care to a delicate fossil, the amateur fossil-hunter should never attempt the task alone. He might ruin a valuable specimen and end up with a heap of hopeless fragments. He should locate the nearest paleontologist, usually in the nearest museum or university, and ask him to inspect the find. As a reward, if the fossil prove to be of some unknown species, he just might find a Latinized version of his surname worked into the new creature's name.

One of the most famous collectors was Charles Hazelius Sternberg (1850–1943), an upstate New Yorker. In the 1860s, young Sternberg went to Kansas to work on his brother's ranch. In those days in Ellsworth City, "the dead-cart used to pass down the street every morning to pick up the bodies of those who had been killed in the saloons the night before, and thrown out on the pavement to be hauled away."[1]

Fascinated by fossils, Sternberg made a collection of fossil leaves and sent it to the Smithsonian Institution. During a year of study at the Kansas State Agricultural College in 1875–76, he vainly tried to join a fossil-hunt financed by Marsh. Sternberg then wrote an impassioned letter to Cope, asking for $300 wherewith to buy a wagon, a team, and a camp outfit and to hire a cook and a driver. Back came the money by return mail, and Sternberg set to work for

Cope. He continued to hunt for fossils all his active life—he lived to be 93—under the most rigorous physical conditions, despite the fact that he was a slight man, deaf in one ear, and lame as a result of a boyhood accident.

On this first expedition, Sternberg found some good specimens of the mosasaur *Platecarpus*. He also narrowly missed running into a war party of Indians led by the famous chief Crazy Horse, on their way to the campaign that ended with the destruction of Custer and his force at Little Bighorn.

Sternberg's greatest danger, however, was not hostile Indians but falling off cliffs, since many of the fossils lay exposed on precipitous slopes. In the autumn of that same year, Sternberg went with Cope to the Bad Lands of Montana. Cope asked Sternberg to climb up on a high ridge and examine a slope that overhung a sheer thousand-foot drop. Sternberg

. . . concluded that I should have no difficulty in crawling across the smooth space, for I reasoned that if I began to slip, I could drive the sharp end of my pick into the soft rock and thus stop myself. So climbing up the slope through the loose earth to the base of the upper ledge, I started to cross. When I was halfway over I began to slip, and confidently raising my pick, struck the rock with all my might. God grant that I may never again feel such horror as I felt then, when the pick, upon which I had depended for safety, rebounded as if [the rock] had been polished steel, as useless in my hands as a bit of straw. I struck frantically again and yet again, but all the time I was sliding down with ever-increasing rapidity toward the edge of the abyss. . . .

To this day I do not know how I escaped. I suddenly found myself lying on the ledge, on the side I had left a moment before. Probably some part of my clothing, covered with dust as it was, had acted as a brake upon the polished surface. I lay for an hour with trembling knees, too weak to make my way back to camp.[2]

On a later occasion, his party sighted a good saber-tooth skull on top of a slender erosion pinnacle. The pinnacle was too delicate to set a ladder against; for, if it were broken, the skull would be smashed. The problem was solved by cutting notches in the sides of the pinnacle, whereby one of the men scaled it to the top and broke off the skull.

The most pressing problem was water. Vast areas of prairie, mountain, and desert either had no water at all or contained a few alkaline springs, almost undrinkable. In those days, too, the fossil hunter was limited to regions in which there was not only potable water but also natural fodder to sustain his horses or mules. Besides these difficulties, collectors faced scorching heat, cold rains, gales, dust storms, gnats, mosquitoes (and the malaria they brought), rattlesnakes, and mud. Digging in the Cretaceous formation called the Kansas Chalk, Sternberg told how:

> Then comes the work in the hot sun, whose rays are reflected with added fervor from the glaring surface of the chalk. Every blow of the pick loosens a cloud of chalk dust, which is carried by the wind into our eyes. But we labor on with unfailing enthusiasm until we have laid bare a floor space upon which I can stretch myself out at full length. Lying there on the blistering chalk in the burning sun, and working carefully and patiently with brush and awl, I uncover enough of the bones so that I can tell what I have found, and so that when I cut out the rock which holds them I shall not cut into the bones themselves.[3]

Sternberg was describing the work done on his first season in the field for Cope. In 1878, Cope sent him to hunt the John Day River region of Oregon. Here he almost ran into the Bannock War, but luck saved him from an encounter with Chief Egan's 300 hostile Snake warriors. Later, he worked for Marsh and for Karl von Zittel of the University of Munich. After 1911, he dug fossils for the Geological Survey of Canada, collecting dinosaurs from the rich badlands of western Alberta. In the course of a fossil-hunting career of over half a century, Sternberg recovered many specimens that are leading attractions in the world's great museums of today.

The fossils that men like Sternberg so laboriously quarried out of the cliffs, however, did not always reach their destinations. Many dangers still threatened them. A beautifully complete turtle was smashed to smithereens when the table on which Sternberg had placed it collapsed. While one of his sons was preparing a seven-foot *Triceratops* skull they had found in Kansas, a tornado blew down the building in which they were working and shattered the specimen beyond repair. And in 1914, two duckbilled dinosaurs, on their way to the British Museum, were sent to the bottom of the Atlantic by a German submarine.

Other paleontologists suffered similar exasperations. Scott had a whole season's collection stolen by a wagon train of Mormons, who threw them away when they found that the bundles contained nothing of value to them. His prize collection from the John Day River was stored in boxes in the cellar of Nassau Hall at Princeton. When steam heat was being installed in this building, the workmen "rifled the boxes, carrying off what struck their fancy and wantonly destroying the rest."[4]

Sternberg, however, not only persevered but also reared three sons, who became famous fossil hunters like their sire.

One afternoon in June, 1876—the year that saw Sternberg's first field work for Cope—three undergraduates at Princeton were lying under the trees on the canal bank, making a languid pretense of preparing for an examination. One was Francis Speir, Jr., later a noted lawyer; the other two were budding scientists, William Berryman Scott and his lifelong friend Henry Fairfield Osborn. Osborn (1857–1935) son of a president of the Illinois Central Railroad, became in his time one of the world's leading paleontologists.

The elder Osborn owned a house near Garrison, New York, near that of a prosperous New York importer named Theodore Roosevelt, the father of President Teddy Roosevelt. After the Civil War, a young scientist named Albert Bickmore came to the senior Roosevelt with a scheme for a great natural history museum in New York City. The two pressed bankers like J. Pierpont Morgan for money and politicians like Boss Tweed for the legal authority to build the museum. Both Morgan and Tweed came through handsomely.

In 1874, the cornerstone of the American Museum of Natural History was laid in the presence of President Grant, the governor, the mayor, and other notables. Joseph Henry, Secretary of the

Smithsonian Institution, made a speech. He said that, fine as the new facility undoubtedly would be, it could serve best if it actively explained to the public the wonders of the natural world. This idea of public service was new at the time; but the American Museum of Natural History has led the world in museum techniques ever since.

On that June afternoon in 1876, however, the Museum, consisting of a few odd collections, was still housed in an old arsenal building in Central Park and in a half-built edifice of red brick with red sandstone trim on Manhattan Square. Lying on the canal bank near Princeton, Scott remarked:

"Fellows! I have just been reading in an old *Harper's* an account of a Yale expedition to the Far West in search of fossils; why can't we get up something like that?"

"We can; let's do it," said the others.[5]

The three young men went to Philadelphia to ask advice of Cope; but he, fearing that they were Marsh's spies, was politely evasive. Nevertheless, the next year, after the trio had graduated, the expedition got under way. A Professor Brackett was in charge of the technical side of the expedition; and a retired Polish general named Kargé had command of camping, marching, and fighting. To get ready for possible battles with the Indians, the general drilled his sixteen students. When he went to Washington to obtain the coöperation of the War Department, he told General Sherman:

"General, in a fight with Indians, I would rather have my boys than your regulars."[6]

William Tecumseh Sherman thumbed his nose.

The Indians gave no trouble; but the expedition split up because the professor could not get along with the general. The general took his students through Wyoming, where they found some promising fossils and some of the world's most spectacular scenery. As a result, Osborn and Scott determined to make paleontology their careers.

Osborn went to England for graduate study under Francis M. Balfour, the biologist, and under Thomas Huxley, the biologist and educator. One day Osborn was cutting up a lobster in the laboratory when Huxley came in with Darwin, then sixty-nine.

Young Osborn got the thrill of his life when Huxley paused to introduce him to Charles Darwin as "an American who has already done some good paleontological work in the other side of the water." Osborn wrote in his diary:

> I gave Darwin's hand a tremendous squeeze (for I shall never shake it again) and said, without intending, in an almost reverential tone, "I am very glad to meet you." He stands much taller than Huxley, has a very ruddy face, with benevolent blue eyes and overhanging eyebrows. His beard is long and perfectly white and his hair falls partly over a low forehead. . . . He smiled broadly, said something about a hope that Marsh with his students would not be hindered in his work, and Huxley, saying "I must not let you talk too much," hurried him into the next room. . . . The instant Huxley closed the door I was mobbed as the "lucky American" by ninety less fortunate students of Great Britain and other countries.[7]

Osborn and Scott became professors at Princeton. In 1891, Osborn shifted to Columbia University, where he taught for nearly twenty years. He held various posts there and at the American Museum of Natural History, now a flourishing institution, to which new wings had been added.

While Osborn taught at Columbia, Roy Chapman Andrews, William Beebe, William K. Gregory, and Richard S. Lull—all outstanding names in the biological sciences—studied under him. Osborn became president of the Museum in 1908 and so remained until he retired in 1933. His presidency saw the greatest growth of the Museum. Osborn never tried to make money; instead, he used a good deal of his large private fortune in scientific work.

In maturity, Osborn was a tall, mustached, heavy-featured man of ducal dignity. He was a class-conscious aristocrat with a candid appreciation of his own accomplishments. Those who liked him—and there were many—called him a gentleman of the old school. Those who did not like him—and there were quite a few of these, also—called him a pompous, self-important snob. After William Gregory had become a professor at Columbia, he took some graduate students into Osborn's office to meet the great man. Beaming benignly, Osborn said:

"When I was a young man, I studied in England. There I once had the opportunity of seeing Darwin and was greatly inspired. Now you young men can see me, and I hope you'll be equally inspired."[8]

Although a grandee, Osborn was a kindly and affable one when given his own way. He was generous with his juniors, even taking them to live with him when they were hard up. He led an exemplary home life and even in his old age kept a youthful zest for science and an interest in young scientists.

Although Osborn's critics accused him, with some justice, of obscurantism and of proposing purely verbal solutions to scientific problems, his solid achievements were great. Aside from encouraging the vast growth in the Museum, he put into practice the modern museum technique of assembling fossil skeletons and mounting them in lifelike attitudes.

For many years, an artist named Charles R. Knight worked under Osborn's direction. Knight, who had become an artist despite the handicap of one bad eye, started as an assistant to Cope and became the world's greatest restorer of extinct animals. Although such restoration is bound to include much educated guesswork, few have ever equaled Knight in making prehistoric monsters look lifelike and plausible. His misty primaeval landscapes decorate the walls of several museums, and his dwellers of the past are scattered through many books on paleontology.

Osborn wrote prodigiously. Three great treatises—*The Age of Mammals, The Origin and Evolution of Life,* and *Men of the Old Stone Age*—brought together all the facts then known about these subjects. Since these works are now dated, scientists value more highly Osborn's monographs on the ancestry of groups of animals like the elephants (*Proboscidea,* in two volumes of elephantine size). These monumental monographs are all untidy, exhaustive, and exhausting.

Osborn shrewdly prophesied that the elephant's ancestors would be found in Africa. Sure enough, they were. In Egypt, in 1907, he himself found fossil animals ranging from the piglike little *Moer-*

itherium up through tapirlike forms to creatures bearing at least a faint resemblance to modern elephants.

Osborn thought that the ancestors of most other mammals would be found in Asia and sent the Third Asiatic Expedition (1921–32) to Mongolia. He also expanded Cope's pioneer work on the classification of mammals by their teeth and devised the modern system of names for the bumps and hollows on the chewing surfaces of these teeth.

In the 1920s, Osborn got mixed up in the controversy over evolution, which, despite its scientific triumph, was still a long way from popular acceptance. With most people, deeply ingrained childhood beliefs are not to be banished merely by presenting evidence that these beliefs are wrong. In fact, the masses usually come to believe some revolutionary scientific discovery only when a younger generation, brought up on the new idea since childhood, reaches maturity and replaces the older generation that was shocked and antagonized by it.

In the early twentieth century, when nearly all biologists had accepted evolution, many influential people in the United States and Europe continued to oppose its teaching in schools. Some people objected to evolution on religious grounds, since it can be reconciled with the Hebrew creation myth of Genesis only by giving the creation story a far-fetched, figurative interpretation. Other people were simply horrified by the thought of being akin to monkeys, mice, and mushrooms, no matter how long ago.

In the United States, this opposition reached its height in the 1920s. In several states, laws were passed forbidding the teaching in public schools of the theory of evolution. The furor reached its climax with the famous trial of John Thomas Scopes in 1925 at Dayton, Tennessee. Scopes and his friends, who planned the trial as a test case, hoped the young teacher would be convicted of teaching evolution so that they could appeal this conviction and persuade a higher court to declare Tennessee's new "monkey law" unconstitutional.

Osborn helped the defense with advice about scientific witnesses and offered to send them affidavits upholding the soundness of the theory. He had earlier urged William Jennings Bryan, the famous politician who joined the case as one of the attorneys for the prosecution, to come to the Museum to see for himself the evidence for evolution; and when he declined, Osborn suspected publicly that Bryan refused for fear of having his convictions shaken. Bryan retaliated by calling Osborn "a tall professor coming down out of trees who would push good people not believing in evolution off the sidewalk."[9]

After the spectacular Monkey Trial, most Americans became gradually familiar with ancient eras and prehistoric life through books, magazines, and movies like *The Lost World* (1925) wherein rubber dinosaurs lumbered jerkily about the scene. Opposition to the idea of evolution abated, and all three Southern monkey laws were either repealed or invalidated. In recent decades, however, Fundamentalist antievolutionism has revived under the deceitful name of "Scientific Creationism," causing textbook publishers to omit evolution from their books for fear of losing sales to antievolutionist school boards. This reaction began in California under the governorship of Ronald Reagan, who fostered it.

Despite his quarrel with Bryan, Osborn was a religious man. In later years, his earnest if abstract piety led him to insist that man must have split off from the general primate stock earlier than most scientists now believe that he did—perhaps in the Oligocene Period. All modern biological scientists believe that men and modern apes descend from a common ancestor. They also agree that this forebear was a small, hairy primate which, although not the same as any existing species, could reasonably be called an ape. Osborn found it easier to accept man's apelike ancestor if he assumed that man's family tree branched off from that of the apes as early as possible.

In his seventies, Osborn retired from the presidency of the Museum to travel before he died. Despite his quota of faults and foibles, Osborn was a great man. The American Museum of Natural History, although the product of many minds and hands, is in a sense his monument; and a nobler monument few men have ever had.

During his presidency, Osborn sent many expeditions into the field. One of his most successful fossil-hunters was Barnum Brown (1873–1963). Born in Kansas, Brown attended Kansas University, where he came under the influence of Samuel W. Williston, a leading paleontologist. Brown arrived in New York in 1897 to complete his graduate studies and to work part time at the American Museum of Natural History. Two years later, Osborn called him into his office at nine o'clock one morning and said:

"Brown, can you go to Patagonia with the Princeton party? The boat sails at eleven o'clock and you will probably be away a year and a half."

"That's rather short notice, Professor, but I'll be on that boat."[10]

After a year, the Princetonians returned; but Brown stayed on for months, tirelessly collecting. Later, he hunted fossils in many parts of the earth, including Greece and India. During the First World War, he doubled as an oil geologist and a diplomat.

A heavy, moon-faced man with a grave expression and a manner of coolly polite reserve, Brown was an unreconstructed individualist. He was fearless to the point of rashness when he hoped to get a specimen. At the age of sixty, on a ground-sloth hunt in New Mexico, he nearly died when he lost his grip on a rope by which he was lowering himself into an extinct volcanic crater. On another occasion in India, his associates panicked when a snake slithered into camp. Aware that it would make a fine specimen, Brown grabbed the reptile, only to discover after it was safely pickled in alcohol that he had caught a king cobra. This same man had the curious distinction of having once been named one of the Five Best Husbands in the United States by the Divorce Reform League.

Brown's most spectacular find comprised two gorgeous skeletons of *Tyrannosaurus* from the Hell Creek badlands of Montana. One of these, mounted in the Hall of Cretaceous Dinosaurs of the American Museum of Natural History, dominates that hall today. The other dinosaur specimen still rears its vast height above visitors to the Carnegie Museum in Pittsburgh. Brown spent two long summers digging out these fossil bones and guarding them as they journeyed 130 miles by wagon to the nearest railroad station.

Furthermore, Brown obtained a fine skeleton of the sauropod *Barosaurus* for the American Museum. This unfortunate fossil had been portioned out among the National Museum, the Carnegie Museum, and the University of Utah. Brown reunited the separated sections by trading other fossils for them.

The most famous of all the American Museum's enterprises was the Third Asiatic Expedition to Central Asia. The hero of this tale is Roy Chapman Andrews (1884–1960), a native of Wisconsin who made the whole world his home. As a young graduate of Beloit College, Andrews got a job in the American Museum by offering to clean the floors if necessary.

Andrews' first big job was literally big—to salvage the skeleton of a whale. A blue whale, the largest animal of all time, had washed ashore on Long Island. Andrews and another man were sent to measure the colossal cadaver and to fetch back the skeleton. It was truly a labor of Hercules, but they accomplished it.

The Museum directors decided to put the blue whale on exhibition. Because it was not practical to skin and mount such a creature in the usual manner, a light, life-size model was suggested. Andrews solved the problem by using wire and papier-mâché. The resulting model still floats above one of the Museum's vast halls.

Then the trustees decided that the Museum needed a whole series of whales, with a proper account of their nature and habits. This knowledge did not then exist; for practical whalers, like most hunters everywhere, cared nothing about the animals they slew, save for such knowledge as helped them better to kill or exploit their prey.

Andrews—a tall man, strikingly handsome despite extreme baldness, and a friendly, enthusiastic extrovert—traveled the world for eight years seeking whales and facts about them. In 1908, he worked out a local whaling station in Vancouver, suffering horribly from seasickness. The following year, he collected white whales in the St. Lawrence and Saguenay rivers.

Andrews next went to the Far East, lived in Japan, and rediscovered the gray whale, once common off the coast of California but then believed extinct. It turned out that a surviving pod of gray whales migrated annually between the Bering Sea and the Korean coast. Another group, which traveled between the Bering Sea and Lower California, also survived the onslaught of the whalers and now, under government protection, is making a comeback.

Between trips, Andrews found time to get his doctorate at Columbia with a thesis on the gray whale. After studying tigers in Korea and fur seals on the Pribilof Islands, Andrews persuaded certain men of means to send him exploring into southwestern China. This was the First Asiatic Expedition of the American Museum, during which Andrews almost died of an infected hand. He collected some rare Chinese relatives of the American mountain goat and laid the groundwork for a second, larger expedition to test Osborn's theory that Central Asia had been the center of radiation for many lines of evolution.

Andrews spent the First World War working in Peking as a U. S. Naval Intelligence operative. He played polo and drove automobiles into the Gobi Desert, proving that even the chugging contraptions of the time could travel over roadless wastes. In 1919, he headed the Second Asiatic Expedition to Mongolia. Although he narrowly escaped being killed in his sleep by Mongolian dogs, a kind of man-eating, long-haired mastiff, Andrews discovered that indeed many species of animals had started from Asia for their journeys over the face of the earth.

The Third Asiatic Expedition arrived in Peking in 1921 and set up house in the former palace of a Manchu prince. Thence they went out on a series of combined automobile, truck, and camel forays into the Gobi Desert, which reaches eastward to within 200 miles of Peking.

Excitement stirred when Walter Granger found the unmistakable tooth of a titanothere. These were massive beasts, related to the horses and rhinoceroses. A titanothere of a later and larger species looked much like an oversized rhinoceros with two horns side by side on its nose. Although titanotheres swarmed across North America early in the Age of Mammals, aside from some doubtful fossil fragments from the Balkans, the animal was not theretofore known in the Old World.

The very next day, Granger found the first Cretaceous dinosaurs from Central Asia.

Another striking discovery of that year was the skull of a *Baluchitherium,* the largest known land mammal. A few odd bones had been found eleven years before in Baluchistan; but the Third Asiatic Expedition recovered enough bones to give a good idea of what the creature really looked like. A gigantic hornless rhinoceros, it resembled a tapir half again the size of an elephant; for it stood eighteen feet high at the shoulder.

Then, on July 12, 1922, the Expedition camped on the brilliantly colored sandstone bluffs of Shabarakh Usu, which they called the Flaming Cliffs. While the cooks got to work on apple pies, the fossilhunters wandered off. Presently, one man ran back for his tool box, saying he had found a dinosaur's skull. Soon all the paleontologists were chipping out the skulls of several individuals of a small, hornless ceratopsian dinosaur, *Protoceratops,* related—perhaps ancestral to—the huge American *Triceratops.* As Andrews told the story:

Our real thrill came on the second day, when George Olsen reported at tiffin that he was sure he had found fossil eggs. We joked him a good deal, but nevertheless all of us were curious enough to walk down with him after luncheon. Then our indifference suddenly evaporated; for we realized that we were looking at the first dinosaur eggs ever seen by a human being. We could hardly believe our eyes. But even though we tried to account for them in every possible way as geological phenomena, there was no shadow of doubt that they really were eggs. That they must be those of a dinosaur we felt certain. True enough, it was never known before that dinosaurs did lay eggs, but since most modern reptiles are oviparous, it was considered probable that their ancient ancestors followed this method of reproduction. Nevertheless, although hundreds of skulls and skeletons of dinosaurs had been discovered in various parts of the world, never had an egg been brought to light.

The eggs could not be those of a bird. No birds are known from the Lower Cretaceous, the geological horizon in which the eggs were found, and all the Jurassic and Upper Cretaceous birds were much too small to have laid eggs of this size. The elongate shape of the eggs is distinctly reptilian. A bird's egg usually is much larger at one end than at the other, because it is deposited in a nest, from which it might roll out unless it revolved on its point. Reptile eggs, which are deposited in shallow depressions scooped out of the sand, usually are elongate and similar in shape to the specimens we found. These eggs were in a great deposit full of dinosaur skeletons and containing, so far as we could discover, no remains of other animals or of birds.

Three of the eggs were exposed and evidently had broken out of the sandstone ledge beside which they were lying. Other shell fragments were partially embedded in the rock. Just under the low sandstone shelf we could see the projecting ends of two more eggs. While all the members of the expedition were on their hands and knees about ten-million-year-old eggs, George Olsen began to scrape away the loose rock on the summit of the shelf, and to our amazement he uncovered the skeleton of a small dinosaur, lying four inches above the eggs. It was a toothless species and we believe that it may have been overtaken by a sandstorm in the very act of robbing the dinosaur nest. Professor Osborn has named it *Oviraptor* (the egg seizer) *philoceratops* signifying "fondness for ceratopsian eggs."

We believe that the eggs were originally buried in fine sand, which would be particularly suitable for the preservation of delicate objects. The first specimens found by George Olsen are about eight inches in length and seven inches in circumference. They are rather more elongate and flattened than is usual in the case of the modern reptile eggs and differ greatly in shape from the eggs of any known bird.

The preservation is beautiful. Some of the eggs have been crushed, but the pebbled surface of the shell is as perfect as if the eggs had been laid yesterday instead of ten million years ago. The shells are about one-sixteenth of an inch thick and doubtless were hard and not membranous. Fine sand has filtered through the breaks, and the interior of all the egg is solid sandstone. In the photographs, the bits of broken shell partially embedded in the rock are plainly to be seen, and it needs no stretch of imagination to realize that the objects pictured are really eggs. In fact, we tried our best to think of any geological phenomena that could have produced a similar result, but try as we would, we could never get away from the fact that "eggs is eggs" and that these were laid by a dinosaur.

A few days after the discovery, five eggs were found in a cluster. Albert Johnson also obtained a group of nine. Altogether twenty-five eggs were taken out. Some of them, as in the case of the original group, were lying upon the surface of the ground, exposed by the erosion that had worn away the sandstone in which they were embedded; others were enclosed in the rock, with only the ends in sight. The eggs of Johnson's "clutch" were considerably smaller than the original lot and were unbroken. They may have been laid by a "pullet" dinosaur, and the larger ones by a full-grown "hen." But more probably they are the eggs of an entirely different species.

Most interesting of all was the fact that in two of the eggs that had been broken in half we could plainly detect the delicate bones of the embryonic dinosaurs. Never before in the history of science has it been possible to study paleoembryology! Not only did we discover the eggs, but we obtained during our five days in this locality a complete developmental series of *Protoceratops*. Baby dinosaurs, which probably had been hatched only a few days, and others in all stages of development up to adults nine feet long, with completely developed frills were added to our collection.

The nights when we lay about a camp fire of tamarisk branches (a desert bush from the sand dunes near the tents), our talk was of dinosaurs and eggs. The deposit was unbelievably rich. Seventy-five skulls and skeletons were discovered, some of them absolutely perfect. Obviously the Flaming Cliffs were a region of great concentration of dinosaurs during the breeding season. Like living reptiles, dinosaurs scooped out shallow holes and laid their eggs in circles with the ends pointing inward; sometimes there were three tiers of eggs, one on top of the other. The lady dinosaur covered her eggs with a layer of sand and left them to be hatched by the sun's rays. She didn't sit on them like a hen. It was necessary for the covering sediment to be loose and porous in order to admit warmth and air, and it is possible that the exceedingly fine sand at this spot was particularly well adapted to act as an incubator.

I have been asked a thousand times since then if we expected to find dinosaur eggs when we went to the Gobi. I suppose that nothing in the world was farther from our minds. As a matter of fact, we didn't even know that dinosaurs laid eggs. We supposed they did, for dinosaurs are reptiles and most reptiles lay eggs, but in the whole history of paleontology no evidence of how dinosaurs produced their young ever had been found. We discovered the eggs purely by chance, in the examination of a deposit which we knew was rich in dinosaur remains.

Most of my friends seem flatly disappointed because our eggs are so small. They are only nine inches long and I've had a lot of explaining to do. Few people realize that there were big dinosaurs and little dinosaurs just as today there are pythons and tiny grass snakes. When the public sees a nine inch egg it is horribly disgusted. It demands something about the size of an office safe. It visualizes only the great sauropod dinosaurs, *Diplodocus* or *Brontosaurus,* reptiles which could have looked into a second story window if there had been houses at that time. Those dinosaurs must have laid eggs, of course, and if they are ever found the public should be satisfied, for they ought to be a lot bigger than a football. But until that time the one we have must do. After all, a nine foot dinosaur, mostly tail, could not be expected to do much better than a nine inch egg. That's a ratio of an inch to a foot of dinosaur.[11]

Just after the discovery of the dinosaur eggs, Osborn arrived to visit the Expedition. He took the eggs home to America, where they made a journalistic sensation. Andrews later staged an auction of one egg to raise money to continue his work. Many explorers find it harder to raise money for their expeditions than to bear the chill of polar ice or the bites of swarming tropical bugs; but, as most expeditions are privately supported, this is just one more onerous task that explorers have to undertake.

In 1925, the Expedition went to work again and found eggs of dinosaurs of several kinds. Other discoveries were a huge, doglike carnivore, *Andrewsarchus,* with a skull three times as long as that of a grizzly bear, and some of the oldest known placental mammals—mouselike creatures of Cretaceous age.

These journeys were made hazardous by wars and disturbances. At first it was the backwash of the Russian Civil War. The defeated White Guardists retreated into Mongolia; the victorious Bolsheviki pursued them thither, massacred the people of Urga, and set up a puppet Communist regime in Outer Mongolia. Later, there were incessant clashes among the Chinese warlords, one of whose soldiers almost shot Andrews in 1925. On another occasion, Andrews traded rifle shots with Mongolian bandits. When Chiang K'ai-shek's Kuomintang armies conquered all of China in the late 1920s, Chinese nationalists calling themselves a "Cultural Association" began harassing the Expedition. They confiscated all the specimens and returned them only under diplomatic pressure. In 1929, the nationalists not only made Andrews take a pair of untrained Chinese "experts" into the field but also forbade the Exposition to make maps.

Seeing that scientific work would soon become impossible, Andrews spent the summers of 1931 and 1932 in Peking, writing up the results of his work. Then he returned to the United States, became director of the American Museum, and finally retired to his farm in Connecticut to devote himself to writing.

Despite the prominence in the dinosaur story of American fossil-bearing sites and American collectors, scientists of many nations have taken part in the hunt for fossil reptiles. For example, after the departure of the Third Asiatic Expedition from China, a joint Swedish-Chinese expedition under the Swedish explorer Sven Hedin hunted fossils in Mongolia and Kansu. Except for some good turtle shells, the collections were all more or less fragmentary. Nevertheless, they were valuable because they indicated the existence in Asia of reptiles somewhat like the American *Brontosaurus, Stegosaurus,* and *Tyrannosaurus.*

The latest exploration into the secrets of the Gobi Desert has been made by a Polish-Mongolian group under the leadership of the Polish woman paleontologist Zofia Kielan-Jaworowska. Her fossil-hunting team, which spent the summers of 1963–65 in Outer Mongolia, made significant finds. In the Flaming Mountains of the Gobi, near the place where Andrews found his dinosaur eggs, they discovered eighteen skulls of rodentlike, leaf-eating mammals that lived in the Cretaceous Period when dinosaurs still roamed the earth, and twelve well-preserved skulls of insectivores that eventually evolved into the higher mammals that rule the earth today. They also found the nearly complete skeletons of eleven dinosaurs, one a large carnivore with forelimbs eight feet long.

As so often happens in the history of science, it turned out that Andrews' eggs were not really the first dinosaur eggs to be collected. The first such eggs were found in France but had failed to become generally known. In the 1950s, the botanist Raymond Dughi, director of the Musée d'Histoire Naturelle of Aix-en-Provence, in Southern France, was reading an article in an old periodical. He left the book open when he went to answer the telephone. When he returned, he found that the wind had flipped the pages to an 1869 article by Philippe Matheron. Matheron reported that near Aix-en-Provence he had found fragments of eggs, which, he opined, might be the eggs either of some large bird or of a local sauropod dinosaur, *Hypselosaurus*.

The article inspired Dughi to search the neighborhood in his turn. He found many whole eggs and thousands of fragments, undoubtedly laid by the sauropod in question. At the suggestion of a visiting American scientist, the Musée gave one of its eggs to the Museum of Comparative Zoology at Harvard. This egg is a little under 8 inches long, with about twice the volume of an ostrich egg. Although of good size compared to a hen's egg, it is absurdly small compared to the size of the animal that laid it.

One of the best collections of native British fossils was amassed between 1867 and 1917 by two brothers named Leeds, who lived in the eastern Midlands.

As a lawyer in York, Charles Leeds began the collection; his younger brother Alfred, a farmer near Peterborough, carried it on after Charles emigrated. Most of their fossils were obtained from clay pits being quarried by brick companies. For decades on end, Alfred Leeds periodically made the rounds of the pits near Peterborough in a dogcart, asking whether any new bones had turned up and generously tipping workmen who rescued fossils from the grinding mills. At home, he enlisted the help of his wife and five sons in cleaning and piecing together the bones.

Among Leeds' finds were a partial skeleton of *Cetiosaurus,* a British sauropod; *Omosaurus,* a British stegosaur; and *Leedsia,* a Jurassic fish, which, judging by its 9-foot-long tail, must have been at least 30 feet long in life. The head was too fragmentary to restore, but some of the creature's relatives resembled a modern swordfish. Alfred Leeds found some plates, which for a while he thought belonged to his stegosaur. However, O. C. Marsh visited his collection in 1888 and proved that they were parts of another huge fish.

In time, all these fossils were sold or given to public institutions, mostly to the British Museum and the University of Glasgow. The mechanization of brick-clay quarrying has put an end to this fine source of fossils, because a digging machine cannot be stopped so easily as a man with a crowbar or a shovel whenever a delicate 100-million-year-old bone comes to light.

One of the most celebrated European paleontological projects was the German expedition to Africa in 1909–14. In 1907, a German mining engineer named Sattler, searching for a source of commercial garnets in what was then German East Africa and is now Tanzania, came upon fossils near Tendaguru Hill.

This hill is a low knoll in the middle of a wide, flat plain in the Mbenkuru River watershed. Although Tendaguru Hill would seem scarcely worthy of notice, it is the only elevation for miles in all directions, save for a row of conical hills to the west. To reach Tendaguru Hill, one had to hike 70 miles northwest from the small port of Lindi, walking for three to five days. No beasts of burden could be used because the region was infested by the tsetse fly, whose bite implanted microörganisms fatal to all such animals.

The plain was covered with a tropical scrub forest of bush, bamboo, and small trees. In the wet season, it was hard to hack one's way through the bush and harder yet to see where one was going. In the dry season, vision and movement were easier, but the water sources dried up until a camp had to depend upon a few tiny trickles, scattered miles apart about the plain. Because of a lack of permanent water, only a few natives lived on the plain.

A German geologist working in German East Africa, Eberhard Fraas, heard of Sattler's find and visited the site. Although sickness and lack of transportation kept him from collecting more than a few fossils, he sent word of this treasure to colleagues in Germany, where it aroused much enthusiasm and talk of "national honor."

An expedition was organized in the spring of 1909 under the direction of Werner Janensch, curator of the Berlin Museum of Geology and Paleontology. With two young assistants, Hennig and von Staff, he set out.

Sattler accompanied the German scientists to the site and served as interpreter until they learned enough of the native tongue to manage. Their native diggers were WaNgomi, an active, warlike people of Zulu stock who had revolted against German rule only four years before. The paleontologists originally hired 170 men; but, as the years passed, this work-crew grew to 500. Janensch and Hennig were pleasantly surprised to find these Africans honest, hard-working, and capable of taking an intelligent interest in their work. Some became expert at identifying dinosaur bones as ribs, leg bones, vertebrae, and so on. Others drew sketches of the way they thought the creatures looked in life. Hennig said he wished that some of the cheerfulness of these people could be exported to the *Mutterland*.

The WaNgomi were much puzzled as to why the white men should go to so much trouble and expense to collect such useless objects as bones. Their favorite theories were that the bones were to be sold for money, or to be traded for clothing, or to be ground up for magical potions.

The dinosaur-bearing beds consisted of three layers of marl, a soft rock containing both clay and lime of Upper Jurassic to Lower Cretaceous Age. Marine strata separated the three marl beds from each other, showing that the sea had advanced and retreated during the time when these beds were laid down. The uppermost of the dinosaur-bearing beds comprised the top of Tendaguru Hill; the two lower beds cropped out on the sides of the hill and spilled out over the plain. Most of the dinosaur remains lay in the upper and middle marl beds.

Besides the hardship of having to depend for water on a few

widely scattered mudholes, often fouled by animals, the paleontologists had to cope with the swarming African fauna. Big beasts were not much of a problem. The scientists never saw lions, although they heard them roaring often enough; and they caught sight of an elephant only once.

Nevertheless, on one of their periodic safaris to and from Lindi, the line of porters was charged by a rhinoceros. Since the animal is not native to that part of Africa, this one must have wandered in from some other region. Hennig yelled:

"Drop the loads! Up the trees!"

But the Africans merely stood staring while the rhino plunged through the line, luckily without hitting anybody, and crashed off into the bush. When Hennig asked them why they had acted so stupidly, they explained that they had never seen such an animal before and had taken it for a locomotive.

A *locomotive?*

Yes, bwana, a locomotive. They explained that they had never seen a locomotive, either, but had heard about it. Some had even heard it from a distance, snorting along the government railway. They understood that it was a great, barrel-bellied beast, which the whites had tamed to their service. So, when an animal answering this description appeared, making similar snorting noises, they assumed that it was nothing but a locomotive that had slipped its tether and wandered off into the bush.

The worst problem for the expedition was that of insects. If a man left his boots on the ground at night, in the morning he found that termites had eaten away the soles. If he left a sugar bowl on the table, in no time a million ants cued up to take their turn at it. The defense against this was to stand the legs of the table in small vessels, such as tin cans, filled with either water or oil. Water was less successful than oil; for, if one forgot to keep the cups of water filled, the water evaporated and the ants swarmed up. Even cups of oil were not entirely satisfactory, Hennig averred; for some ants were clever enough to climb to the roof above the table and drop on it. Sometimes the entire camp had to be routed out at night to fight off an invasion by a horde of stinging ants.

The site contained an enormous number of fossils—far more than could be carried off by one expedition. As in most of such sites, the greater part of the remains were fragmentary. One of the most spectacular finds was a sauropod *Brachiosaurus,* one of the largest of all dinosaurs, measuring 74.5 feet long. While its tail was shorter than that of *Brontosaurus,* its neck was longer. Its lifted head rose 39 feet into the air; if it lived today it could easily look into a third-story window. Probably weighing forty to fifty tons, this was the largest dinosaur of which a good skeleton has been collected. Altogether they found six species of sauropods: two species each of *Brachiosaurus, Gigantosaurus,* and *Dicraeosaurus.*

The expedition uncovered over fifty specimens of a dinosaur named *Kentrurosaurus,* an African relative of the armored *Stegosaurus.* There were also a small iguanodont and one slender little flesh-eater, a flock of small pterosaurs, and a few sea shells imbedded in this ancient marsh.

Since all these fossils tended to crumble, Janensch and his assistants prepared the fossils with bandages and plaster of Paris for their long journey back to the coast. Although the crew widened the trail, big limb bones had to be deliberately broken in order to enable the bearers to carry them on their heads. Smaller bones were taken out in carrying cases made of bamboo stems.

In Lindi, the bones were repacked in stout wooden chests made of wood that had been shipped all the way from Finland via the Cape of Good Hope. Then they were loaded aboard a native dhow, carried by water to steamy Dar-es-Salaam, and transferred to an ocean-going steamer. Finally, they were transferred once again to a canal boat for the trip up to Berlin, where they arrived safely amid great rejoicing in German scientific circles.

There was much speculation as to how the remains of so many dinosaurs came to be concentrated in beds otherwise rather poor in fossil remains. Some German scientists suggested that the animals had been overwhelmed by a natural catastrophe. Some thought they had been trapped on sinking, shrinking islands along the coast.

Hans Reck, who also dug in Africa in later years, thought that the site had been a great salt marsh; and that the dinosaurs, crossing the marsh in search of food or in the course of a migration, had broken through the thin crust and been trapped by the slimy mud beneath. Other students, equally competent, feel sure that the massive carcasses were carried to their final resting place by some prehistoric river.

Encouraged by a gift from the Kaiser that assured the proper display of the specimens, German paleontologists began to clean and assemble the *Brachiosaurus* in the Museum für Naturkunde in Berlin. The First World War interrupted this project; so did the political and economic upheavals that followed that war. Altogether it took twenty-six years to complete the mounting.

The job was finished in 1937—two years before the outbreak of the Second World War. When hostilities started, the paleontologists hastily took their monster apart and buried it in the cellar to protect it from the devastating Allied air raids, which smashed so many of Berlin's splendid museums. The dinosaur survived. After the war, the brachiosaur was brought out and reassembled, and there it stands to this day in the museum in the eastern sector of Berlin.

In the 1920s, a series of British expeditions hunted dinosaurs at Tendaguru—a task then somewhat lightened by the use of motor trucks. The first expedition, in 1924–25, was headed by the Canadian paleontologist W. E. Cutler and his youthful assistant, Louis S. B. Leakey, later famous as the finder of the ape-men of Olduvai Gorge. After Cutler died in 1925, other Britons continued his work for a number of years.

Earlier, in 1909, a young British paleontologist, D. B. Piggott, went to Lake Victoria to look for fossil mammals but had the misfortune to be eaten by a crocodile. As Dr. Simpson, the American paleontologist, remarked: "One might say that he did not collect reptiles—*au contraire!*"

In recent decades, the flow of dinosaur skeletons into museums has tapered off. There are several reasons for this. For one thing, many of the most obvious and accessible skeletons have already been collected. This is not to say that the world's fossil-bearing deposits are becoming exhausted; far from it. But when the most visible remains have been dug up, we must either hunt for the less evident prehistoric reptiles or wait for erosion to strip away more of the soil and rock that covers them.

For another thing, collecting a dinosaur skeleton requires much hand labor; and hand labor, as everybody knows, has been rapidly rising in cost the world over. It takes months to dig a skeleton out and years to prepare it for exhibition. Moreover, in any museum a few dinosaur skeletons go a long way. A museum that collects them wholesale soon finds that it has no place to mount them, unless it can afford to build a new wing.

Furthermore, additional specimens are increasingly likely to duplicate, or nearly duplicate, specimens already on exhibit. All sauropods, for example, look pretty much alike. Hence there is little point in mounting more than two, or at the most three, sauropods in any one museum.

Finally, scientists prefer to spend the money and man-hours at their disposal on the solution of unsolved problems. It is far more meaningful to trace an animal's pedigree back to its remote ancestors than merely to collect more skeletons of the same type of creature. Ancestors common to widely varying groups of descendants are likely to be small, nondescript animals, whose fossils are harder to find and less impressive than those of the later colossi. But finding one such ancestral animal repays the effort more abundantly, in scientific terms, than digging up another massive *Brontosaurus*.

Still, as nations grow in wealth and population, more and more cities and universities will decide that they, too, should have first-class museums of natural history. Thus dinosaur-hunting, on a modest scale, is likely to continue for many years to come.

As the art of fossil-collecting has changed greatly during the past century, so also has the art of preparing and mounting the specimens. In fact, modern museums owe much of their popularity to the skill with which animals are mounted and displayed. A look at what goes on behind the scenes in every great museum will give the reader an idea of what it is that makes the dinosaur of a hundred million years ago seem almost alive today.

It is now extremely rare for the same man to dig up a fossil, take it to a laboratory, separate it from the rock, prepare it for exhibition and study, and write a description of it for the scientific publications. Specialization has come to paleontology as it has to other human activities.

Separating bones from their rocky matrix and mounting them is now done by an expert craftsman called a preparator. Parts of the bone may have been separated from the matrix in the field and treated and bandaged. If so, the preparator has to remove this bandage without damaging the fragile bones, which could easily disintegrate in the air. Those bones that are still encased in rock must be chipped free with delicate tools like small hammers, chisels, awls, dentists' drills, and a tiny sandblasting nozzle. Sometimes limestone is removed from around the bones by dissolving it in acid.

If a bone is merely to be studied, the preparator separates the bone from the rock, puts it back together if it is broken, but otherwise leaves it as it is. If the bone is to form part of a skeleton on exhibition, however, he may have to do a great deal more. Since even a good fossil skeleton is seldom complete, the paleontologist has to judge how far he should go in restoring missing parts.

Sometimes this is not much of a problem. If the right thigh-bone is present but the left is missing, he can make a plaster left thigh-bone that is a mirror image of the right one. If a single rib or vertebra is wanting, it can be made to resemble the ribs or vertebrae before or behind it. If an important part like the skull or the pelvis is missing, the missing part can sometimes be copied from the corresponding parts in another animal of the same species, or at worst of a closely allied species.

A century ago, the men in charge of museums tended to put all the museum's material on display. Hence the halls of a museum were crowded with cases, and the cases were crammed with closely ranked specimens identified by tiny, illegible labels. Unless he were himself a scientist, the visitor soon gave up his quest for knowledge from fatigue, eyestrain, and museum feet.

Nowadays a museum displays only a fraction—often less than a tenth—of all its specimens. The rest are packed away, labeled and preserved, so that scientists can study them. The general public sees comparatively few exhibits; but these are carefully chosen, artistically mounted and lighted, and explained by clear, informative captions in large lettering.

In many museums, however, there is still room for improvement in the wording of the captions. This is often done by the scientist responsible for the specimen, who writes a technical, polysyllabic, Latinized professorese that baffles the layman. We have seen sentences like: "The astralagus is convex on its distal surface," without any explanation of the words "astralagus" and "distal" or for that matter of the significance of this fact.

If a museum decides to put a whole skeleton on exhibition, this can be done in two ways. One is the open mount, in which the bones are completely separated from the rock and assembled in the positions that they would have had in life. They are held in place by an iron framework, to which each bone is attached by clamps. The other method is the slab mount, in which the bones are only half picked out of the rock, so that the skeleton appears in relief.

Each kind of mount has certain advantages. The slab mount is best when the original skeleton is fairly complete and lies in a lifelike attitude, with the bones still in their proper relative positions. On the other hand, if the bones are badly scattered or if the skeleton is twisted out of shape, the open mount is best, so that each part can be properly reassembled. Museums like to have slab mounts for the sides of the hall and open mounts for the center.

Interesting as the skeletons are, people prefer to see what the animal looked like in life. Making pictures or statues of what a prehistoric animal is thought to have looked like is called "restoration." Although restoration is not very important from a strictly scientific point of view, it is helpful for education and for gaining public support of scientific museum projects.

Restoration is no great problem with such animals as the northern mammoth, of which frozen carcasses have been found as well as excellent drawings and paintings made by cave men in Europe. But, alas! no cave man ever saw a live dinosaur, since dinosaurs became extinct millions of years before our ancestors came down out of the trees.

Restoring animals that became extinct before human times takes educated guesswork. The skeleton defines the general size and shape of the animal, while the form of the bones gives a clue to its general build. For example, an animal with massive, pillarlike leg bones obviously stood on massive, pillarlike legs that supported a bulky, barrel-shaped body. By studying the roughened surfaces of bones to which muscle tendons were once attached, the restorer can learn how these muscles ran and can get an idea of how big they were. In this way, he can build up an image of the creature's outer surface.

The most speculative part of any restoration is the skin and its covering. Save in extremely rare cases—such as the skin of Sternberg's hadrosaur, the fins of Hauff's ichthyosaur, and the feathers of *Archaeopteryx*—such soft parts vanish without a trace. Consider such prominent features as the zebra's stripes, the lion's mane, the camel's hump, the skunk's scent glands, and the peacock's tail. If we knew these animals only from their fossils, we should not be aware of these distinctive ornaments. While anyone can tell a living lion from a tiger, the skeletons of the two are almost identical. If nobody had ever seen a live elephant, a restorer, working from a skeleton alone, would probably fail to conjure up its huge ears and long, serpentine trunk.

The best that a restorer can do is to follow the rules that apply to living animals. In general, mammals have hair. Arctic mammals have long hair and tropical mammals short hair—albeit there are exceptions. Large tropical mammals, like the elephant and the rhinoceros, are almost hairless because their ratio of mass to surface enables them to generate all the heat they need. Likewise birds have feathers, while reptiles have skins that are either bare or armored with scales or plates.

When an armored reptile's plates are preserved, the restorer can do a fairly accurate job. Some dinosaurs had scaly or warty skins, of which impressions have been found. Dinosaurs that lived much of the time in water are restored with smooth skins, because such is the hide of a hippopotamus. Yet, it is more than likely that some dinosaurs had dewlaps or other flaps and frills about which we know nothing. They may have used these appendages as heat radiators. Neave Parker's drawing of an iguanodon (Plate 50) shows such a dewlap, but this is educated guesswork.

In the matter of color, we are almost completely at sea. Since in our world the largest reptiles—the crocodiles, the Komodo monitor lizard, and the Galápagos tortoises—are all clad in dark, drab coats, ranging from slate gray to charcoal brown, it seems natural to show dinosaurs similarly colored. Some paleontologists, however, surmise that dinosaurs wore bright coats in gay patterns, as do so many small snakes and lizards today. We shall probably never know the true colors of dinosaurs. Looking at one of Knight's beautiful murals, showing several kinds of Mesozoic reptiles disporting themselves, we must remember that probably fewer than half the creatures there bear a reasonable likeness to the giant reptiles who walked this earth so very long ago.

In restoring a fossil life form, the paleontologist tries to imagine the creature's behavior and picture its natural surroundings. Like a skilled detective, he can infer many facts from the skeleton itself. The most obvious distinction is between land and water animals, even though both kinds may have been transported by water after death and thus come to rest among the remains of aquatic life. In general, land animals have legs; water animals, fins or flippers. Animals at home in both elements, like the hippopotamus or the sea lion, may have either.

Moreover, it is not hard to guess that a large fresh-water dweller like a sauropod dinosaur must have lived in a clime where lakes did not freeze over in winter. Likewise, reef corals are limited to warm ocean water that stays above 70 degrees Fahrenheit; at least, all the reef corals known today are so limited. A climbing animal like a monkey or a squirrel must have lived where there were trees, not on a desert or a prairie. A very large plant-eater, needing a lot of food, must have lived among lush vegetation, which in turn indicates a fairly high rainfall.

The animal's teeth, likewise, tell much about its habits and habitat. Anybody can distinguish the flesh-eater's fangs from the plant-eater's grinders; it is the difference between a dagger and a millstone. Details of the structure of the teeth offer further clues.

Animals that graze eat a lot of sand with their grass and thus wear down their teeth. Grazers, therefore, bear teeth of a special design. Sometimes, as in horses, the molars are unusually long and keep growing up from the root throughout most of the animal's life. When an animal has teeth of this kind, we may infer a grass diet, and this in turn suggests an open prairie with only a few trees and a modest rainfall.

We can also tell something about an animal's behavior from the details of its build. If a beast has long, slender legs, it probably ran fast; if it was a low, squatty creature covered with heavy armor, it shuffled slowly along. Very large animals did not burrow, climb, or fly. If their brains were small in proportion to their bodies, as with dinosaurs, their actions were ruled by a few simple instincts, like those of a modern frog or alligator.

Little by little, the paleontologist puts together, like a mosaic, his picture of the life of a former era. He knows that, in any fauna, the small animals vastly outnumber the large, and the plant-eaters vastly outnumber the flesh-eaters. It takes, on the average, about ten pounds of vegetable food to make one pound of adult herbivore, and about ten pounds of herbivore to make one pound of carnivore. Also, the size of the carnivores is neatly adjusted to that of their prey; the tiger cannot live on mice, nor can the weasel prey upon buffalo.

Yet, despite the best of detective work, much is still conjecture. We do not know for sure how some of the bipedal dinosaurs carried their tails in walking or what caused the great waves of extinction, like that which closed the Age of Reptiles. There are enough enigmas of this sort to keep the world's paleontologists busy for many years to come.

11

The Heritage of the Dragons

At the end of the Cretaceous Period, some seventy million years ago, the last of the giant Mesozoic reptiles vanished. The winds that blew over the lands no longer carried the reptilian roars, bellows, grunts, and hisses that had resounded for nearly two hundred million years. The mammals inherited the earth, and all that remains from the Age of Reptiles are the lizards, snakes, turtles, crocodiles, and tuatara of today.

Yet this does not mean that the dragons passed from the scene without leaving a trace or without exerting an influence upon the modern world. For the dinosaurs formed a part—and, in fact, the most spectacular and picturesque part—of the pageant of the evolution of life on earth. The discovery of the fact of evolution, and the spread of the acceptance of this fact, was the biggest revolution in the thought of man since Copernicus and Galileo proved that the earth goes round the sun.

The discovery of the Age of Reptiles helped this revolution along in two ways. First, the reptiles themselves evolved according to the same laws and principles that governed the evolution of other life forms, thus confirming the truth of the evolutionary hypothesis. Second, by their very size and grotesqueness, they aroused public interest. They lured generations of young people into the study of the life sciences and made evolutionists of them. Most of all, they furnished paleontologists and museums with excellent free publicity and charmed the public into supporting these scientists and institutions with the funds they needed to carry on their work. Without the dinosaurs, the evolutionary revolution would have taken longer and met with even stronger opposition than it did.

At least a hundred men before Charles Darwin had thought of evolution. Anaximandros of Miletos, a Greek philosopher who lived more than five centuries before Christ, suggested "that man was, originally, similar to a different animal, that is a fish." Six hundred years later, the Roman poet Lucretius wrote a poem on nature, which not only preached a doctrine similar to evolution but even dimly grasped the idea of natural selection:

> And in the ages after monsters died,
> Perforce there perished many a stock, unable
> By propagation to forge a progeny.
> For whatsoever creature thou beholdest
> Breathing the breath of life, the same have been
> Even from their earliest age preserved alive
> By cunning, or by valor, or at least
> By speed of foot or wing.[1]

In 1589, the aged Bernard Palissy, a famous French potter and naturalist, died in the dungeons of the Bastille because, among other crimes, he speculated about evolution. In 1619, Lucilio Vanini was burned at the stake in Toulouse on similar charges.

Then why do we credit Charles Darwin with the theory of evolution? We give him most of the credit because earlier evolutionists merely surmised that evolution had taken place. They did not prove that all forms of life had evolved or show why the various forms had to evolve as they did. Darwin did these things, and he gathered such an overwhelming mass of evidence and arranged it in such a logical way as to convince all whose minds were not hopelessly trapped in tradition.

Of the evolutionists before Darwin, Lamarck—the French biologist who founded invertebrate zoology—was the most important. He not only believed in evolution, but he also drew the first of those tree-shaped diagrams to show how the higher forms of life had developed from the lower. He and his colleague Cuvier, the founder of vertebrate paleontology, each got hold of part of the puzzle of evolution. If they had put their pieces together, they might have solved the enigma; but fallible men seldom do things that way.

For one thing, Lamarck not only believed in evolution; he also believed that no species ever became extinct. Several scientists of the time—including Thomas Jefferson, a pretty good amateur paleontologist—shared this belief. They argued that such extinction would spoil the symmetry of Nature, or that God would not permit it.

On the other hand, Cuvier did believe in extinction. In his great *Recherches sur les ossemens fossiles,* he proved that remains had been found of at least 150 extinct species. But he did not believe in evolution. He argued that no fossil links had been found to connect living with extinct forms, and that the animals mummified and sculptured in ancient Egypt belonged to the same species as those of today. He did not realize the immense length of geological periods, compared to which the time from ancient Egypt to the present is a mere jiffy.

In Cuvier's time, only a few fossil-bearing formations were known, and these had been laid down at widely different times. Cuvier accounted for these seeming gaps in the record by saying that the earth's history had been punctuated by several great catastrophes. The earth's axis had shifted, so that the oceans splashed out of their beds, drowning the plants and animals of whole continents. Then the waters settled back into their basins, and the devastated lands were repopulated by immigrants from continents that had escaped the flood. The last of these calamities was the biblical Deluge. This theory became known as Catastrophism.

Cuvier influenced many people of his day, including the poet Shelley. He temporarily won his argument, both with his correct belief in extinction and with his mistaken theory of Catastrophism, not because he was any nearer right than Lamarck, but because he was forceful, energetic, eloquent, and self-confident—a logical thinker and a clear writer. Lamarck, on the other hand, was shy, nervous, modest, and self-effacing, and he wrote a good deal of nonsense. However, on the one vital question of evolution, Lamarck turned out to be right and Cuvier, wrong.

Cuvier's Catastrophism seemed reasonable when only a few geological periods were known. But, as the nineteenth century wore on, geological discovery closed up the gaps between the known periods, and paleontologists began to find "missing links" between extinct and modern life forms by the thousands. So the rival theory of Gradualism, put forth by the English geologist Charles Lyell, took the place of Catastrophism.

Lyell taught that the form of the earth's surface today is due to the gradual, day-by-day action of wind and water, such as we see about us all the time. There had been no catastrophes. Yet even Lyell's Gradualism was modified by the Swiss naturalist Louis Agassiz's discovery of the Pleistocene Ice Age, showing that the earth had undergone drastic climatic change. If the Alvarez cosmic-collision theory is generally accepted, Gradualism will be still further revised.

In a sense, we may say that Darwin combined the correct parts of the theories of Cuvier and Lamarck to form his theory of evolution. In addition, he not only asserted that evolution had taken place and produced convincing evidence of this fact; but he also conceived a correct explanation of *how* evolution works. This mechanism, which Darwin was the first fully to recognize, was his theory of natural selection—"Darwinism" in the narrow sense of the word.

The foundation of Darwin's theory of evolution by natural selection was laid down by Benjamin Franklin among other people. In 1750, Franklin wrote a letter, explaining how organisms increase to fill all the space available for them:

I had for several years nailed against the wall of my house a pigeon-box that would hold six pair; and, though they bred as fast as my neighbours' pigeons, I never had more than six pair, the old and strong driving out the young and weak, and obliging them to seek new habitations. At length I put up an additional box with apartments for entertaining twelve pair more; and it was soon filled with inhabitants, by the overflowing of my first box and of others in the neighbourhood. . . .

A year later, in a short treatise, Franklin applied the lesson of the pigeons to people:

There is, in short, no bound to the prolific nature of plants or animals but what is made by their crowding and interfering with each other's means of subsistence. Was the face of the earth vacant of other plants, it might be gradually sowed and overspread with one kind only; as, for instance, with fennel. And were it empty of other inhabitants, it might in a few ages be replenished from one nation only; as, for instance, with Englishmen. Thus there are supposed to be now upwards of one million English souls in North America. . . . This million, doubling but suppose once in twenty-five years, will in another century be more than the people of England. . . .[2]

An English clergyman, Thomas Malthus, read Franklin's pamphlet and carried the idea farther. People, he said, tend to increase until there is not enough food to go round. Then their numbers stop growing because they are destroyed by starvation, war, or disease as fast as they are born. When wild country is settled or an advance in farming makes possible bigger crops, people increase for a while. But, sooner or later, population catches up with food supply and people go hungry again. This, said Malthus, was man's tragic "struggle for existence."

In 1798, Malthus put these arguments into a pamphlet, *An Essay on the Principle of Population* . . . When a storm of abuse descended upon him, he calmly gathered more data and expanded his pamphlet into a book. Malthus's ideas have been hotly debated ever since. They have been denounced by people who thought his a hardhearted doctrine, or who disapproved of population control, or who wished to blame all the ills of mankind on capitalism. Nevertheless, most modern scientists who study human populations find Malthus's ideas still basically sound.

In 1831, Charles Robert Darwin (1809–82) was a tall, round-faced, bushy-browed, button-nosed youth who had studied medicine at the University of Edinburgh and religion at Cambridge without showing much talent or enthusiasm for either. His career as a biological scientist began when he secured a post as naturalist on a British naval vessel, H.M.S. *Beagle,* which was about to set out on a five-year cruise of exploration and research around the coast of South America and across the Pacific Ocean.

Darwin dug for fossils in Argentina. He met the primitive Fuegian Indians, a race of big, powerful, potbellied men with tangled mops of coarse black hair, who painted their huge flat faces in weird designs and wore only caps and cloaks of fur against the shrieking wind and driving rain of their bleak Antarctic home.

He observed the giant tortoises and iguanas plodding about the Galápagos Islands and examined the birds of those isles and the colorful coral reefs of the vast Pacific.

Throughout the whole voyage, Darwin suffered horribly from seasickness and remained in poor health for the rest of his life. Constant headaches, nausea, indigestion, and exhaustion kept him from working more than a couple of hours a day. His illness was never diagnosed, but some investigators have thought that he suffered from Chaga's disease, caused by the bite of *Triatoma,* a large, squashy, black bug, which attacked him in hordes when he camped on the pampas.

Home from the sea, Darwin spent a few years in London, married, and moved to a country house. There he remained for the rest of his long life, supported by a legacy, which he inherited from his father and which he built into a tidy fortune by shrewd investments. He wrote as many scientific books and papers as his feeble health allowed. Although he made other important contributions to the sciences of biology and geology, his evolutionary theory was his major work.

Darwin studied the abundant notes he had made during his Pacific voyage and thought long and hard about the differences he had observed among animals. These differences, he felt sure, furnished the key to the way the different species had developed.

In 1838, Darwin read Malthus's *Essay on Population*. Here, in Malthus's phrase "struggle for existence," lay the clue he sought. Each species, Darwin saw, increases until its homeland can support no more of its kind. Thus, in each generation, many individuals perish.

Now, no two individuals of a species are exactly alike. They vary in size, in shape, in strength, in fertility, in intelligence, and in resistance to disease. Therefore, some are better equipped than others to survive the hazards of life and to engender offspring.

On the whole, those survive that are best fitted to do so. Their offspring, more often than not, inherit their useful qualities. In this way, nature selects the fittest to survive; this is the meaning of Darwin's term "natural selection." As Darwin saw it, natural selection is an automatic process, working according to coldly impersonal natural laws. And, because the best-fitted individuals tend to survive and breed, a species very slowly changes to adapt itself, quite unconsciously and mechanically, to the life it leads.

Being an extremely shy and modest man, Darwin delayed the publication of his great theory for twenty years, while he wrote and rewrote his essay and gathered more and more evidence to support his ideas. In 1858, he was dumbfounded to receive a manuscript from a young naturalist acquaintance, Alfred Russel Wallace. Wallace, too, had read Malthus and had been struck, while lying ill on a trip to the Molucca Islands, by the idea of evolution by natural selection. Now he wanted to know what Dr. Darwin thought of his idea.

For all his modesty, Darwin was dismayed by the thought of losing the credit for all his careful work. So he permitted his friends Lyell and Hooker to write a joint paper on the subject of evolution, based upon Wallace's article and fortified with material Darwin had written. When this paper was presented, it aroused much interest among scientists but made not a ripple in the thinking of the general public.

Spurred to action at last, Darwin in 1859 published his most famous book: *On the Origin of Species by Means of Natural Selection, or the Preservation of Favoured Races in the Struggle for Life,* a work known to most people simply as *The Origin of Species*. This closely reasoned study caused a sensation. It became a best-seller, ran through a number of editions, and was heatedly denounced far and wide because it contradicted the story of Creation as told in the Bible.

In the late nineteenth century, some people complained that Darwin had not completely explained evolution. And, in fact, he had not. Three questions about evolution called for answers: Why do individuals in a species vary? How are these variations inherited? And, how do these variations bring about changes in a species? By his theory of natural selection, Darwin had answered the last of these questions only.

A contemporary of Darwin answered the second question: How are variations inherited? By a strange mischance, however, his answer was overlooked for more than thirty years.

Johann Mendel (1822–84) was born in Austrian Silesia, the son of a family of poor but honest and kindly peasants. Although an intelligent man, Mendel's father had no chance of rising out of his class. Under the feudal laws of the Austro-Hungarian Empire, the older Mendel had to work without pay for three days a week on the estate of the local countess. And young Mendel could afford to attend only the neighborhood elementary school.

The local elementary school did, however, teach science, although the school inspector considered this fact a scandal. Johann Mendel early learned to love scientific experiment. His family did their best to get him a higher education; but Mendel's schooling had to stop when his father was crippled by an accident. Mendel tried teaching school but could not earn enough to pursue a university career. Eager to complete his education and religiously inclined, he decided to become an Augustinian monk. So, taking the religious name of Gregor, he entered the monastery of the Moravian city of Brünn (now Brno, Czechoslovakia) not far from his birthplace.

From 1854 to 1868, Mendel taught at a school near Brünn and tested some of his scientific ideas by breeding garden peas. From this experiment, he made an unexpected discovery. When he crossed tall peas with short peas, he did not get plants of medium height, as one might expect. The peas of the second generation were all tall.

But, when he interbred the peas of the second generation, Mendel obtained a lot of mixed offspring. One quarter of this third generation were tall peas that behaved, when interbred, like any other tall peas of pure ancestry. Another quarter were short peas, which behaved like any other short peas.

The remaining peas—half of the peas of the third generation—were tall peas, which acted just like the hybrid, mixed peas of the second generation. That is to say, when interbred, they gave rise to plants of three different kinds, in the ratio of 1:2:1. That is: one-quarter were true-breeding tall peas, one-half were tall but did not breed true, and one-quarter were true-breeding short peas.

Other plant breeders, including Darwin, had noticed similar variations, but Mendel was the first to show that these variations occurred in simple numerical proportions. He crossed many other plant varieties to check his findings. He learned that such characters as the colors and shapes of flowers, seeds, pods, stems, and leaves of peas followed the same rules of inheritance as did the height of the plants. But each part followed the rules independently, so that a multitude of different combinations of sizes, shapes, and colors could be obtained in the same species of plant.

In February, 1865, Mendel read a paper on his experiments before the Natural History Society of Brünn. The members listened in polite incomprehension. The next year, Mendel published his report, *Experiments in Plant Hybridization,* in the *Proceedings* of this society and sent copies to various European libraries and to leading scientists everywhere.[3] Three years later, he published another report.

Nothing happened. Nobody wrote Mendel or tried the same experiment to see if it worked. Mendel wrote about his experiments to the one important botanist he knew, Nägeli. The latter sent a condescending reply, which showed that he neither understood Mendel's discovery nor took it seriously.

Meanwhile, Mendel had been elected abbot. His botanical work dwindled away, especially after his monastery became embroiled in a quarrel with the government over taxes. Moreover, in his later years he became quite stout and so, no doubt, found stooping down to peer at plants a burdensome task. When one visitor asked Mendel about his work with peas, Mendel changed the subject as if it embarrassed him.

A few scientists may have glanced at Mendel's articles. But, although Mendel had expressed himself clearly enough, none really understood what he had done, let alone realized its importance. Then in 1900, when Mendel had been dead for sixteen years, his reports were rediscovered by three amazed European biologists.

Mendel was now hailed as the founder of genetics, the science of heredity. He had discovered that certain qualities in living things, such as height and color of flowers in sweet peas, are passed on either completely or not at all. This is called the inheritance of unit characters.

Mendel also found that a quality can be passed on invisibly, so that it misses an entire generation but pops up again in a later generation. His tall but non-true-breeding peas possessed some quality that caused shortness, which they had inherited from their short parents and could pass on to their offspring. These peas, Mendel reasoned, had inherited both a tallness-character and shortness-character from their parents. The tallness-character, however, determined the height of the plant. As he expressed it, tallness was *dominant* over shortness. The hidden shortness of the hybrid peas he called a *recessive* character.

When Mendel's work was rediscovered, biologists at once began to extend the new science. They found, for instance, that the human eye obeys the Mendelian rule. Brown is dominant over blue, so that two blue-eyed parents cannot (with rare exceptions) beget a brown-eyed child. But two brown-eyed parents, each carrying a recessive blue-eye character, can beget blue-eyed children. This does not mean that if two such brown-eyed parents with the recessive blue-eye character have three brown-eyed children, the fourth is certain to be blue-eyed, any more than if one flips a nickel four times, one always gets two heads and two tails. It merely means that, of a thousand children born of such unions, a number very close to 250 will be blue-eyed.

Other scientists, who investigated the mechanism of heredity, learned that all the more complex many-celled organisms are made up of cells of two kinds: body cells, and sex cells or gametes. To start any individual on the road to life and growth, a male gamete or spermatozoön must be united with a female gamete or ovum to form a single cell, called a *zygote*. When the ovum and spermatozoön (or egg and sperm) have been united, the single resulting zygote divides, grows, divides again, and so on until a complete working body is made. When the body matures it, in turn, gives rise to gametes.

Although many plants and lower animals combine both sexes in one individual, the higher animals all have separate sexes. By combining the hereditary factors from two parents instead of one, more variations in the offspring are possible. Thus, natural selection can operate more effectively among these variations and thus a species can respond more sensitively to its environment and evolve more rapidly in whatever direction is to its advantage.

For those interested in how variations creep into a species, a brief account of the reproductive process is in order. Every cell is made up of two parts. Except in bacteria and blue-green algae, most of the machinery for running the cell is contained in a small central part called the *nucleus*. In the nucleus are microscopic threadlike particles called *chromosomes*. The number of chromosomes in a cell varies. It is, for instance, eight in a vinegar fly and forty-six in a man.

When a cell divides to make two cells, each of its chromosomes manufactures a duplicate of itself, so that each of the daughter cells gets a full complement. In sexual reproduction, the body produces special sex cells or gametes, each of which has but half the normal number of chromosomes. When a male sex cell or spermatozoön unites with a female sex cell or ovum, the combined cell that results possesses the normal number of chromosomes again.

Each chromosome is a long chain of complex molecules called *genes*. The genes control the growth of the various parts of the body.

Each gene affects the development of one or more organs, while several genes, acting together, may control the growth of a single organ. A human body cell has been estimated to contain about 40,000 genes. Each gene in turn consists of thousands of atoms in a particular arrangement.

Now and then a change occurs in a gene. An atom is knocked off or added, or a group of atoms is twisted askew, or the gene is doubled, misplaced, or lost. If the change occurs in a gamete or sex cell that is destined to give rise to a new organism, the new gene pattern is passed on to the offspring, which grows up with the new trait or *mutation*. A living thing affected by a mutation in one of the gametes from which it sprang is called a *mutant*. A certain number of mutations take place all the time in any species. In addition, the rate of mutation has been greatly speeded up, in experimental insects and bacteria, by X rays, by chemicals like formaldehyde, and even by sudden changes of temperature.

These discoveries made it possible to answer the question about evolution that puzzled Darwin and furnished his critics with ammunition: Why do organisms of one species vary? They vary when penetrating radiations, chemicals, or other influences cause alterations in their sex cells. Unless these variations, called mutations, are so harmful that the creatures never live to reproduce, these changes are passed on to the next generation.

Most mutations involve so small a change that the change can hardly be detected. For example, some mutations might make our digestion a little better or a little worse, our eyesight a little keener or a little dimmer, or our arteries harden a little sooner or a little later.

In point of fact, nearly all the mutations we know about are harmful. They make our eyes and digestions and arteries worse, not better. Constructive or beneficial mutations cannot be more than a small fraction of one per cent of the total. The bigger the mutation, the less is the chance that it will be a good one. Most drastic mutations are lethal, slaying the offspring in embryo or in infancy.

The reason for this is simple. A gene is an extremely complicated little bit of chemical machinery. It is precisely fitted to its task of controlling, in coöperation with other genes, the growth of some part of the body. To expect a big random mutation to make the body better is like trying to improve your watch by hitting it with a hammer. The over-all effect of mutation is harmful to the species, because the great majority of mutations are destructive.

Although the number of possible mutations is enormous, and any gene may mutate in many different ways, some genes mutate more frequently than others. Many undergo certain mutations over and over, just as an automobile of a given model may have a particular weakness in the design that causes a certain part to break down in many cars of this model. Geneticists estimate, for instance, that the mutation causing hemophilia (bleeder's disease) occurs once in every 50,000 human births. The hemophilia that Queen Victoria of England passed on to her descendants in the Russian and Spanish royal families was probably such a mutation.

Although rare, constructive or beneficial mutations do take place. That is how evolution operates. In a wild state, living things with destructive mutations tend to die young, while those with constructive or useful mutations have more than their share of offspring.

In the wild state, then, the species is kept healthy and sometimes improved by the action of mutation and selection together. When destructive mutations arise, they are worked out of the species by the process of selection. Many geneticists worry about the fate of man under civilized living conditions, since civilization enables the victims of hereditary defects to live and breed about as well as anybody else. If such human beings are near-sighted, they wear glasses; if they have flat feet, they wear arch supports; if they have allergies, they take injections.

Since unfavorable mutations continue to take place, rain or shine, they pose an ominous question: What will happen to the human race after a few thousand years of civilized life? There will not be much advantage to having to work for, say, only three hours a week, if one must spend all the rest of one's time at the clinic, being treated for a dreadful load of hereditary defects.

A common type of mutation deprives a creature of an organ or function. If this organ is not needed, the mutation occurs again and again until the variant without the organ eventually becomes the standard type. This is the process of *rudimentation*. Rudimentation results in eyeless, colorless cave animals. It results in nearly hairless, tailless men as well. For, at some stage in their evolution, our ancestors dwelt in tropical forests where hair was not needed for warmth; therefore repeated mutations got rid of most of it.

Any organ or function not needed for living is apt to be lost by rudimentation, or at least reduced to a vestige, even when lack of the organ confers no positive advantage. But, once the genes that built up the organ disappear completely, the organ rarely can be regained. For instance, our forebears failed to re-grow their pelts when they moved to colder climates; they had to invent clothing and discover fire instead.

Another illustration of rudimentation was the development of the very successful order of reptiles called snakes. During the Cretaceous Period, it is believed, certain lizards took to a burrowing habit. To such a burrowing animal, wriggling its way underground after worms and grubs, neither eyes nor ears nor legs are of much practical use. Hence, probably, the process of rudimentation caused all three sets of organs to degenerate.

However, not all of these lizards stayed underground. When legs had been completely lost, some of the legless ones returned to the surface. In certain places, such as in heaps of stones and tangles of underbrush, they could get around by sheer wriggling (helped by the movement of broad belly scales attached to the ends of their ribs) in quite as lively a fashion as lizards with legs. But, in this new environment, eyes were useful again. Therefore, the eyes of snakes regained their former power. However, it would seem that their ears had degenerated too far to be restored, so snakes remain deaf to this day.

These principles explain why the Mesozoic reptiles that took to the water acquired a streamlined form: there was a positive evolutionary advantage to such a form, in that it enabled them to swim faster; so the forces of selection constantly pushed the species in that direction. They explain why the pelvic bones of some kinds of these reptiles shrank or disappeared: since the animals no longer walked, these bones were no longer needed for muscular attachments; so rudimentation got rid of them. And finally, they explain why these reptiles failed to re-grow the gills of their remote water-dwelling ancestors: the genes that would stimulate the growth of such gills had long since vanished from the gene pool of the species; so there was nothing for the selective process to work on. Thus mutation, selection, and heredity work together to give the biotas (the floras and faunas combined) of different environments their distinctive forms.

Any environment offers opportunities for new species, just as a city affords commercial opportunities for new businesses. Whether any new species will arise to take advantage of these opportunities depends upon many things. Since beneficial mutations are always small, the opportunity must be one that some existing species can approach by small steps, unless it can immigrate ready-made from another continent or sea.

Also, the number of possible mutations, while vast, is not unlimited. Although living tissue can produce an immense variety of forms and structures, there are many that it cannot produce. One can, for instance, amuse oneself by designing an imaginary animal with wheels. But, unless wheels could be evolved step by step, through possible mutations, from existing organs, they could not be attained. And there is no known method by which an animal could evolve its fins or legs, by small stages, into wheels. Such a wheel could not rotate if connected to the rest of the animal by nerves and blood vessels.

When an environment offers an opportunity, this opportunity will be taken by the first species to make the change. This species may hold its place in the scheme of things indefinitely, unless the environment itself suffers a sharp shift or unless another species, better adapted, moves in and crowds the first arrival out. This happened when the placental carnivores from North America crossed the Panama land bridge and crowded out the carnivorous marsupials they found in possession of South America.

Edward D. Cope (1840–97), the
nbuckling American paleontologist of
te nineteenth century. *Photo from the
rican Museum of Natural History.*

67.   O. C. Marsh (1831–99), Cope's rival
in nineteenth-century paleontology. *Photo
from the American Museum of Natural
History.*

68.   A paleontological expedition of the Carnegie Museum, collecting
fossils in Utah, on the site of the present Dinosaur National Monument,
about 1913. *Photo from the Carnegie Museum.*

69.   Henry Fairfield Osborn. *Photo from the American Museum of Natural History*

70.   A still from the 1925 motion picture *The Lost World*, made from Sir Arthur Conan Doyle's novel of that name. *Photo from the Bettmann Archive, Inc.*

Roy Chapman Andrews examining a [nest?] of dinosaur eggs in Mongolia in 1922. [Pho]to from the American Museum of Nat[ural] History.

72. Egg of the sauropod dinosaur *Hypselosaurus*, with a hen's egg for comparison. *Photo from the American Museum of Natural History.*

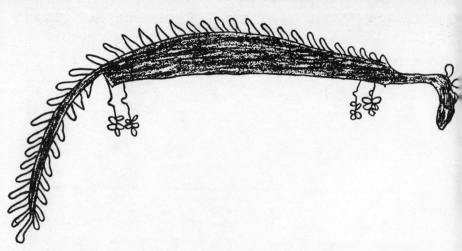

73. Sketch by a native worker for the German Tendaguru expedition (1909–14), Sefu ben Abdullah, of how he thought a dinosaur looked in life. (After Hennig.)

74. Skeleton of *Brachiosaurus* in the Museum für Naturkunde, Berlin. *Photo from the Museum für Naturkunde.*

75. Charles R. Darwin at about the time he wrote *The Origin of Species. Photo from the American Museum of Natural History.*

76. The Crystal Palace Park, showing some of Waterhouse Hawkins's statues of fossil reptiles. A group of plesiosaurs, with an ichthyosaur just visible to the right of them (center foreground) and a group of iguanodons on the hill behind them. *Photo from the London County Council.*

77. Model by Hawkins of the ankylosaur *Hylaeosaurus* in Crystal Palace Park. *Photo from the London County Council.*

78. Models by Hawkins of the ancestral crocodile *Teleosaurus*, with a plesiosaur in the background, in Crystal Palace Park. *Photo from the London County Council.*

DINNER IN THE IGUANODON MODEL, AT THE CRYSTAL PALACE, SYDENHAM.

79. Banquet given by Hawkins to his scientific friends in the nearly finished model of one of his iguanodons, 1853. *Courtesy of the Illustrated London News.*

80. Illustration from Thomas Hawkins's *The Book of the Great Sea Dragons* (1840), showing plesiosaurs, ichthyosaurs, and pterosaurs as they were thought at the time to have looked.

81. The Swiss hero Vietor slaying an Alpine dragon, in Athanasius Kircher's *Mundus subterraneus* (1678).

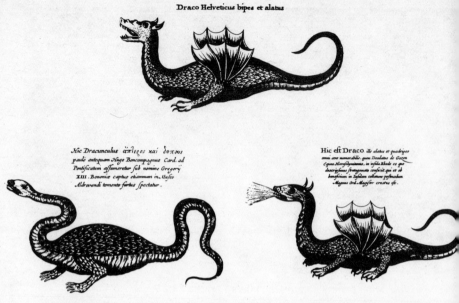

Draco Helveticus bipes et alatus

Hic Dracunculus ἄπτερος καὶ ὁόπους
paulo antequam Hugo Boncompagnus Card. ad
Pontificatum assumeretur sub nomine Gregory
XIII. Bononiæ captus etiamnum in Musео
Aldrovandi tomento fartus spectatur.

Hic est Draco ille alatus et quadripes
omni ære numerabilis, quem Dædalus de Gozen
Eques Hierosolymitanus, in insula Rhodo 300 quo
descripsimus stratagemate confecit: qua et ob
benefacta in Insulam collatam postmodum
Magnus Ord. Magister creatus est.

82.   Dragons of various kinds, illustrated in Athanasius Kircher's *Mundus subterraneus*.

83.   The sea serpent said to have been seen from H.M.S. *Daedalus* in 1848. *Courtesy of the Illustrated London News*.

In any biota, we rarely find two species occupying exactly the same niche. If they do, then one is crowding the other out, and the latter is disappearing. This does not necessarily mean that members of one species actually attack those of the other. A species can oust a competitor by means of its higher birth rate, or more efficient digestion, or greater resistance to disease, or any of many other evolutionary advantages.

Conversely, when we see two or more similar forms coexisting over a long period, we can surmise that they are separated by some difference of habit or habitat that keeps them from competing too severely with each other. In Africa, for instance, the black and the white rhinoceros (both of which are actually slate gray) do not compete, for the first is a browser (eating leaves) and the second a grazer (eating grass). Likewise, several genera of sauropods coexisted in the fresh waters of the Jurassic Period. Although we do not know the details, we may assume that similar differences of habit and habitat applied to them, too.

The speedy acceptance by the general public of the concept of evolution was one of the gifts of the dragons of old; for educated Victorians fell under the spell of the giant reptiles that came to light in the nineteenth century. By the 1880s, the term "dinosaur" had become a household word, and news of new discoveries was the talk of the day, not only in England but also on the continents of Europe and North America.

In the early 1850s, a large exhibition hall, the Crystal Palace, was built in London. Designed by Joseph Paxton and made entirely of iron and glass, it led the way to modern skyscraper construction. When the building was moved from its original site in Hyde Park to Sydenham Park, southeast of the city, the anatomist Sir Richard Owen suggested that the decorations include a set of life-sized "antediluvian monsters." The idea was approved, and the sculptor B. Waterhouse Hawkins, working under Owen's direction, created the statues out of iron-braced, stucco-covered brick.

Near the new site of the Crystal Palace stretched a little lake with two islands and a group of rocky islets. Several Palcozoic rep-

tiles and amphibians were set up on the islets. On the larger of the
two main islands, a swarm of Mesozoic reptiles took form. These
included a megalosaur, a hylaeosaur, a mosasaur, two iguanodons,
and a number of pterosaurs, ichthyosaurs, and plesiosaurs. The
remaining large island held the later Cenozoic mammals, like the
ground sloth *Megatherium.*

The statues were ingenious and colorful but not very accurate.
In those days, the iguanodon and the megalosaur were known from
fragments only. Therefore Owen and Hawkins assumed that, since
the iguanodon had teeth like the modern iguana, it must have looked
like an oversized iguana. The megalosaur, they assumed, was similar
but with flesh-eater's fangs. Both were shown as walking on all
fours, to the later scornful amusement of O. C. Marsh, who snorted
that so to treat these reptiles "would be almost as incongruous as
to do this by the genus Homo."[4] But, then, he had the advantage of
living when more complete specimens of iguanodon had been discovered.

On December 31, 1853, when the group was nearly finished,
Hawkins gave a dinner for Owen and twenty other savants inside
one of his iguanodons. On June tenth of the following year, Queen
Victoria officially opened the building and grounds to the public.
Since there were no signs explaining the sculptures, visitors who had
not provided themselves with Owen's guide book were mightily
puzzled by these nightmarish apparitions. One man surmised that
the statues were erected by some temperance society to warn top-
ers of what they would see if they kept on guzzling.

Not to be outdone by her sister metropolis, New York determined to have a Crystal Palace and a herd of monster reptiles, too.
A copy of the Palace was duly built; but five years later, in 1858, it
was destroyed by fire. Still, the monsters were so popular among
New Yorkers that in 1868, the Commissioners of Central Park hired
Waterhouse Hawkins to make a set of statues like those in London
for a planned "Paleozoic Museum." Hawkins set up a studio in
the Park and, with Herculean zest, began work on a new set of
restorations, based upon fossils of prehistoric American animals.

Alas! Two years later, Boss Tweed and his gang of grafters seized control of the Park Commission. They canceled Hawkins's contract, scrapped plans for the museum, and caused Hawkins's casts and molds to be buried in Central Park, where they will, no doubt, perplex some future archaeologist.

Although New York never got her plaster dinosaurs, the fossil fauna of London has survived to the present day. In 1936, the Crystal Palace—like its American copy—burned. The park was allowed to run down during the Second World War, leaving the monsters battered and hidden by brush. In recent years, however, the London County Council has spruced up the Crystal Palace Park. Hawkins's statues have been patched up and given new coats of paint, so that they once more present an imposing—if inaccurate—picture of former geological ages.

12

Dinosaurs in the World of Today

Long before the discoveries of Hofmann's mosasaur, Mary Anning's ichthyosaur, and Gideon Mantell's iguanodon, men believed in the existence of gigantic, scaly monsters similar in many ways to the real reptiles of the Mesozoic. So, perhaps, we should look into the source of these beliefs. Have any such animals ever shared the earth with man?

When our forefathers tried to think up the most terrible beast they could, they imagined the dragon. One of the simpler dragons, for instance, was Python, whom the god Apollo slew at Delphi. Python was just an enormous snake, and we call a family of real snakes after him today. To other dragons, imagination added lizard's legs, or bat's wings, or a sting at the end of the tail, or a fiery breath, or the power of thought and speech, or some combination of these.

Ancient legend creeps with these supersaurians: Apepi in Egypt, Tiamat in Babylonia, the Ashi Dahaka in Iran, and the wise *lung* of China. Heroes like Bellerophon and Beowulf, Sigurd and St. George slay a dragon as their crowning deed of dought. Warriors from Agamemnon on down painted dragons on their shields; kings like Richard the Lion-hearted embroidered them on their standards. The learned Konrad von Gesner in the sixteenth century and the equally learned Father Athanasius Kircher in the seventeenth devoted whole chapters of their books to dragon lore.

For evidence, men produced fossil bones, which they attributed not only to dragons but also to giants. The "giants" were usually remains of the extinct kin of the elephant: mammoths and mastodons. If one looks at the skull of an elephant, one sees that it does look a bit like the skull of a monstrously hideous man, five or six times natural size. If one had never seen an elephant and did not know about its trunk, one might easily make this mistake. As for the "dragons," they could be the bones of almost any large beast that did not possess the high, short, manlike skull of the elephant. In Europe, dragon tales were often based upon the skull of the extinct woolly rhinoceros or the great cave bear.

The skeptical eighteenth century taught educated men that there were no dragons. European explorers had traveled far and wide through the Americas, Asia, and Africa. Although they heard rumors of dragonlike beasts, nobody ever caught one. To be sure, Asia and Africa harbored pythons and crocodiles of formidable size, which may in ancient times have given rise to dragon myths. These, however, were now well-known animals, without a trace of fiery breath or batlike wings.

So people, with a little sigh, gave up their dragons. The dragon took refuge in fairy tales. Here he comes to such ludicrous ends as that of the Purple Dragon in L. Frank Baum's *The Magical Monarch of Mo,* who is stretched out thin and cut up into violin strings.

Or rather, people *thought* they had given up their dragons. No sooner had the legend been banished than—thanks to the work of Cuvier, Buckland, Leidy, and other pioneers in paleontology—the dragons popped into view again. Whether or not they still lived, they *had* lived once upon a time. This time there was no question of mistaking the skull of a bear or a rhinoceros for that of a dragon. Scientists now knew enough about bones to tell the skull of a reptile from that of a mammal, and these were unmistakable reptiles.

Soon, popular books about fossil organisms appeared, such as *The Book of the Great Sea Dragons* (1840) by the geologist-poet Thomas Hawkins. These books were illustrated by engravings of Mesozoic scenes, showing reptiles of land, sea, and air, drawn with splendid inaccuracy and engaged in frightful battles under gloomy

Gothic skies. These pictures look so much like those from medieval dragon lore that one half expects an armored knight to clatter into the scene on his destrier.

Naturally, all this talk about real dragons brought up the question: Did any such creatures still exist? A hundred years ago, this question was not so foolish as it sounds today. At that time, despite the heroic journeys of European explorers, the map of the world still showed many large blank spaces marked "unexplored."

Since one would expect to find dinosaurs in a hot, damp climate like that of Mesozoic times, unknown Central Africa seemed an especially hopeful place to look for such survivals from the past. In fact, several sizable animals were first brought to light there by white men after the turn of the century. There was the okapi, which Sir Harry Johnston discovered in the Congo in 1900; the giant forest hog, collected by Lieutenant Minertzhagen in 1904; the pygmy hippopotamus, which Hans Schomburgk found in Liberia in 1912; and the Congo peacock, not definitely identified until 1937.

Schomburgk, who discovered the pygmy hippo, collected live animals for Carl Hagenbeck, the wild-animal dealer of Hamburg. In Liberia, Schomburgk was told of a beast in Lake Bangweolo, which killed hippopotami. Hearing the tale, Hagenbeck sent an expedition to Lake Bangweolo, but this group could not even find the lake.

Nor was this all. In 1913, a German expedition under Captain von Stein, to the then German colony of the Cameroons,[1] heard tales of a similar hippopotamus-killer called the *mokéle-mbêmbe*. The outbreak of the First World War ended this expedition before the searchers could run down the rumors. According to the tale, the *mokéle-mbêmbe* had a smooth skin, a long neck, and a single large tooth or horn. A German woman, Ilse von Nolde, repeated stories of a similar animal, the *coje ya menia* or water lion, in Angola. There have been other accounts as well, including one alleged sighting a pair of iguanodons.

Despite all these fascinating tales, no dinosaurs materialized. The rapid opening up of Africa by road and rail has gone on apace during the last half-century, together with the dwindling of the wild life, until today most of Africa is not much wilder than Ohio. It is scarcely credible that any animal large enough to kill hippopotami could have survived undiscovered. The same must be said of the jungles of tropical South America and southeast Asia.

The African dinosaur tales, then, are but the last stage of a process that has gone on ever since Europeans began to learn about the other continents. First came the stage of wild rumors. At this time, explorers and natives did not understand each other beyond a few words, and the explorers themselves did not believe in spoiling a good story for the sake of a few facts. Hence the wildest yarns were brought back to Europe, to arouse the awe and wonder of stay-at-homes. Sometimes the stories were made up of whole cloth; sometimes they were an exaggeration or a misunderstanding of something real; and sometimes they turned out to be true.

The classical Greeks heard, for instance, that in Africa lived snakes 150 feet long, which looked like hills when coiled up; and also a red carnivorous bull with movable horns. In India, they were told, dwelt the *martichora,* which

. . . has a face like a man's, a skin red as cinnabar, and is as large as a lion. It has three rows of teeth, ears and light-blue eyes like those of a man; its tail is like that of a land scorpion, containing a sting more than a cubit long at the end. It has other stings on each side of its tail and one on the top of its head, like the scorpion, with which it inflicts a wound that is always fatal. If it is attacked from a distance, it sets up its tail in front and discharges its stings as if from a bow; if attacked from behind, it straightens out and launches its stings in a direct line to the distance of a hundred feet. The wound inflicted is fatal to all animals except the elephant. The stings are about a foot long and about as thick as a small rush . . . it kills and devours a great number of human beings. It fights with both its claws and stings, which . . . grow again after they have been discharged. There is a great number of these animals in India, which are hunted and killed with spears or arrows by natives mounted on elephants.[2]

Here we can recognize a fantastic account of the Indian tiger and also, perhaps, the origin of the legend of the porcupine's shooting its quills. Early explorers in the Americas brought back stories quite as bizarre. In North America, they heard of the Great Salt Mountain, 180 miles long; of live mammoths; and of animals like the side-hill gouger, whose legs were longer on one side than on the other as an adaptation to its habitat.

In South America, they tramped through jungles and over the pampas in search of the golden city of El Dorado. They looked for tribes of warrior women, for a race of headless men with faces in their chests, and for the succarath or su, described as having "the head of a woman, the forelegs of a tiger, the hindlegs of a wolf and a voice like a broken calliope."[3]

Besides the monster tales that have resulted from misunderstanding, credulity, exaggeration, and plain lying, many such yarns have arisen from the natives' honest beliefs in mythical monsters. Most primitive peoples harbor such beliefs; so, before the modern age of science, did everybody, savage or civilized. Sometimes the monster was merely a small beast writ large. The Maoris of New Zealand, for instance, told legends of a dreadful dragon called the *taniwha*. This was nothing but the harmless two-foot tuatara envisioned the size of a whale. Or, the animal might be a composite of several known animals.

Many early dragon legends are plainly based upon reports of pythons and crocodiles by people who heard about them at second hand. The salt-water crocodile, which is believed to exceed 30 feet in length, is certainly as formidable a monster as any reasonable man could want. What, however, are the actual possibilities of the survival into historic times of any large land reptile, other than a crocodile or a giant snake?

Of dinosaurs, the chance is negligible. If dinosaurs had survived as late as the Pleistocene, the paleontologists would certainly have come upon their remains among the vast masses of Cenozoic fossils they have collected during the past century.

The true lizards, however, have reached a formidable size. The largest living lizards are the monitors of the genus *Varanus*. Of these, about thirty species are scattered about the tropical parts of the Old World. They are of rather slender form, most species reaching a length of 3 to 6 feet, with forked tongues like those of snakes. Some live in deserts, some in jungles. They are active predators with a special relish for crocodiles' eggs, and they climb and swim with agility.

The champion monitor is the Komodo dragon, *Varanus komodensis,* first discovered by Europeans in 1912. This mighty lizard, which dwells on three small Indonesian islands and has been doubtfully reported from New Guinea, reaches a length of 10 feet and may weigh as much as a large man. Among other prey, it kills wild pigs for its dinner. There are even tales of its pulling down deer and buffalo, although we should want strong evidence before believing that. When hunting, it now and then stands up on its hindlegs, like a bipedal dinosaur, to look about for possible prey.

Men who have caught the Komodo dragon for zoos have found it a formidable captive. The lizard is as powerful as an alligator of similar size and even more active. When snared, it leaps furiously about, hissing like a steam engine and trying to bite and claw its captors. Moreover, it has the disagreeable habit of vomiting all over them. Yet, after a few months in captivity, it becomes so tame that it will affectionately climb up on its keeper.

Early travelers' tales of the Komodo monitor may have gone into the general stock of tales from which the dragon legends were fabricated. It would not take much exaggeration to make the Komodo monitor into a story-book dragon. In the case of the related fossil genus *Megalania,* from the Pleistocene of Australia, no exaggeration would be needed; this lizard reached a length of 20 to 30 feet.

One is tempted to ask if the last survivors of *Megalania* may not have been seen by men and embroidered into dragon legends. . . . But alas, the fossils of *Megalania* go back long before historic time, and Europeans did not certainly sight Australia until Luis Vaez de Torres glimpsed Cape York in 1606. So no connection between *Megalania* and any mythical dragon is likely.

There remains, however, the question of the sea serpent. Whereas the hope of finding live dinosaurs has faded with the opening up of the world's last unexplored lands, interest in the sea serpent has remained lively down to the present. Sea-serpent enthusiasts, like the late Godfrey Cabot, come close to forming a cult; like those of believers in Plato's Atlantis, the Lost Ten Tribes of Israel, or the occult wisdom of the Great Pyramid.

Moreover, there is enough apparently sober testimony about the sea serpent to imply that some unknown monster might, after all, lurk in the vastnesses of the ocean. At least, the possibility merits serious thought. The sea serpent comes into our story because a common interpretation of sea-serpent stories makes the beast a plesiosaur. It therefore qualifies as a Mesozoic reptile, if not as a dinosaur.

The sea-serpent legend begins with an imaginative sixteenth-century Swedish archbishop, Olaus Magnus,[4] who spent his last decades in retirement in a monastery in Rome, writing. His main work was a *History of the Northern Nations* (1555).[5] In this book, Olaus devoted a section to the sea monsters said to haunt the coasts of Norway. He told of ship-eating whales. He told of the kraken or giant squid, whose existence, long doubted, was finally admitted in the 1870s. And he told of the sea serpent. One of the copper engravings in Olaus' book portrayed such a serpent attacking a ship. This picture was copied and recopied in subsequent books of natural history, such as Konrad von Gesner's *Historia animalium.*

Figure 52.   Sea serpent, as illustrated in Konrad von Gesner's *Historia animalium* (1586).

Once the sea-serpent tales of Olaus and his successors were in print, stories of encounters with marine monsters became more and more frequent. The monsters, also, became more and more serpentine. One of the most celebrated sea-serpent stories was Captain Peter M'Quhae's report of 1848:

> Her Majesty's Ship *Daedalus*
> Homoaze, Oct. 11

Sir,— In reply to your letter of this day's date, requiring information as to the truth of a statement published in *The Times* newspaper, of a sea-serpent of extraordinary dimensions having been seen from Her Majesty's ship *Daedalus* under my command, on her passage from the East Indies, I have the honour to acquaint you, for the information of my Lords Commissioners of the Admiralty, that at 5 o'clock p.m. on the 6th of August last, in latitude 24° 44′ S., and longitude 9° 22′ E. [in the South Atlantic], the weather dark and cloudy, wind fresh from the N.W., with a long ocean swell from the S.W., the ship on the port tack heading N.E. by N., something very unusual was seen by Mr. Sartoris, midshipman, rapidly approaching the ship from before the beam. The circumstance was immediately reported by him to the officer of the watch, Lieut. Edgar Drummond, with whom and Mr. William Barrett, the Master, I was at the time walking the quarter-deck. The ship's company were at supper.

Our attention being called to the object it was discovered to be an enormous serpent, with head and shoulders kept about four feet constantly above the surface of the sea, and as nearly as we could approximate by comparing it with the length of what our main-topsail yard should show in the water, there was at the very least 60 feet of the animal *à fleur d'eau,* no portion of which was, to our perception, used in propelling it through the water, either by vertical or horizontal undulation. It passed rapidly, but so close under our lee quarter, that had it been a man of my acquaintance I should have easily recognized his features with the naked eye; and it did not, either in approaching the ship or after it had passed our wake, deviate in the slightest degree from its course to the S.W., which it held on at the pace of from 12 to 15 miles per hour, apparently on some determined purpose.

The diameter of the serpent was about 15 or 16 inches behind the head, which was, without any doubt, that of a snake, and it was never, during the 20 minutes that it continued in sight of our glasses, once below the surface of the water; its colour a dark brown, with yellowish white about the throat. It had no fins, but something like the mane of a horse, or rather a bunch of seaweed, washed about its back. It was seen by the quartermaster, the boatswain's mate, and the man at the wheel, in addition to myself and officers above mentioned.

I am having a drawing of the serpent made from a sketch taken immediately after it was seen, which I hope to have ready for transmission to my Lord's Commissioners of the Admiralty by tomorrow's post.

> I have, etc,
> Peter M'Quhae, Captain[6]

To Admiral Sir W. H. Gage, G. C. H., Devonport

After Mesozoic reptiles became well known, the reports of sea serpents, which until then had tended towards the serpentine, began to describe the monster as more and more resembling a Mesozoic marine reptile like a plesiosaur or a mosasaur. These reports have continued right down to the present. A whole flock of stories took wing in the 1930s about a monster in Loch Ness, Scotland; more recently a team of Russians is said to have searched Lake Vorota in Siberia for a similar creature.

Some of these tales are, undoubtedly, either hoaxes or hallucinations. One must read something of the literature of hoaxes to realize how often apparently sober, upright, solid citizens perpetrate them. Sometimes they do it for money, sometimes for momentary fame, sometimes to persuade people of some pet theory, and sometimes just for the fun of fooling the gullible.

Other cases, such as that of the *Daedalus,* do not seem to be thus explicable. With so many people in on the hoax, one or another would surely betray the secret. Hence many cases remain where the witness must have seen something, although not necessarily a sea serpent in the usual sense.

Several marine animals can easily be mistaken for sea serpents. These include the finback whale and its smaller cousin the sei whale. Both are long, slender whales of almost serpentine form. Others are the kraken, the basking shark, the whale shark, and the ribbonfish, which rarely comes to the surface and which reaches a length of 30 feet. Groups of smaller animals, such as sea lions, porpoises, or killer whales, may give the impression of a sea serpent when moving in a single column and simultaneously breaking the surface, one behind the other.

That *still* leaves cases, like that of the *Daedalus,* unaccounted for. To consider them, we must bear a couple of cautions in mind. For one, we ought to keep an open mind on such doubtful questions until they are cleared up. By "cleared up" we mean until somebody recovers an actual specimen, or until the oceans have been so thoroughly explored, from shore to shore and from top to bottom, that no unknown monster could still exist.

The other caution is that, in the absence of a specimen, mere testimony is never enough to establish the improbable, no matter how detailed the accounts or how respectable the witnesses. The reason is that, if the testimony of sane and sober witnesses were enough to establish a fact, then we should have to believe not only in sea serpents but also in witches on broomsticks, ghosts, devils, angels, elves, gnomes, mermaids, dragons, gryphons, unicorns, bleeding statues, magical spells, miraculous cures, prophetic powers, flying saucers, and dozens of other wonders for which volumes of convincing testimony can be mustered.

However, let us suppose that some of the sea-serpent witnesses have in fact seen something that is neither a whale, nor a shark, nor a squid, nor a floating log, nor a school of porpoises, nor any of the other things commonly used to explain sea-serpent sightings. Let us assume that there is a large, undescribed animal at large in the sea, which has caused these reports. What would it be?

Two obvious answers are a plesiosaur or a mosasaur. Then such an animal must have survived all those seventy million years since the Mesozoic. It should have left its bones in some Cenozoic marine fossil-bearing bed. Neither beast has done so.

The Age of Mammals furnished a creature that would make at least as good a sea serpent as any Mesozoic reptile. This is the primitive whale *Basilosaurus*. The fore part of this whale looked much like that of one of the smaller toothed whales of today. The after part, however, was drawn out into a long, serpentine tail with a pair of flukes at the end, so that the animal ranged up to 60 feet in length. Since *Basilosaurus* swam by rippling that snaky tail up and down, it would, on the surface, look much like the conventional picture of a sea serpent.

As a modern sea serpent, however, *Basilosaurus* encounters the same difficulty as that met by Mesozoic reptiles. The remains of whales of this family all come from Eocene and Oligocene deposits, and none from any later period. The indication is, therefore, that the Basilosauridae have been extinct at least for thirty to forty million years.

Professor A. C. Oudemans, who three-quarters of a century ago investigated the sea serpent and devoted a book to it, suggested that the Great Unknown of the sea was a pinniped: a member of the suborder that includes the seals, the walruses, and the sea lions, but with a much longer neck and tail than any of these. We may picture it as a kind of fur-bearing plesiosaur.

Aside from the lack of fossil remains from late geological periods, the fatal flaw in theories of reptilian and mammalian sea serpents is that all these beasts would be air breathers. Therefore, they would have to surface to breathe. In these days, when the oceans are stitched and webbed by ship and airplane routes, and the great whales have been nearly exterminated by Norwegian, Russian, and Japanese whalers who hunt their prey with the help of helicopters, the chances that any large surface-dwelling marine animal would be overlooked are negligible. In the modern world, there just is not enough undisturbed space for Great Unknowns to hide any more.

We suspect that the most plausible candidate for the rôle of sea serpent is something else. The common eel lives most of its life in the fresh waters of western Europe and eastern North America. When the urge comes upon it, it swims downstream to the ocean and thence to the Sargasso Sea. There the eels lay their eggs and die. From the eggs come leaf-shaped, transparent larvae, which set out upon the landward journey at a speed of about a thousand miles a year. Eventually, the offspring of American eels return to American rivers; those of European eels, to European rivers.

These larvae reach a length of 4 inches and then turn into conventional eels, losing height from top to bottom, thickening from side to side, and acquiring color. About that time they reach their ancestral rivers, which they ascend. Then they grow to their full size of 3 to 5 feet long. The conger eels and the morays pass through similar stages but live all their lives in the sea.

But sea serpents? Well, on 31 January, 1930, the Danish research ship *Dana,* off the Cape of Good Hope, caught an eel larva. Like other eel larvae, it was flat, leaf-shaped, and transparent. But, instead of being 3 or 4 inches long, it measured 6 feet, ½ inch in length.

Now, it may be that eels of this particular species grow to maturity without getting any longer than the one caught by the *Dana;* they simply shrink vertically and thicken until they become 6-foot eels. On the other hand, if the adult bears the same ratio to the larva as with fresh-water eels, the adult would be 60 to 100 feet long. To us, that will make a quite satisfactory sea serpent until a better one comes along.

This supposed giant eel, however, does not explain the case of the *Daedalus,* for two reasons. Eels do not swim with their heads out of water, as this beast was said to have done. And eels swim by wriggling from side to side, whereas Captain M'Quhae specifically said that his monster did not wriggle.

The senior author has a theory (or at least a guess) as to what this serpent might have been. If one looks at the *Illustrated London News* picture (Plate 83) squint-eyed, one sees that the "serpent" looks like a dugout canoe, of the kind used in primitive lands for fishing. The dark color of the "serpent's" back would be the shadowed interior of the canoe, and the "head" the expanded bow platform on which a fisherman places his foot in shooting or spearing a fish.

Our surmise, then, is that some fishermen, fishing from their dugout off the coast of West Africa or eastern South America, rashly harpooned a whale shark. The harmless whale shark is the largest living fish, reaching 45 feet, and is fairly common in tropical waters. The fish, naturally, took off. The harpoon line was belayed to the canoe. Failing to untie or cut the line, the fishermen dove overboard and swam for shore, leaving the shark to tow the boat about the South Atlantic for weeks or months until the line broke or the harpoon head tore out. This is just a guess, which can never be proved one way or another. But who has a more plausible one?

If the prospect looks dim for Mesozoic reptiles in the flesh, the last century has certainly seen an imposing resurrection of these animals in the form of fiction. Dinosaurs and other Mesozoic monsters have become standard plot elements in the science-fiction story. As in so many branches of imaginative fiction, the first steps in this direction were taken by Jules Verne (1828–1905). In one of his early science-fiction novels, *A Journey to the Centre of the Earth* (1864), his explorers of the network of underground caverns, with which the author assumed the earth to be riddled, witness a fearful fight between an ichthyosaur and a plesiosaur in the waters of an underworld sea.

Since then, dinosaurs and other ancient reptiles have been brought on stage in scores of tales. Sometimes the monsters have survived down to the present day in some out-of-the-way place, as in Sir Arthur Conan Doyle's *The Lost World* (1912). Sometimes the story is laid back in the Mesozoic. It may simply narrate the doings of the reptilian denizens of that world; or it may bring a crew of people back to the Mesozoic Era by time machine.

Most exasperating, to people who know anything about dinosaurs, are the many stories, comic strips, and movies in which our skin-clad cave-man ancestors are shown as battling dinosaurs. One of the first things that one learns about Mesozoic reptiles is that they all became extinct about seventy million years before man evolved from his apish ancestors. Therefore, to show early men and dinosaurs as contemporaries is as glaring an anachronism as Julius Caesar in a derby hat.

For the benefit of readers who would like to read stories about Mesozoic reptiles, we have included in the bibliography a separate fiction division, listing some typical stories of this class. Most of them contain glaring scientific errors of one kind or another; but, on the other hand, most of them furnish good, rip-snorting entertainment.

Suppose, just for fun, that we *could* travel back in time to the Mesozoic to hunt dinosaurs. What would such a safari be like?

For one thing, transportation would be a problem. Even if the time machine were big enough to hold a jeep, such a vehicle might prove more trouble than it was worth, since in the Mesozoic Era there were no roads and no sources of gasoline. Most of the ground would be very rough, since there was no grass between the trees and shrubs to retard erosion. Grass first appeared around the end of the Cretaceous and became really widespread only in the Cenozoic Era. On some plains, a caterpillar-tracked vehicle might be useful; for the most part, however, one would have to walk.

Moreover, one could not whistle up a hundred native porters to carry one's gear on their heads for a dime a day. Therefore, one would probably take along some pack asses or mules. In most places where there was enough forage for herbivorous dinosaurs, there would also be enough to keep one's animals healthy, if one did not push them too hard and if something with 6-inch fangs did not take a fancy to them.

Human food would not present much of a problem. In most places in the Jurassic and Cretaceous, there would be enough small dinosaurs, such as camptosaurs or boneheads, to furnish fresh meat.

As for guns, hunters of modern thick-skinned big game, such as elephant and rhinoceros, argue over the question of the best kind of gun. Some are satisfied with a heavy repeating rifle of the kind used for large thin-skinned game, like moose, buffalo, grizzly bear, or lion. A typical gun of this sort is the .348 Winchester 71, a lever-action rifle. There are also a number of magnum rifles in .300, .330, and .375 calibers. A "magnum" is a rifle designed for an oversized cartridge with an oversized powder load, to give higher velocity than is usual in that caliber. These guns can be had in lever, bolt, pump, and automatic action; bolt action seems to be the most popular for heavy rifles nowadays. They are larger than those used for deer and black bear but smaller than real elephant guns. They have muzzle energies in the range of 1000 to 2500 foot-pounds.

Some hunters also prefer these rifles for elephant and rhinoceros, citing the following advantages: The rifle itself is lighter; it kills the animal just as dead if the bullet hits a vital spot; and it gives the hunter more than two shots at a time. Sometimes the smaller guns are defended as "more sporting."

Others, however, prefer a real elephant gun for thick-skinned large game. This is a double-barreled rifle, which looks rather like a shotgun. Elephant guns come in .465, .475, .500, and .600 calibers, firing cartridges the size of bananas. With such a gun, one need not hit an elephant in a vital spot to knock it off its feet. It works the other way round, too. If the hunter is a small man or is not used to heavy guns, it may knock *him* off his feet. All these guns are made to order in Britain, and most of them cost over a thousand dollars apiece.

For shooting large dinosaurs, consider: A rhinoceros weighs about one ton, a hippopotamus two or three, an elephant two to ten. In the Mesozoic, one would hunt animals weighing as much as several elephants. Moreover, being reptiles, they would cling more stubbornly to life than a mammal. To make things harder, it does no good to shoot them in the brain, because they have none. This is to say, they have a little lump of tissue, the size of a golf or tennis ball, on the top of their spines; but one would have little chance of hitting that lump inside a skull 3 to 7 feet long.

Therefore, the heaviest rifle is none too powerful. That means the daddy of all elephant guns; the Continental .600. This is the most powerful sporting arm made, weighing 14.5 pounds. It packs 7600 foot-pounds of muzzle energy, which almost puts it in the anti-tank gun class. Therefore, one had better be a pretty solidly built man oneself, to drag this weight around rough Mesozoic country and not be knocked arsy-varsy by the recoil. Several other makes come fairly close to this gun in power, such as Holland & Holland's .500 double express with 5700 foot-pounds. We understand that there are now magazine rifles with muzzle energies in the same range as these double-barreled guns.

We already have some idea of Mesozoic climate and flora. The Cretaceous would seem rather exotic, although many plants like magnolias, pines, sequoias, and willows would be familiar. There are clumps of palmetto and giant fern, but little or no grass. Hence erosion would gouge the land into millions of gullies. The Jurassic would seem like another world.

Of the dinosaurs, the duckbills and other large ornithopods would provide good trophies with little risk. They would be hard to approach, having keen senses. The smaller ornithopods, such as the camptosaurs and the boneheads, would furnish meat but little else.

The armored dinosaurs—stegosaurs in the Jurassic, ankylosaurs in the Cretaceous—might as well be left alone. There is no sport in shooting them, since the ankylosaurs simply curl up on the ground when approached, and the stegosaurs turn their backs and lash their tails in the hope that one will impale oneself on the spikes. And those small, blunt heads are not impressive trophies.

The ceratopsians (Cretaceous only) furnish the biggest heads of all. In fact, these heads are sometimes so large as to be practically uncollectible. A 7-foot *Triceratops* head may weigh over a ton. This may be too much to get back to the time-machine site, or too big to go into the machine. If one does get it back to the present, one may find that, when one has mounted such a head in a living room of modest size, there is no space left in the room for anything else.

Being unused to men, such dinosaurs should not be very hard to stalk. On the other hand, the animals' lack of fear would have its dangerous side. While it would be easy to walk up to one's game and knock it over, the game would also be readier to charge if wounded or annoyed than it is today. Nowadays most wild animals, even the biggest, run away from men if given the chance.

A charging ceratopsian, outweighing an elephant, would be almost impossible to stop from the front, even with a Continental .600. One would have to dodge the charge like a matador and shoot the beast from the side as it blundered past.

Sauropods one might as well let be. They are so stupid and sluggish that there is no sport in shooting them, and they are almost unkillable. The small head, swaying about on that long neck, is hard to hit, and for a body shot one needs a bazooka or an anti-tank gun. If one kills a sauropod in the water, it sinks and cannot be recovered. If one kills it on land, one has no trophy but that silly little head and thirty tons of meat, which one cannot possibly eat up before it spoils and draws hungry carnosaurs by its stench.

Lastly one has the theropods, from lively little predators the size of a stork up to colossi like *Allosaurus* and *Tyrannosaurus*. Of the theropods, the larger carnosaurs would be the most dangerous game of all time. In dealing with such as these, one wants the heaviest gun, an iron nerve, and some other hunters to back one up. The moment when one faces a carnosaur is no time to panic, or to turn an ankle, or to catch a twig in the action of one's gun, or to forget to take the gun off safety, or to climb a tree small enough for the carnosaur to reach up and pluck one out of. There is no use running away in the open. Although the large carnosaurs' movements look slow and clumsy, their legs are so long that they cover ground faster than a man can, even with their slow, ponderous strides.

People who have heard about dinosaurs' tiny brains sometimes think that they must have dim senses as well. This is not necessarily so; the ornithopods and the theropods, in particular, have keen senses. True, they have little memory. Hence, out of sight, out of mind. When a carnosaur comes slavering after one, if one can dodge behind a bush or into a gully the dinosaur may forget one and wander off. But one should not count upon it.

In dealing with carnosaurs, there is no nonsense about "Your shot, old boy!" Everybody lets the dinosaur have it and keeps on shooting until the brute is down for good. If brain shots are a waste of rounds, the dinosaurs have big hearts, weighing 50 to 100 pounds. A shot through the heart will at least slow them up. Several will kill them, although it sometimes takes them fatally long to realize that they are dead—fatally, that is, for the hunter.

Not much modern hunting is really dangerous. Primitive men, facing big game with spears, needed much more nerve than a modern man with a high-powered rifle. As we have explained, primitive men never hunted dinosaurs, because there were none to hunt in their time. But, if we could hunt dinosaurs with the best modern guns, we should find ourselves in a position like that of a tribesman facing a lion with a spear. That would be a *real* thrill. Best of all, on such a hunt one would not have to worry about depleting some rare species, because they are all extinct anyway!

Such was the splendid spectacle of the Age of Reptiles. What lessons, if any, can we learn from this drama? It is easy to pontificate that, since the dinosaurs became extinct, we shall do likewise unless we prove ourselves more intelligent and adaptable than they. But such generalities really mean very little. Since human beings differ from dinosaurs in many important respects, the effects of natural forces upon us are likely to differ to an equal degree from the effects of those forces upon the dinosaurs.

However, we can say this much. We know now that numerous and apparently well-adapted species can disappear, and we do not really know why. That is, we know some possible causes, but we do not know for certain what cause or combination of causes brought about the Great Deaths of the Cretaceous and the Pleistocene. There is, in fact, a lot that we do not know about the process of extinction.

The reader may have heard dogmatic prophecies to the effect that an atomic war, or the use of pesticides, or some other human action will or will not exterminate mankind. Will it? Probably not; but we do not know. And, until we know a lot more about the process of extinction, it would be rash to be too cocksure about the destiny of our own species.

Our other closing point is this. The reader may have shared the wish of many people that some samples of the life of the Mesozoic could have been reserved intact for us to admire. This has not happened and cannot happen, since time travel is a flat impossibility.

However, let us remember that the earth is now undergoing another Great Death, as drastic as those of the Cretaceous and the Pleistocene. This is the extermination of animals by man. A hundred or more species have disappeared in the last century, and over a hundred others like the California condor, the Arabian oryx, the blue whale, and the Galápagos tortoises are in dire straits.

Conservationist societies struggle to save what wild life they can, but the fight can never be finally won. In fact, the front cannot even be stabilized so long as the human species continues increasing at its present horrible rate. Moreover, the conservationists are mostly idealistic amateurs. They are opposed by professional exploiters, who stand to make material gain from the destruction of the animals and the conversion of their lands to profitable use. Guess who has the advantage in such a struggle!

Well, why protect wild life? There are several reasons. With the growth of the world's population and the demand for a higher standard of living everywhere, it is important to conserve every natural resource that we can. Moreover, scientists like to save every possible species for study.

But the real argument for keeping some lands in their natural state, with their native beasts and birds, goes beyond material things. If all the large wild animals were wiped out, mankind would no doubt get along. But what a dull world it would be, like the Paleocene just after the extinction of the dinosaurs!

If you heard that some dinosaurs had survived on an island, but that somebody had just shot them all for their hides, you might well feel a furious resentment, for some of the color and variety would have gone out of the world. Our descendants may feel the same about us if we casually allow all five species of rhinoceros to be exterminated because aging, superstitious orientals think that powdered rhinoceros horn will revive their sexual energies, or if we let all the large whales be turned into lubricating oil and canned meat.

If the world were all tamed and civilized into a worldwide mosaic of city, suburb, and farm, with no life but man and his domestic animals, it would be almost as monotonous as a jail. Nobody wants to live in even the nicest jail, because of the monotony. The existence of the wilderness with its wild life is one of the things that makes the world interesting. If it is right to prefer freedom to imprisonment, variety to monotony, and color to drabness, then it is right to save as much as we can of the wilds and their dwellers.

Notes

Chapter 1, THE DAY OF THE DRAGON
1. Gilbert & Sullivan: *The Mikado,* Act I.

Chapter 2, THE FINDING OF THE DRAGONS
1. Strabo, I, iii, 4; Herodotus, II, 12.
2. Born Georg Bauer, he Latinized his name in accordance with the usage of the time.

Chapter 3, OUT OF THE SEA
1. Cuvier's opossum, like his mosasaur skull, may still be seen at the Musée d'Histoire Naturelle in the Jardin des Plantes in Paris.
2. Formerly spelled "Solenhofen."

Chapter 5, THE RISE OF THE DINOSAURS
1. Meaning "plant saurian"—a misnomer perpetrated by an early paleontologist who, on the basis of fragmentary remains, mistakenly thought that the animals were herbivores.

Chapter 6, THE REPTILIAN MIDDLE AGE
1. The equations for the strength of a column in compression are complex, but the rule we give is a good enough approximation.
2. The largest known modern elephant, the Fénkövi elephant killed in 1955 in Africa and now mounted in the National Museum of Natural History in Washington, stands 13 feet 2 inches at the shoulder and is estimated to have weighed twelve tons in life. Some species of Pleistocene mammoths attained a slightly larger size, although most were smaller.
3. Stokes (1964).

4. For some reason—perhaps because it is easy to spell and pronounce—journalists are in the habit of mentioning this animal by its full species name, *Tyrannosaurus rex,* although they never give the species names for other dinosaurs, like *Iguanodon mantelli.* Since there is no logical reason for using the full species name for one extinct animal but not for others, we shall omit the *rex.*

5. G. E. Ray, p. 36.

6. Quoted in Colbert (1945–51), p. 78, & Swinton (1962), pp. 20 ff.

Chapter 7, REPTILES OF SEA AND AIR

1. Hall & Hall, p. 10. Cabot (who seems to have been an otherwise rather unattractive character) is the subject of a recent biography: *Only to God,* by Leon Harris (N.Y.: Atheneum, 1967).

2. Cf. C. Ray. Dr. Ray reached conclusions almost identical with ours, albeit he devoted most of his attention to the "true" seals and walruses, which—unlike the fur seals and sea lions—rely mainly upon their hind flippers for propulsion.

Chapter 8, THE DOOM OF THE DRAGONS

1. Some paleontologists consider *Deinodon* simply a larger species of *Gorgosaurus.*

2. In 1890, Marsh bestowed this name on fragmentary specimens he found in Colorado and Montana, from the Lance formation at the end of the Cretaceous. Later, Osborn's diggers turned up several nearly complete specimens of a similar form from the earlier Belly River and Judith River beds, to which—largely because of the gap in time between those formations and the Lance—he gave the separate genus name of *Struthiomimus* ("ostrich-mimic"). Some paleontologists accept *Struthiomimus* as a separate genus, while others do not. We follow the latter course to spare the reader a technical name.

3. Suborder Ankylosauria or Nodosauria; usage differs.

4. Colbert (1961), p. 164.

5. Hotton, pp. 165–71.

6. Cloud.

Chapter 9, THE GREAT FOSSIL FEUD

1. Osborn (1913–25), p. xix.

2. Schuchert & Le Vene, p. 42; Jaffe, p. 282.

3. Schuchert & Le Vene, pp. 246 f; Jaffe, p. 291.

4. Opinions differ as to whether these two specimens should be placed in the same species or whether the second and smaller specimen

should be put in a separate species or even a distinct genus, *Archaeornis*. Present opinion tends to the belief that both birds are of the same species.

5. Jaffe, p. 292.

6. Osborn, *op. cit.*, p. 144.

7. According to some, *Eohippus* should instead be called *Hyracotherium*, the name of a similar and earlier-discovered European form.

8. Osborn (1931), p. 178.

9. Osborn (1913–25), pp. 135 ff.

Chapter 10, DIGGERS AND DINOSAURS

1. Sternberg (1909), p. 14.

2. *Ibid.*, pp. 72 ff.

3. *Ibid.*, p. 42.

4. Scott, p. 174.

5. *Ibid.*, p. 48.

6. *Ibid.*, p. 55.

7. Osborn (1913–25), p. 57.

8. This story has been told us by several of Osborn's former associates. In some versions, Osborn named Huxley as the man who had inspired him.

9. Osborn, *op. cit.*, p. 142, & interview with R. C. Andrews, 1953.

10. Barton, p. 309.

11. Andrews (1926), pp. 228–31; (1943), pp. 214 ff. Two of Andrews' statements are not quite correct. The eggs were laid, not ten million, but something like a hundred million years ago; and the baby dinosaurs were not the first known fossil embryos—the baby ichthyosaurs from the Solnhofen slates were.

Chapter 11, THE HERITAGE OF THE DRAGONS

1. Hippolytus: *Refutation of all Heresies*, I, v; Lucretius: *De rerum natura*, V, 538–44.

2. Franklin, p. 70; Van Doren, p. 217.

3. Gregor Mendel: "Versuche über Pflanzenhybriden," in *Verhandlungen der naturforschenden Vereinigung in Brünn*, Abhandlung iv, 1865; Moulton & Schifferes, pp. 579–86.

4. Schuchert & Le Vene, p. 385.

Chapter 12, DINOSAURS IN THE WORLD OF TODAY

1. The Germans spelled it *Kamerun*.

2. Ktesias: *History of India*, in Photius, p. 112. For the African animals mentioned, see Diodorus Siculus, II, XXXV–XXXVI. *Martichora* (later

corrupted to *manticora*) is from the Old Persian *martiya*, "man," +
khvar, "eat."

3. "Mythical Monsters," in *Life*, 23 Apr., 1951, p. 115.
4. A Latinization of his original name, Olaf Stora.
5. *Historia de Gentibus Septentrionalibus.*
6. Quoted in Carrington, pp. 32 ff, & Ley (1950), pp. 221 ff.

Bibliography

Non-Fiction

ADAMS, Frank Dawson: *The Birth and Development of the Geological Sciences,* Baltimore: Williams & Wilkins Co., 1938; N.Y.: Dover Pubs., 1954.

ANDREWS, Roy Chapman: *On the Trail of Ancient Man (A Narrative of the Field Work of the Central Asiatic Expeditions),* N.Y.: G. P. Putnam's Sons, 1926.

—— *Under a Lucky Star (A Lifetime of Adventure),* N.Y.: Viking Press, 1943.

AUGUSTA, Josef, & BURIAN, Zdeněk: *The Age of Monsters (Prehistoric and Legendary),* London: Paul Hamlyn, 1966.

—— *Prehistoric Animals,* London: Spring Books, n.d.

—— *Prehistoric Reptiles and Birds,* London: Paul Hamlyn, 1961.

—— *Prehistoric Sea Monsters,* London: Paul Hamlyn, 1964.

BARNETT, Lincoln: "The Pageant of Life," Part V, in *Life,* 7 Sept. 1953, pp. 54–74.

BARTON, D. R.: "Father of the Dinosaurs," in *Natural History,* XLVIII, 5 (Dec. 1941), pp. 308–12.

BEECHER, Charles E.: "Othniel Charles Marsh," in *Amer. Jour. of Science,* 4th Series, VII (June 1899), pp. 403–28.

BEERBOWER, James R.: *Search for the Past (An Introduction to Paleontology),* Englewood Cliffs, N.J.: Prentice–Hall, 1960.

BELLAIRS, Angus d'A.: *Reptiles: Life History, Evolution, and Structure,* London: Hutchinson & Co., 1937; N.Y.: Harper & Bros., 1960.

BERNER, Lloyd V., & MARSHALL, Lauriston C.: "Oxygen and Evolution," in *New Scientist,* 11 Nov. 1965, pp. 415–19.

BOCK, Wilhelm: "Triassic Reptilian Tracks and Trends of Locomotive Evolution," in *Jour. of Paleontology*, XXVI, 3 (May 1952), pp. 395–433.

BOHLIN, Birger: *Fossil Reptiles from Mongolia and Kansu (Vol. 6 of Reports from the Scientific Expedition to the North-Western Provinces of China under the Leadership of Dr Sven Hedin)*, Stockholm: Statens Etnographiska Museum, 1953.

BROWN, Barnum: "The Last Dinosaurs," in *Natural History*, XLVIII, 5 (Dec. 1941), pp. 290–95.

—— "The Mystery Dinosaur," in *Natural History*, XLI, 3 (Mar. 1938), pp. 190–202, 235.

CAMP, Charles L.: "Geological Boundaries in Relation to Faunal Changes and Diastrophism," in *Jour. of Paleontology*, XXVI, 3 (May 1952), pp. 353–58.

CARRINGTON, Richard: *Mermaids and Mastodons (A Book of Natural and Unnatural History)*, N.Y.: Rinehart & Co., 1957.

CLOUD, Preston E., Jr.: "Paleoecology—Retrospect and Prospect," in *Jour. of Paleontology*, XXXIII, 5 (Sept. 1959), pp. 926–62.

COLBERT, Edwin E.: *The Age of Reptiles*, N.Y.: W. W. Norton Co., 1965.

—— *The Dinosaur Book (The Ruling Reptiles and their Relatives)*, N.Y.: McGraw-Hill Co., 1945–51.

—— *Dinosaurs (Their Discovery and their World)*, N.Y.: E. P. Dutton & Co., 1961.

—— *Evolution of the Vertebrates*, N.Y.: John Wiley & Sons, 1955.

—— *Men and Dinosaurs*, N.Y.: E. P. Dutton & Co., 1968.

COWLES, R. B.: "Comments on the Schatz Theory of Dinosaurian Extinction," in *Proc. of the Pennsylvania Acad. of Science*, XXXII, 1958, pp. 265 ff.

CROMPTON, Z. W., & CHARIG, A. J.: "A New Ornithischian from the Upper Triassic of South Africa," in *Nature*, CXCVI, 4859 (15 Dec. 1964), pp. 1074–77.

CUVIER, Baron G.: *Recherches sur les Ossemens Fossiles, où l'on Rétablit les Charactères de Plusieurs Animaux dont les Révolutions ont Détruit les Espèces*, 3d ed., Paris: G. Dufour & E. D'Ocagne, 1825, 7 vols.

DACQUÉ, Edgar: *Grundlagen und Methoden der Paläogeographie*, Jena: Fischer, 1915.

DALY, Reginald Aldworth: *Architecture of the Earth*, N.Y.: Appleton-Century, 1938.

DARWIN, Charles: *The Autobiography of Charles Darwin and Selected Letters* (ed. by Francis Darwin), N.Y.: Dover Pubs., 1957.

—— *The Voyage of the Beagle* (ed. by Leonard Engel), Garden City, N.Y.: Doubleday & Co., 1962.

DE BEER, Sir Gavin: *Charles Darwin,* Garden City, N.Y.: Doubleday & Co., 1964.

DIBNER, Bern: *Darwin of the Beagle,* Norwalk, Conn.: Burndy Library, 1960.

DIETZ, Robert S.: "The Sea's Deep Scattering Layers," in *Scientific American,* CVII, (2 Aug. 1962), pp. 44–50.

DUNBAR, Carl O.: "A Half Century of Paleontology," in *Jour. of Paleontology,* XXXIII, 5 (Sept. 1959), pp. 909–14.

ELIAS, Maxim K.: "The State of Paleontology," in *Jour. of Paleontology,* XXIV, 2 (Mar. 1950), pp. 140–53.

FAUL, Henry, & ROBERTS, Wayne A.: "New Fossil Footprints from the Navajo Sandstone," in *Jour. of Paleontology,* XXV, 3 (May 1951), pp. 266–74.

FENTON, Carroll Lane, & FENTON, Mildred Adams: *The Fossil Book (A Record of Prehistoric Life),* Garden City, N.Y.: Doubleday & Co., 1958.

—— *Giants of Geology,* Garden City, N.Y.: Doubleday & Co., 1952.

FRANKLIN, Benjamin: *Benjamin Franklin's Autobiographical Writings* (ed. by Carl Van Doren), N.Y.: Viking Press, 1945.

GORDON, Mrs.: *The Life and Correspondence of William Buckland, D.D.* . . . N.Y.: D. Appleton & Co., 1894.

HALL, Elizabeth, & HALL, Max: *About the Exhibits,* Cambridge, Mass.: Museum of Comparative Zoology, 1964.

HAWKINS, Thomas: *The Book of the Great Sea Dragons, Ichthyosauri and Plesiosauri* . . . London: William Pickering, 1840.

HENBEST, Lloyd G.: "Significance of Evolutionary Explosions for Diastrophic Division of Earth History—Introduction to the Symposium," in *Jour. of Paleontology,* XXVI, 3 (May 1952), pp. 299–318.

HENNIG, Edwin: *Am Tendaguru (Leben und Wirken einer deutschen Forschungs-Expedition zur Ausgrabung vorweltlicher Riesensaurier in Deutsch-Ostafrika),* Stuttgart: E. Schweizerbart'sche Verlagsbuchhandlung, 1912.

—— *Gewesene Welten (Auf Saurierjagd im ostafrikanischen Busch),* Ruschlikon, Switz.: Albert Muller Verlag, 1955.

HOTTON, Nicholas, III: *Dinosaurs,* N.Y.: Pyramid Pubs., 1963.

HUXLEY, Julian: *Evolution in Action,* N.Y.: New American Library, 1953.

INGERSOLL, Ernest: *Dragons and Dragon Lore,* N.Y.: Payson & Clarke, 1928.

IRVINE, William: *Apes Angels and Victorians (A Joint Biography of Darwin and Huxley)*, London: Weidenfeld & Nicolson, 1956.

JAFFE, Bernard: *Men of Science in America*, N.Y.: Simon & Schuster, 1944–46.

JARDINE, Sir William: "Memoir of *Cuvier*," in *The Naturalist's Library*, vol. 16, n.d.

JEFFERSON, Thomas: *The Writings of Thomas Jefferson*, Washington: Thomas Jefferson Memorial Assn., 1904, 2 vols.

JELETZKY, J. A.: "The Allegedly Danian Dinosaur-Bearing Rocks of the Globe and the Problem of the Mesozoic-Cenozoic Boundary," in *Jour. of Paleontology*, XXXVI, 5 (Sept. 1962), pp. 1005–18.

—— "Some Nomenclatural and Taxonomic Problems in Paleozoology," in *Jour. of Paleontology*, XXIV, 1 (Jan. 1950), pp. 19–38.

JOLEAUD, Léonce: *Atlas de Paléobiogéographie*, Paris: Lechevalier, 1939.

JOLY, John: *The Surface-History of the Earth*, Oxf.: Clarendon Press, 1925.

KOLLER, Larry: *The Complete Book of Guns*, N.Y.: Maco Magazine Corp., 1954.

LEAKEY, L. S. B.: *White African*, London: Hodder & Stoughton, 1937.

LEEDS, E. Thurlow: *The Leeds Collection of Fossil Reptiles from the Oxford Clay of Peterborough*, Oxf.: B. H. Blackwell, 1956.

LEY, Willy: "Cause of the Ice Age," in *Galaxy Science Fiction*, V, 3–5 (Dec. 1952–Feb. 1953).

—— *The Days of Creation*, N.Y.: Modern Age Books, 1941.

—— *Dragons in Amber (Further Adventures of a Romantic Naturalist)*, N.Y.: Viking Press, 1951.

—— *Exotic Zoology*, N.Y.: Viking Press, 1959.

—— "The Extinction of the Dinosaurs," in *Galaxy Magazine*, XVIII, 3 (Feb. 1960), pp. 107 ff.

—— "The Fatal Coloration," in *Astounding Science Fiction*, XXIX, 2 (Apr. 1942), pp. 98–106.

—— *The Lungfish, the Dodo, and the Unicorn (An Excursion into Romantic Zoology)*, N.Y.: Viking Press, 1941–48.

—— "Tyrannosaurus Was No Killer," in *Astounding Science Fiction*, XXXI, 2 (Apr. 1943), pp. 81–84.

LULL, Richard S.: *Organic Evolution*, N.Y.: Macmillan Co., 1917–27.

MAC LEOD, Roy M.: "Evolutionism and Richard Owen. 1830–1868," in *Isis*, LVI, 3 (Fall 1965), pp. 259–80.

MOULTON, Forest Ray, & SCHIFFERES, Justus J.: *The Autobiography of Science*, Garden City, N.Y.: Doubleday & Co., 1950.

"Mythical Monsters," in *Life*, 23 Apr. 1951, pp. 115–18.

NEWELL, Norman D.: "Crises in the History of Life," in *Scientific American*, CCVIII, 2 (Feb. 1963), pp. 76–92.

OSBORN, Henry Fairfield: *Cope: Master Naturalist (The Life and Letters of Edward Drinker Cope with a Bibliography of his Writings Classified by Subject)*, Princeton: Princeton Univ. Press, 1931.

—— *Impressions of Great Naturalists (Reminiscences of Darwin, Huxley, Balfour, Cope and Others)*, N.Y.: Charles Scribner's Sons, 1913–25.

—— *The Origin and Evolution of Life*, N.Y.: Charles Scribner's Sons, 1916–21.

OWEN, Richard: *Paleontology, or, a Systematic Summary of Extinct Animals and their Geological Relations*, Edinburgh: Adam & Charles Black, 1861.

OWEN, Rev. Richard: *The Life of Richard Owen*, N.Y.: D. Appleton & Co., 1894, 2 vols.

PARKINSON, John: *The Dinosaur in East Africa (An Account of the Giant Reptile Beds of Tendaguru, Tanganyika Territory)*, London: H. F. & G. Witherby, 1930.

PEATTIE, Donald Culross: *Green Laurels: The Lives and Achievements of the Great Naturalists*, N.Y.: Simon & Schuster, 1936.

PHOTIUS: *The Library of Photius*, N.Y.: Macmillan Co., 1920, Vol. I.

PIVETEAU, Jean, *et al.: Traité de Paléontologie*, Paris: Masson & Cie., 1955, Tome V.

PLATE, Robert: *The Dinosaur Hunters (Othniel C. Marsh and Edward D. Cope)*, N.Y.: David McKay Co., 1964.

RAY, Carleton: "Locomotion in Pinnipeds," in *Natural History*, LXII, 3 (Mar. 1963), pp. 10–21.

RAY, Grace Ernestine: "Big for his Day," in *Natural History*, XLVIII, 1 (June 1941), pp. 36–39.

RECK, H.: "Grabungen auf Fossile Wirbeltiere in Deutsch-Ostafrika," in *Geologische Charakterbilde*, Vol. 31, Berlin: Verlag von Gebruder Borntraeger, 1925.

ROMER, Alfred Sherwood: *Vertebrate Paleontology*, Chicago: Univ. of Chicago Press, 1933–62.

—— "Vertebrate Paleontology, 1908–1958," in *Jour. of Paleontology*, XXXIII, 5 (Sept. 1959), pp. 915–25.

RUSSELL, Loris S.: "The Relationships of the Alberta Cretaceous Dinosaur '*Laosaurus*' *Minimus* Gilmore," in *Jour. of Paleontology*, XXIII, 5 (Sept. 1949), pp. 518 ff.

SAWIN, J. J.: "The Pseudosuchian Reptile Typothorax Meadei," in *Jour. of Paleontology*, XXI, 3 (May 1947), pp. 201–38.

SCHATZ, Albert: "Some Biochemical and Physiological Considerations Regarding the Extinction of the Dinosaurs," in *Proc. of the Pennsylvania Acad. of Science,* XXXI, 1957, pp. 26–36.

——— "A Reply to Cowles' 'Comments on the Schatz Theory of Dinosaurian Extinction,'" in *Proc. of the Pennsylvania Acad. of Science,* XXXII, 1958, pp. 267 ff.

SCHLAIKJER, Erich M.: "The Rise of the Dinosaurs," in *Natural History,* XLVIII, 5 (Dec. 1941), pp. 284–87.

SCHUCHERT, Charles: *Outlines of Historical Geology,* N.Y.: Wiley, 1931.

SCHUCHERT, Charles, & LE VENE, Clara Mae: *O. C. Marsh, Pioneer in Paleontology,* New Haven: Yale Univ. Press, 1940.

SCOTT, William Berryman: *Some Memories of a Paleontologist,* Princeton: Princeton Univ. Press, 1939.

SEELEY, H. G.: *Dragons of the Air (An Account of Extinct Flying Reptiles),* N.Y.: D. Appleton & Co., 1901; N.Y.: Dover Pubs., 1967.

SIMPSON, George Gaylord: "The Beginnings of Vertebrate Paleontology in North America," in *Proc. of the Amer. Philosophical Soc.,* LXXXVI, 1943, pp. 130–88.

——— "The Discovery of Fossil Vertebrates in North America," in *Jour. of Paleontology,* XVII, 1 (Jan. 1943), pp. 26–38.

——— "Holarctic Mammalian Faunas and Continental Relationships During the Cenozoic," in *Bull. of the Geological Soc. of Amer.,* LVIII (July 1947), pp. 613–88.

——— *Life of the Past,* New Haven: Yale Univ. Press, 1953–61.

——— *The Meaning of Evolution: A Study of the History of Life and of its Significance for Man,* New Haven: Yale Univ. Press, 1949.

——— "Memorial to Walter Granger," in *Proc. of the Geological Soc. of Amer.,* Annual Report for 1941, pp. 159–72.

——— "Periodicity in Vertebrate Evolution," in *Jour. of Paleontology,* XXVI, 3 (May 1952), pp. 359–85.

——— *This View of Life (The World of an Evolutionist),* N.Y.: Harcourt, Brace & World, 1964.

SIMPSON, George Gaylord; PITTENDRIGH, Colin S.; & TIFFANY, Lewis H.: *Life (An Introduction to Biology),* N.Y.: Harcourt, Brace & Co., 1957.

STERNBERG, Charles H.: *Hunting Dinosaurs in the Bad Lands of Red Deer River, Alberta, Canada,* Lawrence, Kan.: priv. prin., 1917.

——— *The Life of a Fossil Hunter,* N.Y.: Henry Holt & Co., 1909.

STERNBERG, C. M.: "New Restoration of a Hooded Duck-Billed Dinosaur," in *Jour. of Paleontology,* XVI, 1 (Jan. 1942), pp. 133 ff.

——— "Pachycephalosauridae Proposed for Dome-Headed Dinosaurs,

Stegoceras Lambei, N. Sp., Described," in *Jour. of Paleontology*, XIX, 5 (Sept. 1945), pp. 534–38.

—— "Thescelosaurus Edmondensis, N. Sp., and Classification of the Hypsiliphodontidae," in *Jour. of Paleontology*, XIV, 5 (Sept. 1940), pp. 481–94.

STERNBERG, R. M.: "A Toothless Bird from the Cretaceous of Alberta," in *Jour. of Paleontology*, XIV, 1 (Jan. 1940), pp. 81–85.

STOKES, William Lee: "Fossilized Stomach Contents of a Sauropod Dinosaur," in *Science*, CXLIII (7 Feb. 1964), pp. 576 ff.

—— "Pterodactyl Tracks from the Morrison Formation," in *Jour. of Paleontology*, XXXI, 5 (Sept. 1957), pp. 952 ff.

STOVALL, J. Willis, & LANGSTON, Wann, Jr.: "Acrocanthosaurus atokensis, a New Genus and Species of Lower Cretaceous Theropoda from Oklahoma," in *Amer. Midland Naturalist*, XLIII, 3 (May 1950), pp. 696–728.

SUESS, Eduard: *The Face of the Earth* (*Das Antlitz der Erde*), Oxf.: Clarendon Press, 1906, 5 vols.

SWINTON, W. E.: *Dinosaurs*, London: British Museum (Natural History), 1962.

—— *The Dinosaurs* (*A Short History of a Great Group of Extinct Reptiles*), London: Thomas Murray & Co., 1934.

—— *Fossil Birds*, London: British Museum (Natural History), 1958–65.

—— *150,000,000 B.C.* (*The Prehistoric Monsters of Crystal Palace*), London: London County Council, n.d.

TROMP, S. W.: "The Determination of the Cretaceous-Eocene Boundary by Means of Quantitative, Generic, Microfaunal Determinations and the Concept 'Danian' in the Near East," in *Jour. of Paleontology*, XXIII, 6 (Nov. 1949), pp. 673–76.

VAN DOREN, Carl: *Benjamin Franklin*, N.Y.: Viking Press, 1938.

WEGENER, Alfred Lothar: *The Origins of Continents and Oceans*, N.Y.: Dutton, 1924.

WELLER, J. Marvin: "Paleontologic Classification," in *Jour. of Paleontology*, XXIII, 6 (Nov. 1949), pp. 680–90.

—— "The Species Problem," in *Jour. of Paleontology*, XXXV, 6 (Nov. 1961), pp. 1181–92.

WEST, Geoffrey (pseud. of Geoffrey Harry Wells): *Charles Darwin: A Portrait*, New Haven: Yale Univ. Press, 1938.

WILLISTON, Samuel Wendell: *The Osteology of the Reptiles* (ed. by William King Gregory), Cambridge, Mass.: Harvard Univ. Press, 1925.

WILSON, J. Tuzo: "Continental Drift," in *Scientific American*, CCVIII, 4 (Apr. 1963), pp. 86–100.

ZITTEL, Karl Alfred von: *History of Geology and Paleontology* (*To the End of the Nineteenth Century*), London: Walter Scott, 1901.

Fiction

ADAMS, Samuel Hopkins: *The Flying Death*, N.Y.: McClure, 1908.

ASTOR, John Jacob: *A Journey in Other Worlds*, N.Y.: D. Appleton & Co., 1894.

BLISH, James: *The Night Shapes*, N.Y.: Ballantine Books, Inc., 1962.

BRADBURY, Ray: "A Sound of Thunder," in *Collier's* for 28 June 1952; reprinted in *Golden Apples of the Sun*, Garden City, N.Y.: Doubleday & Co., 1953; and in *R is for Rocket*, N.Y.: Doubleday, 1962.

BURROUGHS, Edgar Rice: *At the Earth's Core*, Chicago: McClurg, 1922; N.Y.: Ace Books, Inc., n.d.; N.Y.: Canaveral Press, 1962.

—— *Back to the Stone Age*, Tarzana, Calif.: Edgar Rice Burroughs, Inc., 1937; N.Y.: Ace Books, Inc., n.d.; N.Y.: Canaveral Press, 1963.

—— *Land of Terror*, Tarzana, Calif.: Edgar Rice Burroughs, Inc., 1944; N.Y.: Ace Books, Inc., n.d.; N.Y.: Canaveral Press, 1963.

—— *The Land that Time Forgot*, in *Blue Book* for Aug. 1918; Chicago: 1924; N.Y.: Ace Books, Inc., n.d.; N.Y.: Canaveral Press, 1962; N.Y.: Dover Publications, 1963.

—— *Out of Time's Abyss*, in *Blue Book* for Dec. 1918; Chicago: McClurg, 1924 (as part of *The Land that Time Forgot*); N.Y.: Ace Books, Inc., n.d.

—— *Pellucidar*, Chicago: McClurg, 1923; N.Y.: Ace Books, Inc., n.d.; N.Y.: Canaveral Press, 1962.

—— *The People that Time Forgot*, in *Blue Book* for Oct. 1918; Chicago: McClurg, 1924 (as part of *The Land that Time Forgot*); N.Y.: Ace Books, Inc., n.d.

—— *Savage Pellucidar*, N.Y.: Ace Books, Inc., 1963; N.Y.: Canaveral Press, 1963.

—— *Tanar of Pellucidar*, N.Y.: Metropolitan Books, 1930; Ace Books, Inc., n.d.; N.Y.: Canaveral Press, 1962.

—— *Tarzan at the Earth's Core*, N.Y.: Metropolitan Books, 1930; N.Y.: Ballantine Books, Inc., 1964; N.Y.: Canaveral Press, 1962; London: Four Square, 1959–62.

—— *Tarzan the Terrible*, Chicago: McClurg, 1921; N.Y.: Ballantine Books, Inc., 1963; London: Four Square, 1960–61.

—— *Three Science Fiction Novels*, N.Y.: Dover Publications, 1963.

CARTER, Lin: *Thongor Against the Gods*, N.Y.: Paperback Library, 1967.

—— *Thongor in the City of Magicians*, N.Y.: Paperback Library, 1968.

—— *Thongor of Lemuria*, N.Y.: Ace Books, 1966.

—— *The Wizard of Lemuria*, N.Y.: Ace Books, 1965.

DE CAMP, L. Sprague: "A Gun for Dinosaur," in *Galaxy Science Fiction* for Mar. 1956; reprinted in *The World that Couldn't Be* (ed. by H. L. Gold), N.Y.: Doubleday & Co., 1959; and in L. Sprague de Camp: *A Gun for Dinosaur and Other Imaginative Tales*, N.Y.: Doubleday & Co., 1963.

DOYLE, Sir Arthur Conan: *The Lost World*, London: Hodder & Stoughton, 1912; N.Y.: Doubleday & Co., 1954.

HOWARD, Robert E.: "Red Nails," in *Weird Tales* for July, Aug., Sept., & Oct., 1936; reprinted in Robert E. Howard: *The Sword of Conan*, N.Y.: Gnome Press, 1952; & *Conan the Warrior*, N.Y.: Lancer Books, 1967.

HURLEY, Patrick M.: "The Confirmation of Continental Drift," in *Scientific American*, CCXVIII, 4 (Apr. 1968), pp. 52–64.

HYNE, C. J. Cutcliffe: *The Lost Continent*, N.Y.: Harper & Bros., 1900; reprinted in *Famous Fantastic Mysteries*, VI, 3 (Dec. 1944), pp. 10–115.

KIPLING, Rudyard: "A Matter of Fact," in *Many Inventions*, Garden City, N.Y.: Doubleday, Page & Co., 1911.

LOOMIS, Noel: "The Long Dawn," in *Super Science Stories* for Jan. 1950; reprinted in *Big Book of Science Fiction* (ed. by Groff Conklin), N.Y.: Crown Pubs., 1950.

MARSTEN, Richard: *Danger: Dinosaurs*, Philadelphia: John C. Winston Co., 1953.

MERRITT, A.: *The Face in the Abyss*, N.Y.: Liveright, 1931; N.Y.: Avon Pubs., n.d.

MILLER, P. Schuyler: "The Sands of Time," in *Astounding Stories*, XIX, 1 (Apr. 1937); reprinted in *Adventures in Time and Space* (ed. by R. J. Healy & J. F. McComas), N.Y.: Random House, 1946.

OBRUCHEV, Vladimir: *Plutonia*, N.Y.: Criterion Books, n.d.

ROBERTS, Charles G. D.: *In the Morning of Time*, London: Hutchinson, 1919.

ROUSSEAU, Victor (pseud. of V. R. Emmanuel): "The Eye of Balamok," in *All-Story Magazine* for 17, 24, & 31 Jan., 1920; reprinted in *Fantastic Novels*, III, 1 (May 1949).

TAINE, John (pseud. of Eric Temple Bell): *Before the Dawn*, Baltimore: Williams & Wilkins Co., 1934; reprinted in *Famous Fantastic Mysteries*, VII, 1 (Feb. 1946).

—— *The Greatest Adventure*, N.Y.: Dutton, 1929; reprinted in *Famous*

Fantastic Mysteries, VI, 1 (June 1944); also in John Taine: *Three Science Fiction Novels,* N.Y.: Dover Pubs., 1964.

VERNE, Jules: *A Journey to the Centre of the Earth,* Boston: Shepard, 1874; N.Y.: Charles Scribner's Sons, 1920.

VERRILL, A. Hyatt: *The Bridge of Light,* in *Amazing Stories Quarterly,* II, 4 (Fall, 1929); Reading: Fantasy Press, 1950.

YOUNG, Robert F.: "When Time Was New," in *If Worlds of Science Fiction,* XIV, 7 (Dec. 1964), pp. 6–39.

Index

In the text, extinct animals are called sometimes by their scientific names (e.g. Mosasauridae, *Mosasaurus*) and sometimes by their popular names (mosasaur); but in the Index, for the most part, the scientific names alone are used.